CROSS-BORDER TRANSACTIONS BETWEEN RELATED COMPANIES

CROSS-BORDER TRANSACTIONS BETWEEN RELATED COMPANIES

A Summary of Tax Rules

Edited by

WILLIAM R. LAWLOR

National Tax Partner
Ernst & Whinney, Canada

Chairman, Tax Committee
Ernst & Whinney International

KLUWER LAW AND TAXATION PUBLISHERS
DEVENTER · ANTWERP · LONDON · FRANKFURT · BOSTON · NEW YORK

Distribution in USA and Canada

Kluwer Law and Taxation
190 Old Derby Street
Hingham MA 02043
USA

Library of Congress Cataloging in Publication Data
Main entry under title:

Cross-border transactions between related companies.

Derived from an international tax planning symposium in New York sponsored by Ernst & Whinney.
'Current to January 1985'—Foreword.
1. International business enterprises—Taxation—Law and legislation. 2. Subsidiary corporations—Taxation. 3. Taxation, Double. I. Lawlor, William R. II. Ernst & Whinney.
K4544.C76 1985 341.7′5 85–19810
ISBN 90–6544–232–4 (pbk.)

D/1985/2664/87

ISBN 90 6544 2324

Foreword

Ernst & Whinney holds an annual international tax planning symposium and this topic was the theme of a recent symposium in New York. The following material is current to May, 1985. Many of the underlying principles described herein have been and will likely remain long-standing. However, due to the breadth and complexity of the subject, exceptions to general rules and frequent technical changes on specifics in individual countries, this publication will be most useful as a general guide and quick reference source.

Ernst & Whinney make this work available to assist with international tax planning and the minimization of double taxation. We hope it contributes to more harmonious dealings between all concerned.

Ernst & Whinney

Contents

Introduction and Summary of Rules

William R. Lawlor Canada

INTRODUCTION

Need for International Rules

As the volume of world trade continues to grow strongly and involve an increasing number of participants, and given the vast differences in prosperity levels from country to country, it is not surprising that problems arise when a country tries to determine what a fair burden of taxation should be on its domestic portion of an international transaction.

From a government's viewpoint, many factors must be considered in deciding what type of tax structure to have to finance public services. The taxes on income, sales, value added, imports and exports, Crown Corporations, etc, could all vary significantly from country to country, depending upon the economic strength of that country or the particular industries in it. No doubt a great variety of social, cultural or other national aspirations will also have a significant bearing on the tax mix in any given country. It is, therefore, inevitable that taxpayers engaging in multinational trade will be faced with a wide variety of, sometimes conflicting and sometimes opportunistic, tax regimes.

From the international businessman's point of view, it is only common sense and predictable behaviour that he will structure his affairs so as not to pay taxes unnecessarily. It is also predictable that a number of multinational enterprises will bend the rules a bit in their favour, especially when faced with vague and uncertain tax rules. If the effective tax rates are significantly different in two countries which are party to an international transaction, there will in most cases be a tendency to allocate more of the profit on the transaction to the low rate country. However, many other factors such as exchange controls, customs and tariff laws, government instability, profit incentive plans that may exist in one of those countries, etc, can be the main cause for the multinational enterprise wanting to shift as much of the income on a transaction to one country or the other. There may, for example, be accumulated losses in one country and taxable profits in another and the multinational enterprise is simply trying to achieve a form of international consolidation so as to avoid what it regards as taxation of artificial income in one country.

Some of the problems faced by multinational enterprises might be listed as follows:

1. Tax administrators in different countries taking a different view of the same transaction.
2. The mere review of transactions by assessors can be lengthy and costly and seem to vary greatly from country to country.
3. Often different assessors in different countries (sometimes the same country) will wish to spend time (and, therefore, money) in reviewing the same transactions or the same types of transactions on several occasions.
4. Different tax authorities apply different rules when allocating revenues or expenses from the same transaction to their respective countries.
5. Difficulty in getting one country to accept adjustments to an international transaction initiated by another country. This can be a problem, or at least a costly procedure, even where appropriate tax treaties exist.

Perhaps there is some common ground in governments and multinational enterprises alike wishing for further development of better international standards to which more countries will adhere, not only in their treaties but in their daily practices. Where a dispute does arise, all parties will benefit from a speedy and consistent solution to the problem in all countries concerned. However, it is probably human nature to prefer complexity and delays over a speedy but unsatisfactory solution. Therefore, a certain degree of complexity, double taxation and tax leakage appears still to be inevitable.

Developing International Standards

Some excellent work done by the Organization for Economic Co-operation and Develpment (OECD) in Paris has led to a fairly comprehensive set of international standards for taxing international transactions. These standards now enjoy very wide acceptance amongst member countries of OECD as well as many other countries.

A few countries (United States, Germany) have also made significant strides in codifying what they believe to be acceptable practices in taxing international transactions and in resolving international disputes. The principal publications where these international standards can be found are as follows:

1. 1977 OECD Model Double Taxation Convention – this was an update of an earlier model convention written in 1963 and many countries have closely followed these principles in negotiating new tax treaties over the last two decades. This model convention proposes fairly comprehensive principles of international taxation which cover most aspects of international trade. Most importantly, each of the member countries of OECD have expressed in writing their reservations with particular principles, so that multinational taxpayers are put on notice as to what are the broad principles of a particular member country.
2. Transfer prices and multinational enterprises, a 1979 OECD publication – this booklet actually goes through the more common types of multi-

national transactions and sets down some logical principles and procedures to be followed to avoid international double taxation.

3. UN Draft Model Taxation Convention – this 1979 publication sets out what they believe to be appropriate taxing principles to follow in an international tax convention between a developed and a developing country. This draft tax treaty follows most of the principles in the 1977 OECD model treaty but makes a few important modifications.
4. Draft (Standard) United States International Tax Treaty.
5. EEC Directive 77/799, which provides for the mutual exchange of information, on a general or particular basis, between member states.
6. EEC Draft Directive (*OJ No. C 19/301*, first published in 1976), which dealt with transfers of profits between associated enterprises. It proposed disputes be settled by a simple majority of an arbitration commission, which would be composed of representatives from tax authorities of countries concerned plus an independent country. The proposal has failed so far to gather much support as it reduces each country's sovereignty over tax disputes. However, the proposal is still under active study.

Trends for the Future

Many countries are expanding their tax treaty networks so as to reach agreement on broad taxing principles. Perhaps just as important is a significant increase in the number of meetings, discussions and seminars among the tax administrators in many developed countries so as to better harmonize their administrative practices and interpretations of tax treaties and domestic statutes. Some of the emanations of these efforts are showing up in the form of multiple country and concurrent audits on the same multinational enterprise and, secondly, industry wide audits conducted in an effort to achieve more consistent treatment of several taxpayers in similar situations. There is also a significant increase in the exchange of information between tax authorities in different countries. All of these developments are positive and should be applauded in the hope they will lead to fewer and shorter international tax disputes.

SUMMARY OF RULES IN INDIVIDUAL COUNTRIES

The following is a broad summary of the more important rules in individual countries. The questionnaire following the Introduction was used as a basis for comparison of how different countries treat the same transaction. The large Summary Charts at the end of the book are meant to provide a concise tool for making quick comparisons between countries, and highlighting where a particular country may be applying rules which, based on general international practices, appear abnormal.

The following comments are keyed to the question numbers on the questionnaire and those on the Summary Charts.

PART 1. GENERAL RULES

A.1 General Rules for Allocating Income and Expenses Between Related Companies – Arm's Length Principle

Probably every country in the world adheres, at least in principle, to the belief that transactions between related parties in different countries should be conducted at 'arm's length' prices. Article 9 of the 1977 OECD Model Tax Convention in general states:

> Where conditions are imposed between two associated enterprises (the same people participate directly or indirectly in the management, control or capital of both enterprises) and the commercial or financial dealings between the two are different from what would occur between two independent enterprises, then the enterprise whose profits were understated may have its profits appropriately increased and taxed by the relevant country and, should that occur, the other country will make appropriate downward adjustments in the profits and tax of the enterprise which had initially overstated its profits and taxes.

Different countries describe the arm's length principle with different language such as –

a. Revenues and expenses that are 'reasonable in the circumstances' (Canada).
b. Terms and conditions which deviate from those which unrelated third parties would have agreed upon (West Germany).
c. Will adjust transaction to that which would have applied if the transaction had been between independent parties dealing at arm's length (United Kingdom).

The language to express this principle is very similar in all countries.

A.2 Tax Avoidance or Proper Computation of Income

In most countries the arm's length principle is applied to try and arrive at an appropriate computation of profits in each country and the tax authorities do not have to demonstrate tax avoidance or tax evasion to make the adjustments. Exceptions to this rule appear to be Hong Kong and Brazil.

A.3 Safe Haven Rules

Most countries have not written specific rules to apply the arm's length principle to particular transactions but rather apply a broad, generally worded rule to a vast array of transactions. Exceptions are the United States and, more recently, Germany. The United States was the first to codify its rules in this area and in some detail, to be followed more recently by some German tax regulations.

The specific rules in the U.S. and Germany appear to cover most of the more common types of transactions, whereas a few other countries have written protective rules to cover specific areas where they feel they are exposed. For example, New Zealand and Singapore deem a number of payments to have their source in that country so as to make them subject to the local profits tax unless altered by a tax treaty. Belgium, France and Japan make specific alterations to the rules when there are payments to tax haven countries.

Few countries have created any safe haven rules except for prescribing some minimum interest rates for certain types of transactions (Canada, Japan, Mexico). Perhaps one notable exception is The Netherlands, where it is possible to obtain advance tax rulings even with respect to contentious subjects such as the transfer price for tangible goods.

A.4 Domestic vs International Taxpayers

Most countries apply the same principles to transactions between related domestic taxpayers and those between related taxpayers in different countries. However, the letter of the law is not always the same as administrative practice and the tax authorities in some countries clearly pay more attention to international transactions than they do to domestic ones (United Kingdom, The Netherlands, France, Germany, Belgium, Australia). In addition, some countries go further and give their tax authorities additional powers when dealing with international transactions. For example, New Zealand tax authorities can issue arbitrary assessments against non-residents in particular situations. The same is true in Mexico. In the other extreme, some countries put the onus on their tax authorities to prove that the arm's length principle was not adhered to in cross-border transactions (Japan, Sweden).

B. Related Persons

Some countries can adjust transactions between any two parties, be they related or not, but most countries have a definition of a close relationship between two parties, which relationship makes them subject to the anti-avoidance rules. While the language used to describe this close relationship varies significantly between countries, most of them are attempting to define 'effective control' by one company, person, etc, over another organization. By and large, this means controlling over 50 per cent of the voting power in a company, thus having the ability to elect the board of directors and influence management decisions. A few countries have gone further and defined certain relationships which are less than 50 per cent common control, to be subject to the anti-avoidance rules. For example, Germany and Spain pick up parties with

25 per cent or greater common ownership; Japan picks up parties where 50 per cent or more of the shares are owned by three or fewer unrelated persons; and France picks up all transactions with tax havens, be they related parties or not.

C. Transactions Basis

Virtually all countries apply the arm's length principle on a transaction-by-transaction basis. This, of course, means that tax authorities are looking at groups of similar transactions over a period of time. Very few countries (Belgium, New Zealand) indicate that they would simply look at the net income of the related companies in different countries to see whether a fair share of the total income from these transaction had been reflected in each company. However, while most countries say they would not use the net income approach as their first line of attack (or defence), many countries indicate that the net income approach is an important background fact to be kept in mind when trying to decide if appropriate prices had been charged on particular transactions.

D. Statute of Limitations

Most countries have a statute of limitations which prevent the taxpayer or the tax authorities from opening up earlier transactions. In most situations, the taxpayer is precluded after a very short period from opening up earlier returns. The tax authorities would have, typically, three to six years (twelve in the case of Singapore) to open earlier transactions to properly reflect profits. Where tax avoidance or misrepresentation exists, there is normally no limit on the length of time tax authorities have to make adjustments. In certain countries there are no limits, whether or not misrepresentation exists (Australia, Finland, Japan, Norway).

E. Correlative Adjustments

Where the home country initiates an adjustment in, say, a parent company's taxable income, it appears that no country other than the United States would make any notional adjustments to the foreign related company that was also a party to those transactions. This means that, when dividends ultimately come back from the foreign subsidiary to the local parent, certain funds which have already been taxed in the parent company might bear tax again on the receipt of those dividends. If the home country had insisted that a payment be made back to the parent company to reflect its increased taxable income, then the home country would only tax that income once. The majority of countries simply tax dividends received from foreign subsidiaries with a foreign tax credit for the foreign taxes actually paid.

F. Reaction to Foreign Adjustments

When a foreign country indicates an increase to the taxable income of foreign related parties, that appears to have no immediate impact on the taxation in the home country. The home country may, of course, decide to accept a reduction in domestic income. An exception would exist if the two companies in different countries were being taxed on a consolidated basis as would be the case with a Japanese parent and a subsidiary in a foreign tax haven.

When dividends ultimately flow back from the foreign company (whose profits were adjusted upward), that obviously affects the foreign tax credit calculation in the home country. In some cases, there is still no impact in the home country as certain countries allow dividends to flow home tax-free with no foreign tax credits (Canada, Australia, The Netherlands, etc).

When adjustments to a cross-border transaction are made by the tax authorities of a particular country, that tax authority normally does not insist that payments be made either to their country or out of their country to reflect those adjustments. A few countries do, however, insist that payments be made out of their country (or specific liabilities created in the company's accounts) before they will accept a reduction in the profits in their country in response to an upward adjustment initiated in another country.

G. Underlying Transaction Year Adjusted

When a country's tax authorities make changes to cross-border transactions, most attempt to adjust the year in which the underlying transactions occurred. Belgium and The Netherlands are two exceptions which will frequently adjust a more current year and several other countries occasionally adjust a more current year as a matter of convenience to both the government and the taxpayers involved.

H. Taxpayer can not Initiate Adjustments

In very few countries are taxpayers, by virtue of a request to their tax authorities, able to initiate an adjustment to a cross-border transaction. A few exceptions might be Finland, Sweden and Belgium. In most cases, the taxpayer can only request the tax authorities to make adjustments in response to an adjustment initiated by another country.

PART II. SPECIFIC EXAMPLES

A. Sale of Goods

Assumed Facts

P is a manufacturer which sells finished products to S, which is located in a different country. P sells these products to S at cost. P sells these products to unrelated parties at cost plus 10%. Both S and unrelated parties incur the same selling and promotion expenses and both resell P's products at the same price per unit.

Parent Company

1. Most countries would adjust the income of P so as to reflect an arm's length selling price. The few countries who may not be inclined to do so would be Australia, Hong Kong, Ireland, Saudi Arabia and Sweden.
2. When making adjustments, income would be increased to reflect arm's length selling prices and, to arrive at these prices, most countries would apply principles such as those outlined in the 1979 OECD publication.

If no obviously relevant sales to arm's length parties could be found to use as a guide for making adjustments (often difficult in practice), most countries would still make the best attempt possible to arrive at an estimate of the arm's length price. They might use sales of similar products and even sales between unrelated third parties as a guide to make appropriate adjustments to those prices to reflect the circumstances of the case at hand.
3. If the foreign subsidiary was undertaking a greater amount of selling and promotional expenses, most companies would take this into account in deciding what arm's length prices really were. Many countries would be inclined to take a look at the gross or net income being realized by the foreign subsidiary in an attempt to determine whether that was a fair return for the work being performed by that subsidiary.

Many countries would also allow the transfer price to a foreign subsidiary to be lowered (in some cases even below cost) to establish or protect a market in the foreign country. Some countries, like the United States or Canada, would only lower these prices if it could be demonstrated that the local parent company would act in the same way when dealing with an unrelated party. Other countries would allow the local parent company to lower the transfer prices so as to establish their own foreign subsidiary in a foreign market. There does not appear to be consistent applications of the rules in this area.

Subsidiary

1. No country would automatically accept an offsetting adjustment to one initiated in another country. In some cases, the subsidiary country will simply not accept foreign allocations at all (Hong Kong, Brazil, Mexico, Spain, Sweden). In some cases, it is exchange controls or an otherwise depressed economy which largely explains the reluctance of local tax authorities to accept any foreign adjustments.

2. In many cases, the tax authorities in the subsidiary's country will allow a downward adjustment of S's profits if they believe the adjustment initiated in the foreign country is a fair and reasonable charge. In some cases, this adjustment would only be accepted if there had been a binding contract to pay the higher prices (Japan, Australia). In other cases, the deduction would not be allowed unless it was recorded in the subsidiary's accounts (Denmark, Norway). In some cases, an additional requirement is that the amounts actually be paid by the subsidiary (New Zealand, Norway).

3. If the subsidiary actually makes payments of the allocated amounts to the foreign parent company, in the majority of cases there would be no withholding tax levied by S's country to the extent that the amounts were accepted as a reduction of S's taxable profits. In some cases, there would be no withholding tax even if the amount was not accepted as a reduction of S's profits (Australia, Hong Kong, Ireland, New Zealand).

B. Loans and Advances

Assumed Facts

P and S are manufacturers located in different countries. P loans money on open account without interest so that S can expand its operations. P is not engaged in the business of lending money.

Parent Company

1. Most countries would either impute interest income to the parent company in their country (sometimes at minimum prescribed rates and sometimes at open market rates) or else deny related interest costs to the parent company. A few exceptions to the rule would be Ireland, The Netherlands, New Zealand, Saudi Arabia and Sweden.

2. No country would alter its treatment just because the loan was evidenced by a non-interest bearing note.

3. Most countries would continue to classify the transaction as a loan or advance from the parent company but, in a few cases, the tax authorities of the parent company might regard the transaction as an equity investment in the foreign subsidiary (Finland, Norway, The Netherlands, Switzerland and the United States). Where those countries do treat the transaction as an equity investment, normally the equity can be repaid without any tax implications in the home country. In the case of the United States, however, a repayment of the equity might be regarded as a taxable dividend if the foreign subsidiary had 'earnings and profits' (a U.S. concept).

Subsidiary

1. In all cases, the subsidiary company's tax authorities will assess the characteristics of the transaction independently.
2. Most countries would continue to treat the transaction as a loan, although the same few countries mentioned above would sometimes treat it as an equity investment in the subsidiary. Where it is treated as an equity investment, normally the capital can be repaid without tax burden in S's country. An exception would be The Netherlands and United States, where it could be treated as a dividend payment subject to withholding tax.
3. If P's country imputed interest income to P, then S's tax authorities would sometimes accept the interest expense as a deductible amount in their country if it was felt the charge was fair and reasonable. Several countries would not accept a retroactive interest expense unless there had been a prospective, binding, legal obligation to pay the interest (Australia, Canada, Denmark, Hong Kong, Japan, West Germany).

If S proceeded to make a payment of the allocated interest to P, then normally that payment would be subject to withholding tax either characterized as an interest payment accepted by S's authorities, or as a dividend payment where the payment was not accepted as a deductible expense by S's authorities. A couple of different treatments might be Japan and Singapore, where there appears to be no withholding tax on such payments.

C. Intangibles

Assumed Facts

P and S are manufacturers located in different countries. P performs research and development which has led to P's ownership of patents, trademarks, know-how etc. P gives S exclusive right to use these intangibles in S's country. P does not charge S.

Parent Company

1. Here there is less uniformity in the decision to impute income or disallow relevant expenses to P. Some countries that would not be inclined to make these adjustments might be Australia, Finland, Japan, Mexico, Saudi Arabia and Switzerland.
2. For those countries that do allocate some income to P in their country, the majority would impute an annual royalty to P, whereas a few could also use the

option of imputing a lump sum sale of intangibles to the foreign subsidiary. The form of allocation would appear to depend upon the facts in each case but most countries would look at whether or not P had disposed of an identifiable separate asset. Some would regard the exclusive rights to use intangibles in S's country as a separate asset, whereas other countries would not.

3./4. If P and S had entered a bona fide cost sharing arrangement prospectively then, in the majority of cases, a reasonably drawn contract would govern and not be challenged by tax authorities. Such contracts could not be made retroactively (except where the country was probably open to making such adjustments even without the existence of a contract) in order to arrive at a fair distribution of profit between the relevant countries.

In a few cases, existence of a bona fide cost sharing contract would not have much bearing on a country's willingness to adjust these transactions (Finland).

Subsidiary

1. Once again, in all cases S's tax authorities will make an independent determination of whether or not they wish to accept a reallocation of income inititated by P's tax authorities. In several cases no allocations will be accepted in S (Brazil, normally Germany, Ireland, Mexico, Saudi Arabia, Singapore, Sweden, Spain).

2. Most countries which are willing to make adjustments to S's income will do so if they believe the charges are fair and reasonable. Some name additional requirements such as having a charge made from the parent company, having the expense recorded in the subsidiary's accounts, or even requiring S to pay the income allocated to P. Some countries would not permit the deduction in S unless they felt there had been a prospective, legal obligation for S to pay those amounts.

If S's tax authorities do accept some charge from P, they would normally permit annual royalties to be deducted currently and lump sum charges would have to be amortized over the life of the asset or an arbitrary term of years.

3. If S actually makes payments for the intangibles to P, then the normal rule would be for S to levy a withholding tax. Some variations would be: Australia, which would subject the payment to normal profits tax unless treaties prevented; Canada, which would not levy withholding tax if the payment was regarded as a purchase of an asset rather than an annual usage charge; Denmark, which would simply levy no withholding tax; Germany, which would levy severe taxes on 'hidden distributions of profit' unless the German tax authorities had accepted the payment as a deduction in Germany; Hong Kong, which has virtually no withholding tax; Ireland, which would have no withholding if it treated the payment as a non-deductible dividend distribution; The Netherlands with no withholding; Switzerland with no withholding.

D. Services

Assumed Facts

P is a large multi-national concern which fully owns foreign subsidiary S. Both P and S are engaged in manufacturing and sales activities. P's headquarters performs general management services for P's multi-national operations, including services which directly relate to S. The services include periodic visits by P's executives to review S's operations, financial analysis of S's future requirements, engineering services in connection with S's manufacturing operations and marketing services. P does not charge S.

Parent Company

1. Once again, there is not much uniformity in when P's tax authorities will allocate income to P or deny the relevant costs. While most countries would do one of those two things, some would appear to take no action (Finland, Switzerland). A few other countries would only make allocations for expenses that directly and perhaps exclusively benefit the foreign subsidiary, but would not make allocations for what might be called stewardship expenses (Australia, Belgium, Denmark, Germany, Japan, Mexico).
2. When allocations are made, some countries want to recover only direct costs in P, some would also want to recover indirect costs, while a few would insist on arm's length prices which would probably include a profit margin (Belgium, Norway, Sweden).

Subsidiary

1. Once again the tax authorities in S will always make an independent determination of whether or not they wish to accept some expenses allocated from P.

While most countries will accept allocations of expenses they feel are fair and reasonable as a deduction from local profits, a few will accept no allocations at all (Germany with respect to stewardship functions, Hong Kong, Norway, Singapore, Sweden).

Few countries will explicitly deny a profit element in the charge they are willing to accept. The Netherlands would appear to be sticky on this point.
2. Most countries will also not levy a withholding tax when S makes such a payment to P, to the extent that S's tax authorities had accepted the charge as a deduction against S's profits. In a few countries there would either be withholding tax or profits tax levied against the foreign parent company on the payment, subject to treaty exemption (Australia, Canada if there was a profit element in the charge; Japan if the service was rendered in Japan; Mexico, New Zealand, Spain, Singapore if profit element included in charge). A few

countries would not levy any withholding tax on this type of payment from S to P regardless of whether or not they were deductible in S (Denmark, Finland, Hong Kong, Ireland, Switzerland and the Netherlands).

E. Loan Guarantees and Rentals

Assumed Facts

P is a multi-national company whose main business is manufacturing and selling. P plans to establish foreign sales subsidiary S located in country S. P capitalizes S with $500,000 and guarantees a loan to S of $500,000 obtained from an independent bank. Land and a warehouse which P owns in country S will be used as a site for S's operation. P plans to make this land and warehouse available to S at a fee of $1 per year for 99 years.

Parent Company

1. Very few countries would allocate income to a parent company with respect to the guarantee of S's loan. A few exceptions are The Netherlands, Norway and France.

Nearly all countries would, however, either impute income or deny relevant expenses to P with respect to the real estate which it provided to its foreign subsidiary.

2. Most countries would not regard either aspects of these transactions as an equity investment by P and S. Exceptions are The Netherlands, Switzerland and United States.

Subsidiary

1. Once again all countries will make an independent determination of whether or not they want to accept any allocation of income to P which was initiated by P's tax authorities.

2. Some countries once again will permit no allocation in any circumstances, whereas most other countries will accept a fair and reasonable charge if initiated by P's tax authorities.

3. When S actually makes payments to P for the income allocated to P by P's tax authorities, then S would normally levy a profits tax or witholding tax on those payments (subject to treaties). This comment applies to rentals. Some exceptions where no withholding would apply to rental payments are Hong Kong, Belgium, Denmark, Singapore, Switzerland and The Netherlands.

There appears to be quite inconsistent treatment as to whether or not withholding tax would apply to payments with respect to loan guarantees. In some cases no withholding tax applies even though that payment has a character similar to interest (Belgium, Hong Kong, Ireland, Japan, The Netherlands).

PART III. TAX TREATIES

In terms of the willingness of most tax authorities to adjust cross-border transactions, the tax treaties appear to have more impact in form than they do in substance. One of the more significant aspects of having a treaty in existence between the countries where the transaction occurs, is that the tax authorities are at least willing to discuss the matter with one another and would hopefully exchange sufficient information to allow the competent authorities in these countries to reach a decision based upon common facts.

A. Mutual Agreement Procedures

In the majority of cases, the countries involved have a decent treaty network or are expanding their treaty network. While not all countries have tax treaties (Hong Kong, Mexico, Saudi Arabia), most countries either have mutual agreement procedures under their treaties which they are willing to use or, more importantly, they are receptive to having discussions with the tax authorities of other countries whether or not there is a treaty in existence. Thus, virtually all countries start from the principal of wanting to reach a fair and equitable result for the taxpayers and relevant countries involved.

B. Impact of Treaties

In a number of cases the existence of a treaty can alter the burden of taxation in the particular country. The most common examples of change would be the lowering of the rate of withholding tax or exempting a foreign company from profits tax and replacing it with a normal withholding tax.

In the big majority of cases, while the treaty may take precedence over other domestic tax laws, there is no requirement in the treaty to apply anything other than the domestic tax laws of the country. A few possible exceptions where competent authority procedures might run in different directions from the interpretation of local laws would be Finland and Norway. In the case of Germany, it is found that often a more generous settlement can be obtained from German tax authorities if no formal application is made to use their competent authority procedures. Where such an application is made, the German tax authorities will attempt to maximize the tax burden in anticipation that they might be negotiated down too far in discussions with foreign tax authorities.

C./D. Initiating Competent Authority Procedures

It is normally very easy for a taxpayer to initiate the mutual agreement procedures in a treaty and, in most cases, nothing more than a phone call or an informal request by the taxpayer residing in the competent authority's country is needed. In a few cases, there are time limits (statutes of limitations) imposed for such requests.

In the case of New Zealand the adjustments are initiated by having the taxpayer simply make the adjustments in his tax return and submit them for reassessment.

E. Failure to Reach Agreement

In all cases, if the competent authorities in the relevant countries concerned cannot reach a mutually agreeable position, double taxation will result. In some countries there is a provision in domestic law for making unilateral relief for the taxpayer in their country (Denmark, Singapore, United States).

F. Appeal of Competent Authority Decision

In all cases there is really no legal appeal from a decision reached by two competent authorities. However, this does not mean that the taxpayer is not free to appeal the facts of the case in the domestic courts of his country in addition to seeking adjustment under the mutual agreement procedures.

G. Conforming Adjustments and Payments

When the competent authorities in two countries reach an agreement, virtually all countries will accept conforming adjustments to reflect those reallocations of income. There would obviously be a few exceptions in countries with strong exchange controls such as Brazil.

H. General Experience

In the majority of situations, there has been acceptable if not favourable experience with the mutual agreement and competent authority procedures. As might be expected, there are often long delays as it is very time consuming to ferret out the true facts of many cases and allow appropriate time for discussion between often distant tax authorities.

PART IV. SPECIAL SITUATIONS

In most cases a country would not apply its tax laws differently to cross-border transactions just because one of the parties to the transaction had no gross income or had no net income. In a few cases, expenses would be denied where a company had no gross revenue, as it would be strongly suspect that the expenses were not incurred to earn income.

A country would also not normally apply its rules differently just because the effective tax rates in the two countries involved were either substantially similar (thereby not making much difference to the multi-national enterprise as to which country it paid tax) or whether the tax rates were substantially different (a tax haven). However, there is no question that the majority of developed countries more closely scrutinize transactions with tax haven countries. A few countries go so far as to write special laws to counter transactions with tax haven countries. For example, Japan would require consolidation of a Japanese parent and a foreign subsidiary in a tax haven country.

Questionnaire
Cross-Border Transactions between Related Companies (Tax Aspects)

Note: Each country's paper is geared to answering this questionnaire. It is based largely on one found in volume 56B, 1971, Cahiers De Droit Fiscal International.

PART I. GENERAL RULES

A. 1. What is the general rule for making allocations of income and expenses between related companies? What standard will be used? For example, an arm's length rate?
   2. May such adjustments be made only to prevent tax avoidance or may such adjustments be made to clearly reflect income?
   3. Are any transactions specifically covered? Are any safe havens provided for?
   4. Are different rules applicable to transactions between domestic taxpayers and to transactions between residents and non-residents?

B. What is a related person for purposes of making allocations?

C. Is the principal approach in making adjustments a transactions basis or a net income basis?

D. Is there any statute of limitation applied to the making of allocations?

E. Where an adjustment is made to the income of one of two related companies in different countries, is a correlative adjustment made with respect to the income of the other taxpayer?

F. What effect does an adjustment have when the adjustment is made to a company located outside of your country? For example:
1. Is that company taxed on a consolidated basis with domestic companies?
2. Are dividends from that company or foreign tax credits affected?
3. Is payment of allocated amounts required?

G. Are adjustments made to the tax years in which the underlying transaction took place, or only to the year the adjustment is made?

H. Can a taxpayer initiate an adjustment under the allocation rules by specific request to your tax authorities? If yes, under what circumstances?

PART II. SPECIFIC EXAMPLES

Note: In answering questions related to the Parent (P) it should be assumed that the reporting country is P's country. In answering questions relating to the Subsidiary (S), it should be assumed that the reporting country is S's country.

A. Sale of Goods

Assumed Facts

Assume P is a manufacturer which sells finished products to S which is located in a different country. P sells these products to S at cost. P also sells these products to unrelated parties at cost plus 10% mark-on. Both S and the unrelated parties incur the same selling and promotional expense and both resell P's products at the same price per unit.

As to P:

1. Will income be allocated to P with respect to its sales to S?
2. If yes, how will the allocation be made? What factors are considered?
3. Would your answer differ if there were no sales to independent parties or if S incurred greater selling or promotional expense or resold P's products at a lower price per unit so as to establish a market?

As to S:

1. Will the allocation of income from S to P, determined in P's country, be accepted by S's country, or will S's country make an independent determination?
2. Under what circumstances will S be allowed to deduct the allocation from its taxable income?
3. If S makes a payment of the allocated amount to P, will S's country treat the payment as a dividend subject to withholding?

B. Loans and Advances

Assumed Facts

P and S are manufacturers located in different countries. P loans to S money on open account without interest so that S can expand its operations. P is not engaged in the business of lending money.

As to P:

1. Will interest income be allocated to P? If yes, at what rate will the interest be allocated?
2. Would your answer be different if the loan was evidenced by a non-interest bearing note with a fixed maturity date?
3. If interest income is not allocated, could the loan be considered as an additional equity investment by P in S? If yes, what would be the tax consequences when the loan is repaid?

As to S:

1. Will the characterization of the transaction by P's country be accepted by S's country, or will S's country make a separate determination?
2. If S's country makes a separate determination, will the transaction be characterized as a loan or additional equity investment? Would it make any difference if the loan was evidenced by a non-interest bearing note with a fixed maturity date?
3. If the transaction is characterized as a loan, will interest be allocated? If yes, at what rate will the interest be allocated and will a deduction be allowed for the allocated amount?
4. What would the tax consequences be if P's country allocates a greater amount than S's country and S pays the amount allocated by P's country?
5. If the transaction is characterized as an additional equity investment, what would be the tax consequences of the repayment of the loan? What if P's country characterizes the transaction as a loan and S pays the amount allocated by P's country?

C. Intangibles

Assumed Facts

P and S are manufacturers located in different countries. P performs research and development which has led to P's ownership of certain intangibles consisting of patents, trademarks and know-how. P makes available to S

exclusive right to use in S's country all of P's intangibles. P does not charge S for the use of P's intangibles.

As to P:

1. Will income be allocated to P by reason of S's use of P's intangibles or could P be treated as contributing the intangibles to the capital of S?
2. If income is allocated, will the allocation be in the form of annual royalties or of a lump sum payment? How will the amount of allocation be computed? Does it make any difference if S's country does not allow payments for use of intangibles or if S's country allows payments but does not allow a deduction for tax purposes?
3. Alternatively, could a portion of the research and development costs incurred by P be allocated to S?
4. Would any of your answers change if P and S entered into a *bona fide* cost sharing arrangement with respect to the research and development costs incurred by P?

As toS:

1. If income or expenses are allocated to P by P's country, will S's country accept that allocation or will S's country make a separate determination?
2. If the allocation to P is in the form of a lump sum payment, annual royalty or a reduction of expense will S be permitted a deduction for the amount allocated? How will the amount of deduction be computed?
3. If S makes a payment to P of the amount allocated and the payment is for a lump sum payment, an annual royalty or a sharing of costs, will S's country subject that payment to a withholding tax?

D. SERVICES

Assumed Facts

P is a large multinational concern which wholly owns foreign subsidiary S. Both P and S are engaged in manufacturing and sales activities. P's headquarters division performs general management services for P's multinational operations including services which directly relate to S. The services performed for S include periodic visits by P's executives to review S's operations, financial analysis of S's future requirements, engineering services in connection with S's manufacturing activities and marketing services in connection with S's sales activities. P does not charge S for such service.

As to P:

1. Will income in the form of a charge be allocated to P for the performance of services? If yes, will there be differences in how the charge is calculated depending on the nature of the services?
2. If income is allocated to P, how will the amount of allocation be computed? For example, will P's direct and indirect costs be considered and will a profit be allocated to P?

As to S:

1. If income is allocated to P will the amount determined by P's country be accepted by S's country, or will S's country make a separate determination? If S's country makes a separate determination, how would S's country determine the amount of allocation. In either case, on what amount, if any, would S be allowed a deduction?
2. Will payments by S to P be subject to withholding tax by S's country?

E. Loan Guarantees and Rentals

Assumed Facts

P is a multinational company whose main business is manufacturing and selling. P plans to establish foreign sales subsidiary S located in country S. P capitalizes S with $500,000 and guarantees a loan to S of $500,000 obtained from an independent bank. Land and a warehouse which P owns in country S will be used as a site for S's operations. P plans to make this land and warehouse available to S at a fee of $1 per year for 99 years.

As to P:

1. Will income be allocated to P for P's guarantee of the loan to S or for S's use of P's land and warehouse? If yes, how would the amount of allocation be determined?
2. If income is not allocated, in the alternative could P be treated as having made an additional equity investment in S? If yes, what would be the tax consequences of such treatment?

As to S:

1. Will the characterization of the transaction by P's country be accepted by S's country or will S's country make a separate determination?

2. If S's country makes a separate determination, what would that determination be? If income is allocated to P, how would the amount of allocation be determined?
3. If income is allocated to P and S makes payment of the allocated amounts to P, will S's country subject the payment of a withholding tax?

PART III. TAX TREATIES

A. Do the tax treaties into which your country has entered contain a provision for a mutual agreement procedure concerning the allocation of income and expense between related parties located in the treaty countries?

B. Might the treaty provisions in any way modify your previous answers? If yes, what are the principal modifications? For example, what guidelines does your competent authority use when seeking to negotiate a settlement concerning the allocation of income and expenses? Is he required to apply domestic law?

C. How are these treaty provisions invoked? For example, must the taxpayer seek protection under the treaty or will treaty protection be invoked automatically by your tax authorities when they know that a treaty country is involved?

D. What is the procedure for applying to the competent authority in these situations? Are there any guidelines established which define when the application to the competent authority will be accepted?

E. What is the effect of a failure to reach settlement between the competent authorities of the two treaty countries?

F. Can a taxpayer appeal a settlement made between two competent authorities?

G. Where agreement is reached as to the correct allocation, will conforming adjustments and payments be allowed without further tax consequences?

H. Generally, what has been your experience with competent authority negotiations in this area? Has settlement usually been reached? How long do competent authority negotiations normally carry on?

PART IV. SPECIAL SITUATIONS

A. Are the normal allocation rules described in Part I and illustrated in Part II modified or applied differently in any of the following situations:

1. If either of the related companies does not have any gross income?
2. If either of the related companies has an operating loss for the year?
3. Where the tax rates of the countries involved are substantially equal?
4. Where the tax rate of the country to which the income is to be allocated is substantially lower than the rate of tax in the country where the income was originally reported?

B. Are there any special types of companies or transactions which your tax authorities will closely examine for purposes of allocating income and expenses between related parties? If yes, please describe these situations.

PART V. OTHER CONSIDERATIONS

Please include a description of any additional considerations which you think are important.

Australia

Ian R. Phillips

PART I. GENERAL RULES

A. What is the general rule for making allocations of income and expenses between related companies?

1. Adjustments are made to increase Australian taxable income and, whilst the legislation may be applied to clearly reflect income, the practice is only to make adjustments to correct tax avoidance positions.
2. An arm's length standard is adopted for adjusting transactions between related parties.
3. All types of transaction are covered and no safe havens are proclaimed.
4. The capacity to restate the income of parties to domestic transactions is restricted to demonstrable tax avoidance situations or transactions involving particular classes of assets, such as purchases of depreciable assets or inventories. In contrast, there is no restriction on the application of reallocation rules to transactions between residents and non-residents. This divergence of treatment has not caused any conflict with Australian tax treaties, as the recent Australia–United States treaty was the first to contain a non-discrimination clause.

B. Adjustments can be made when the parties are not dealing at arm's length with each other in regard to the transaction. This is based on the Commissioner reviewing all relevant facts concerning the relationship between the parties, and a close corporate (operational) relationship may be sufficient for a presumption of non-arm's length relationship to be applied.

C. The principal approach in making adjustments is a transactions basis.

D. There is no time limit on making adjustments to non-arm's length transactions. The ordinary statute of limitations provision is expressly excluded from application.

E. Correlative adjustments – if the other company is an Australian taxpayer, there is provision for the making of a correlative adjustment. However, this will not ordinarily be the case.

F. When an adjustment is made to a company located and resident outside of Australia:

1. no consolidation basis or other group relief is available,
2. dividends from that company are not affected and foreign tax credits (if any) are limited to tax imposed directly on dividends, not underlying tax.
3. payment of allocated amounts is not required.

G. The adjustments are ordinarily made in the tax year in which the underlying transaction took place.

H. Apart from competent authority provisions of tax treaties, taxpayers can not initiate an adjustment under the allocation rules by specific request to Australian authorities.

PART II. SPECIFIC EXAMPLES

A. Sale of Goods

Assumed Facts

Assume P is a manufacturer which sells finished products to S which is located in a different country. P sells these products to S at cost. P also sells these products to unrelated parties at cost plus 10 per cent mark-on. Both S and unrelated parties incur the same selling and promotional expense and both resell P's products at the same price per unit.

Parent in Australia

1. The Australian law provides for the allocation of income to P, although in practice this is not common.
2. Arm's length pricing differential as demonstrated by sales to unrelated parties.
3. Yes, the answer would differ if there were no comparable sales to independent parties or if S incurred greater selling or promotional expenses. In the absence of demonstrable arm's length sales, the imputation of an arm's length price is naturally more difficult. Similarly, the circumstances of S's trade may be given weight by the Australian revenue authorities in deciding whether to restate the sales price. If so, this would be done on the basis that an arm's length transaction to a party bearing additional costs may be reduced as a reflection of that fact.

Subsidiary in Australia

1. Australia will wish to make its own determination.
2. S will be allowed to deduct the allocation from its taxable income only if the allocation is charged by P to S and it is open to say that the original contract price was varied so as to be legally binding on S.
3. If S makes a payment of the allocated amount to P and the allocated amount is not deductible in Australia, it will be regarded as a transaction on capital account but not likely as a dividend. Dividends, which are subject to withholding tax, are widely defined in Australian tax law but, to date, Australian tax authorities have not sought to tax the payment of non-deductible allocated amounts as dividends. In general, it is unlikely that Australian courts would accept an upward adjustment in S's purchase price of goods as a dividend paid by S, particularly where the adjustment is a result of proper income allocations in P's country.

B. Loans and Advances

Assumed Facts

P and S are manufacturers located in different countries. P loans S money on open account without interest so that S can expand its operations. P is not engaged in the business of lending money.

Parent in Australia

1. Interest will usually be allocated to P at the prevailing arm's length rate for the transaction. If, however, P can establish that the loan facility will generate assessable income in Australia (for example, through dividends from S), then an interest imputation may not be made.
2. If a non-interest bearing note were signed, interest income would still be imputed to P, but the rate may differ of course. The comments in No. 1. above as to generation of assessable income remain applicable.
3. If interest income is not allocated the loan would still be considered a loan. In addition, there are no major tax consequences as there is no capital gains tax as such in Australia.

Subsidiary in Australia

1. Australia will wish to make its own determination.
2. The transaction would be characterised as a loan.
3. No, interest will not be allocated to S, except if the interest is charged by P to S and it is open to say that the original loan contract was varied so that the

interest charge was legally binding on S. This is unlikely in any event, and could not be done if the loan was evidenced by a non-interest-bearing note. If an interest charge is allowable, the deduction would be limited to an arm's length rate.
4. If P's country allocates a greater amount than S's country and S pays the amount allocated by P's country then, unless the unlikely restatement referred to in 3 can be achieved, the payment would not be deductible to S. The payment may be subjected to withholding tax, however.
5. The transaction would not be characterised as an additional equity investment even if P's country had done so.

C. Intangibles

Assumed Facts

P and S are manufacturers located in different countries. P performs research and development which has led to P's ownership of certain intangibles consisting of patents, trademarks and know-how. P makes available to S exclusive right to use in S's country, all of P's intangibles. P does not charge S for the use of P's intangibles.

Parent in Australia

1. The risk of allocation of income for use of intangibles is not great in the present climate, although it is possible and, with greater sophistication by the Revenue Authorities, an adjustment may be made to allocate income to P.
2. An annual royalty, which will usually be taxable, may be attributed to P. If made, the allocation would be on an arm's length basis, drawing on the information available to Revenue for arrangements between parties at arm's length. The tax position of S would not be a factor in this determination.
3. If the research and development costs are properly incurred by P, they can not be 'allocated' to S. They could be non-deductible if considered incurred in the production of exempt overseas royalty income but, in the absence of a royalty payment, the costs should be deductible on the basis that the capacity of S to pay dividends is enhanced by P assuming these costs. This argument only applies where S is the subsidiary of P, however.
4. If S contributed to costs under a cost sharing arrangement, no question of further allocation of royalties, etc, would arise.

Subsidiary in Australia

1. Australia will wish to make its own determination of acceptable charges to S.

2. S will be permitted a deduction for non-capital outgoings if it can be shown that the allocation was an obligation it had as the user of the patents, trademark and know-how. Strictly applied, this test would be difficult to satisfy but, in practice, is frequently allowed particularly if P is exposed to substantial Australian tax on the transaction. If a lump sum payment for the right to use the intangibles is paid, limited amortization deductions for the costs attributable to patents only would be allowed. Lump sum 'catch-ups' of imputed royalties or expenses are sometimes allowed as deductions in the year of charge rather than against the earlier years to which they refer: this, however, is a result of the imposition of Australian tax on P.
3. If S makes a payment to P of the amount allocated, and the payment is for the use of the intangible, then Australia will subject the payment to normal Australian profits tax as a non-resident deriving Australian source income. This, of course, may be overriden by tax treaties.

D. Services

Assumed Facts

P is a large multinational concern which wholly owns foreign subsidiary S. Both P and S are engaged in manufacturing and sales activities. P's headquarters division performs general management services for P's multi-national operations including services which directly relate to S. The services performed for S include periodic visits by P's executives to review S's operations, financial analysis of S's future requirements, engineering services in connection with S's manufacturing activities and marketing services in connection with S's sales activities. P does not charge S for such services.

Parent in Australia

1. Theoretically, an imputed charge could be included in P's taxable income more especially if P provides comparable services to third parties, thus establishing an arm's length price. In practice, however, it is unlikely at this stage of Australia's development as a capital exporter that any adjustment would be made, particularly for general management, periodic reviews and financial analysis. Engineering and marketing services are more likely to attract attention if they are significant.
2. The test to be adopted is the arm's length price which, in the absence of comparable sales to third parties, can only be established by a buildup of costs, both direct and indirect. The outcome would be the result of negotiation and it may be expected that any profit margin imputed would be minimal.

Subsidiary in Australia

1. Australia may wish to make a separate determination but, in the light of the nature of the services, the charge is likely to be accepted. If the charge was challenged, the imputation of the arm's length consideration would commence with an analysis of the cost of providing the services to which may be added a margin. A deduction would ordinarily be allowed for the allocation charged.
2. There will be no withholding tax as such on payments by S to P, but there will be exposure to Australian tax at non-resident rates on the profit margin to the extent the services have an actual Australian source or a deemed Australian source as royalties.

E. Loan Guarantee and Rentals

Assumed Facts

P is a multinational company whose main business is manufacturing and selling. P plans to establish foreign sales subsidiary S located in country S. P capitalizes S with $500,000 and guarantees a loan to S of $500,000 obtained from an independent bank. Land and a warehouse which P owns in country S will be used as a site for S's operations. P plans to make this land and warehouse available to S at a fee of $1 per year for 99 years.

Parent in Australia

1. In practice, the guarantee of the loan will not attract any income allocation.
The provision of land and warehouse could be expected to generate an income allocation equal to the fair market value of the property; in other words, the arm's length price.
2. P would not be treated as having made an additional equity investment in S.

Subsidiary in Australia

1. Australia will wish to make a separate determination of acceptable charges to S.
2. If the income allocation is charged to S, the Australian taxation authorities would apply an arm's length test. In practice, this would mean the acceptance of the charge for the guarantee but the adjustment of the imputed rental charge to the market value of the lease.
3. If S makes payment of the allocated amounts to P, then P would be liable to Australian tax on the charge for rent which has an Australian source but, arguably, not on the guarantee as the source may be ex-Australian.

PART III. TAX TREATIES

A. Yes, the tax treaties that Australia has entered into contain a provision for a mutual agreement procedure.

B. Yes, the treaty provisions may modify previous answers. The treaty provisions by and large seek to avoid an item-by-item or transaction-by-transaction ascertainment of arm's length trading arrangements and to apply a more equitable global approach. This is all the more so as the Australian domestic law does not facilitate the reduction of taxable income. The Australian competent authority must, therefore, rely on the general provision enabling the domestic law to be overridden in the case of conflict.

C. The Australian taxpayer must apply to have the treaty protection. There are no regulations setting out procedures.

D. No procedure is prescribed for applying to competent authority. However, it is unusual for competent authority provisions to be invoked as part of a protest procedure in which the Australian competent authority is required to exercise his powers under the treaties as a matter of administrative law. No procedural guidelines have been published.

E. We have not experienced a failure to reach a settlement between the competent authorities of the two treaty countries although, in one case, 'negotiations' have been proceeding for 8 years.

F. The only appeal from a settlement made between two competent authorities would appear to be the application of administrative law through, for example, a writ of mandamus. The likelihood of success in such an action is thought not to be good where the Commissioner of Taxation can justify his position on some basis. There are also considerable jurisdictional problems, especially as regards the overseas authority concerned.

G. We can think of no situations where the implementation of an agreement could not be expected to be allowed without further tax consequences.

H. As mentioned above, our experience (and that of Australia as a whole) with competent authority negotiations is quite limited. In our limited experience, considerable difficulties have been experienced in reaching agreement, with consequent delays resulting.

PART IV. SPECIAL SITUATIONS

A. The normal allocation rules described in Part I and illustrated in Part II are normally not applied differently in the following situations:

1. If either of the related companies does not have any gross income;
2. If either of the related companies has an operating loss for the year, although the absence of any immediate Australian tax obligations may cause a lessening of interest by the authorities;
3. Where the tax rates of the countries involved are substantially equal;
4. Where the tax rate of the country to which the income is to be allocated is substantially lower than the rate of tax in the country where the income was originally reported.

B. The transfer pricing arrangements of international oil companies have been the first concern of the Revenue in this area for many years and seems likely to remain so. Transfers in the form of royalties are closely monitored and again, this position is likely to continue. Long-term contracts for the export of minerals and mineral products have also attracted attention in recent years. Revenue authorities also closely scrutinize outward money flows to countries classified in Australia as tax havens. These countries include Hong Kong, Bermuda, the Bahamas, Channel Islands and Switzerland.

Belgium

Roger Couteau

PART I. GENERAL RULES

A. The general rule for making allocations of income and expenses between related companies is the arm's length concept. Companies are deemed related when an enterprise of a Contracting State participates directly or indirectly in the management, the control or the capital of an enterprise of the other Contracting State, or when the same persons participate directly or indirectly in the management, control or the capital of both enterprises concerned.

1. Adjustments are normally made to prevent tax avoidance through excessive transfer of profits.
2. As already stated, the arm's length rate is used.
3. Article 46 of the Internal Tax Law specifies that any amounts paid as interest, royalties, or remuneration for services to a holding company which is located abroad and subject there to an abnormally favourable regime of taxation, will not be considered as expenses in Belgium unless duly justified. The same applies when the said amounts are paid to an enterprise located in a country where the taxes are significantly lower than in Belgium.

   Article 250 of the same law specifies that the sale of shares, bonds, etc, to a holding company located in a country with again an abnormally favourable regime of taxation, is not acceptable to the fiscal authorities unless duly justified.

   Article 24 of the Internal Law and, generally, Article 9 of the treaties concluded by Belgium, are both to avoid abnormal advantages being granted to related enterprises.
4. The already mentioned articles deal with international relations of related enterprises. The Belgian law does not have the same rules between domestic taxpayers with the exception of Article 53 which prevents the granting of abnormal advantages to related enterprises having losses to recoup.

B. The concept of related persons is generally defined as an enterprise of a Contracting State participating directly or indirectly in the management, the control or the capital of an enterprise of the other Contracting State. If the same persons participate in the same manner in both enterprises, the concept of related person is also achieved.

By capital, it is envisaged not only the social capital, but also the providing of financial resources through contribution of capital, loan, credits, etc. In many conventions, the word 'financing' is often used for characterizing the various ways of participation in the capital of a company.

By the same persons it is envisaged the existence of a mutual link, and the possibilities of collusion between the related enterprises, without excluding the existence of family relations between the managers of these enterprises.

C. Normally the first approach in making adjustments is the net income basis. However the transaction basis could also be used.

Article 50 of the Internal Law stipulates that one cannot deduct amounts paid as interest on loans, on credits, on deposits and on other similar items when such payment is higher than the greater of:

- the annual interest rate charged by the National Bank of Belgium, increased by 3 per cent, or
- 9 per cent, when the Bank of Belgium rate is below 6 per cent.

It is to be noted that tax treaties do not impede the application of this Article 50.

D. When an adjustment is made to the income of one of two related companies, no automatic correlative adjustment is made with respect to the income of the other taxpayer.

The adjustment to avoid the double taxation can only take place within the framework of a tax convention. For instance the convention between the United States and Belgium stipulates in Article 25 that the competent authorities of the Contracting States shall endeavour to resolve by mutual agreement any difficulties or doubts arising as to the application of this convention, in particular in the field of allocation of income deduction, credits or allowances.

Generally, however, the Belgian tax authorities accept that changes be taken into account in certain cases. For example, let us suppose that an American parent has made a loan without interest to its Belgian subsidiary and that the IRS insist that interest should be received by the parent for the three latest years. Should the Belgian company pay the interest in one year, the total charge for the three years could be deducted in the year of payment. The time limit for making adjustments to any particular year is normally three years after that year.

E. Effect of an adjustment made to a company located outside of Belgium.

1. For the time being, no consolidation of the accounts of foreign companies with Belgian ones exist.
2. The dividends from that company and foreign tax credits have no special adjustment.
3. Payment of allocated amounts is not required.

F. As mentioned under D, adjustments are only made to the year the adjustment is made.

G. It is possible for an adjustment under the allocation rules to be initiated by a Belgian taxpayer by request either to the ordinary tax authorities or competent tax authority as described under III.D.

H. A Belgian taxpayer cannot initiate adjustments to a transaction in Belgium unless a foreign tax authority has first adjusted the transaction in that foreign country.

PART II. SPECIFIC EXAMPLES

A. Sale of Goods

Assumed Facts

Assume P is a manufacturer which sells finished products to S which is located in a different country. P sells these products to S at cost. P also sells these products to unrelated parties at cost plus 10 per cent mark-on. Both S and the unrelated parties incur the same selling and promotional expense and both resell P's products at the same price per unit.

Parent in Belgium

1. The income of P should be increased by the 10 per cent granted to S which is an abnormal advantage.
2. The 10 per cent will be allocated because it is the normal mark-on between unrelated parties.
3. The answer would not differ if there were no sales to independent parties because the mark-on which would be applicable to eventual third parties would be 10 per cent. Of course, it would probably be very difficult to justify the percentage.

If S incurred greater selling or promotional expenses, the mark-on could be lower. This is also valid if S resold P's products at a lower price. The reason why S has higher charges or resells at lower prices will have to be explained.

Subsidiary in Belgium

1. Belgium will make an independent determination of S's income.
2. S will be allowed to deduct the arm's length profit allocation from its taxable income.
3. Payments by S to P will not be treated as a dividend subject to withholding,

since S should have from P evidence that tax authorities of P have revised its income and so the payment would not be treated as a hidden distribution of profits.

B. Loans and Advances

Assumed Facts

P and S are manufacturers located in different countries. P loans S money on open account without interest so that S can expand its operation. P is not engaged in the business of lending money.

Parent in Belgium

1. Interest income will be allocated to P at open market rates.
2. The answer would not be different if the loan was evidenced by a non-interest-bearing note with a fixed maturity date. This support in itself has no tax consequences.
3. The loan could not be considered as an additional equity investment by P in S since equity is defined in the by-laws of a company. Only a legal increase of capital could create additional equity.

Subsidiary in Belgium

1. Belgium will make a separate determination of S's income.
2. The transaction will remain characterized as a loan and not as an additional equity investment.
3. Interest will be allowed as a deduction providing the interest is not abnormally high.
4. The excess of allocations by P's country over Belgium's allocation will be disallowed in Belgium, and Belgium withholding tax would apply.
5. The transaction would remain classed as a loan and not an equity investment.

C. Intangibles

Assumed Facts

P and S are manufacturers located in different countries. P performs research and development which has led to P's ownership of certain intangibles consisting of patents, trademarks and know-how. P makes available to S

exclusive right to use in S's country all of P's intangibles. P does not charge S for the use of P's intangible.

Parent in Belgium

1. Income will be allocated to P by reason of S's use of P's intangibles. P will not be treated as contributing the intangible to the capital of S.
2. Normally, the allocation will be in the form of annual royalties. Allocation of a lump sum payment would be most extraordinary. The allocation should again be computed on an arm's length basis and generally corresponds to a percentage of the turnover. The fact that S's country does not allow payments for the use of intangibles or if S's country allows payments but does not allow a deduction for tax purposes, should not be taken into consideration. Of course, political consideration could help.
3. Yes, a portion of research and development costs incurred by P could be allocated to S but this portion is normally included in royalties.
4. If P and S entered into a bona fide cost-sharing arrangement with respect to the research and development costs incurred by P, the royalties paid by S to P should be cancelled or reduced.

Subsidiary in Belgium

1. If income or expense is reallocated to P by P's country, Belgium will make a separate determination but will accept P's allocation if it is not found to be excessive.

Indeed, the normal amount of royalties is that which should be determined, in the absence of special relations, between the licensor and licensee.

The criteria to determine an acceptable royalty would reflect the cost of development, improvement and maintenance of the technology plus a normal profit margin.
2. S will be permitted a deduction for a normal amount of annual royalties. If the payment to P is in lump-sum form, the deduction to S can either be taken in the year the payment is made, or spread over the years to which it relates.
3. If S makes a payment to P of the amount allocated, and the payment is for a lump-sum payment, an annual royalty or sharing of costs, Belgium will subject that payment to a withholding tax of 20 per cent. Tax treaties generally exempt such payments from withholding tax. However, this exemption applies only to the normal amount of royalties and is subject to formalities.

The excessive amount will be taxed following domestic rules, subject to withholding tax of 5 per cent, 15 per cent or 25 per cent (sometimes 5 per cent or 15 per cent), and reintegrated to the profits of S.

Tax conventions with developing countries provide for Belgium withholding taxes to be paid even for normal royalties.

D. Services

Assumed Facts

P is a large multinational concern which wholly owns foreign subsidiary S. Both P and S are engaged in manufacturing and sales activities. P's headquarters division performs general management services for P's multi-national operations including services which directly relate to S. The services performed for S include periodic visits by P's executives to review S's operations, financial analysis of S's future requirements, engineering services in connection with S's manufacturing activities and marketing services in connection with S's sales activities. P does not charge S for such service.

Parent in Belgium

1. For the performance of services, a charge will be allocated to P. Of course, the charge will depend on the nature of the service.
2. In allocating income, P's direct and indirect costs are to be considered and increased with a profit. If it appears difficult to measure these costs, the allocation could be made using a proportional rule based on the turnover, the importance of productive facilities, etc.

Subsidiary in Belgium

1. If income is allocated to P, Belgium will scrutinize this amount to determine if it corresponds to real services correctly evaluated. The principle of arm's length remains determining.

It is advisable that S and P conclude a service agreement describing the services rendered and the method of calculating the fee (allocation).
2. Payment by S to P will not be subject to withholding tax in Belgium, even where Belgian tax authorities have denied the payment as a deduction from income.

E. Loan Guarantees and Rentals

Assumed Facts

P is a multinational company whose main business is manufacturing and selling. P plans to establish foreign sales subsidiary S located in country S. P capitalizes S with $500,000 and guarantees a loan to S of $500,000 obtained from an independent bank. Land and a warehouse which P owns in country S will be used as a site for S's operations. P plans to make this land and warehouse available to S at a fee of $1 per year for 99 years.

Parent in Belgium

1. P should normally be remunerated for the risk of guaranteeing the loan to S. However, in normal circumstances, a commission for a bank guarantee is never requested.

On the other hand, the use of P's land and warehouse should be remunerated. The amount of allocation should be determined as being the normal rent which would be obtained from third parties.

2. P will not be treated as having made an additional equity contribution but the normal allocation to be received will be added to its taxable income.

Subsidiary in Belgium

1. Again, the characterization of the transaction by P's country may not be accepted by Belgium and a separate determination could be made.

2. The normal rent which would be obtained from third parties would be allowed to S as a deduction.

3. No withholding tax would be levied when S pays service fees to P, even if they are excessive and not deductible from S's income in Belgium.

PART III. TAX TREATIES

A. The tax treaties that Belgium has entered into do not always contain a provision for a *mutual agreement* procedure concerning the allocation of income and expenses between related parties.

B. The treaty provisions do not change the principles stated in our preceding answers. When mutual agreement procedures are used for transactions between related parties, Belgium tax authorities try to apply arm's length concepts which are required under domestic law.

C. The taxpayer must seek protection under the treaty. The tax authorities will not automatically use these provisions of a tax treaty.

D. Only when a resident of Belgium estimates that he has been taxed contrary to the correct application of a treaty and double taxation results, may he lodge a claim with the Belgian competent authority.

If this authority decides that the request is justified and it can be solved by modification of the taxes to be paid in Belgium (because the taxes do not conform to the treaty), the Belgian authorities decide even without discussions with the other contracting party and adjust the Belgian tax accordingly.

However, when the decision appears to be difficult because the matter is not defined in the convention, or a mutual interpretation is to be reached, the Belgian competent authority will negotiate with the other competent authority. After this consultation it will make a decision, but only corrections for rectifying the double taxation will be made.

E. If the Belgian competent authorities seek the advice of the other contracting authorities they are not obliged to follow this opinion. Indeed, Belgium is not obliged to correct the double taxation. Of course, the advice given is most often adequately treated.

Some treaties, and in particular that with the United States, stipulate that the contracting authorities may contribute to the research of a mutual agreement on similar allocation of income or expenses between a resident of Belgium and a resident of the other contracting state. If the contracting authorities reach an agreement, Belgium will revise the taxation of its resident in conformity with this agreement.

F. A taxpayer cannot appeal a settlement made between two competent authorities.

G. Where agreement is reached as to the correct allocation, conforming adjustments and payments will be allowed without further tax consequences. Moratorium interests will be granted if taxes are refunded.

H. It is very rare that competent authorities are consulted. The length of these consultations is extensive and can last for many years.

The Belgian tax authorities have said that the treaties with Finland, France and Sweden have never been used to apply the mutual agreement rules with respect to determining the existence of a permanent establishment.

PART IV. SPECIAL SITUATIONS

A. If either of the related companies has no gross income or has a loss for the year, the normal allocation rules described earlier would not be modified or applied differently.

The tax rates of the countries involved do not attract modification.

B. The Belgian tax authorities scrutinize most closely:
- royalty agreements,
- interest charges,
- management fees, and
- technical service fees,

to determine if they correspond to real services rendered and to be sure that they are not a transfer of profit from Belgium to other countries.

Brazil

Antonio C. Q. Ferreira

PART I. GENERAL RULES

A. 1. As a general rule, tax authorities in Brazil cannot allocate income or expenses between related or non-related taxpayers.

As strict controls exist in Brazil, a Brazilian company receiving a charge due to an allocation of expenses from its parent or from a related company outside Brazil will normally not be allowed to pay it abroad.

Exceptional adjustments may be made to prevent tax evasion.

When accepted, such adjustments are made to prevent tax evasion.

The Brazilian general tax code (Law 5.172 of October 25, 1966) stating the general rules and principles for taxation, article 148, provides that when calculation of taxes is based on prices or values of assets, rights, services or contracts, the fiscal agent can estimate prices or values via an administrative process whenever the taxpayer information or documents were not reliable. The Income Tax Code states in article 174 that the fiscal agent generally will have the burden of the proof whenever a company maintains its bookkeeping according to the applicable laws.

There are also rules providing for reallocation of income in some transactions between companies and individuals considered to be related parties. Situations when reallocation occurs are as follows:

- Company disposes of assets to the related person at a value substantially below market value.
- Company acquires asset from the related person at a value notoriously above market value.
- Company loses to the related person as a result of failing to exercise its right to acquire assets, the down payment, deposit in guarantee or the amount paid to obtain an option for the purchase.
- Company transfers to the related person without payment or at a value below the market value, the preference right to subscription to securities issued by a corporation.
- Company lends money to a related person at interest rates below

market if, on date of the loan, it has accumulated profits or profit reserves.

- Company pays to a related person rent, royalties or technical assistance in amounts which are substantially in excess of market value.
- Company and the related person enter into any other transaction that is not at arm's length or whose terms and conditions are not those prevailing in the market.

The transactions above also apply to a company and its controlling shareholders. In these cases the transaction will be considered a disguised profit transaction subject to allocation of income to the individual or individuals who directly or indirectly control the company.

Finally, to prevent tax evasion, the law on the value added tax on industrialized products (IPI) specifically requires inter-dependent companies' sales or transfers to be priced at market values.

2. The adjustments generally are to prevent tax evasion.
3. In general, no special rules or safe havens exist. A company lending money to another related company should specify a minimum interest rate equal to the government inflation (ORTN index).
4. The same rules apply to transactions between domestic taxpayers and to transactions between residents and non-residents.

B. A related person for purpose of application of the abovementioned rules for reallocation of income can be an individual or a company, that is a partner, a shareholder of the company, an administrator, those person's spouses or close relatives.

For value added taxes on industrialized products (IPI) purposes, companies are interdependent when:

- one of them by itself, its partners, shareholders, spouse or sons controls the other(s);
- the same individual is a director, partner or administrator of both companies;
- one company has sold to another in the previous year more than 20 per cent (if with exclusiveness) or more than 50 per cent (without exclusiveness) of its sales volume;
- one company sells to another with any side agreement establishing any kind of participation in its sales, results, etc.

C. The principal approach in making adjustments is a transactions basis.

D. For income tax purposes, the statute of limitations is five years, beginning with the first day of the calendar year following the calendar year the return is due. In practice, this can cover up to seven years.

E. Where an adjustment is made by Brazil, no adjustments are made for purposes of subsequent income flows from the foreign company back to Brazil.

F. If the foreign country initiates an adjustment, this has no effect in Brazil. For example:

1. Consolidated returns for income tax purposes in Brazil are not allowed. A law allowing consolidated returns for domestic corporations in 1977 was revoked in 1978.
2. Profits and dividends from foreign corporations are generally exempt of tax in Brazil.
3. Brazil would not allow payments to leave the country.

G. Adjustments, if any, are made to the tax years in which the underlying transaction took place.

H. At any time before a fiscal agent assesses the taxpayer, he can pay a difference of tax due under the rules described above, providing he pays the interest and the monetary correction due. That procedure will avoid penalties. Otherwise, the taxpayer cannot initiate any adjustments.

PART II. SPECIFIC EXAMPLES

A. Sale of Goods

Assumed Facts

Assume P is a manufacturer which sells finished products to S which is located in a different country. P sells these products to S at cost. P also sells these products to unrelated parties at cost plus 10 per cent mark-on. Both S and the unrelated parties incur the same selling and promotional expense and both resell P's products at the same price per unit.

Parent in Brazil

1./2. No income will be allocated to P. Brazil has rigid exchange controls as mentioned before, and this includes imports and exports. A Central Bank department – CACEX – is in charge of the control of all importations and exportations and this control includes pricing.

This means that the export price must be approved by CACEX. This approval is generally granted on a case by case basis under a predetermined policy. An unreasonably low price may be challenged; however, it is our experience that CACEX is liberal in this area.

In any event, tax authorities will not be allowed to allocate to P any income with respect to the sale.

In the case where there are no sales to third parties or where the objective is to establish a foreign market, it will be easier to get CACEX approval of the lower price on the exportation.

Subsidiary in Brazil

1./2. No income will be allocated to S as a result of action in P's country.
3. As a general rule a payment from S to P will not be allowed by Central Bank. If allowed, it would probably be considered as a dividend subject to withholding tax and supplementary tax.

B. Loans and Advances

Assumed Facts

P and S are manufacturers located in different countries. P loans S money on open account without interest so that S can expand its operations. P is not engaged in the business of lending money.

Parent in Brazil

1./2. No income would be allocated to P by income tax authorities. Since P would be subject to Brazilian Central Bank's exchange controls it must get prior approval to remit foreign currency abroad. Our experience is that approval of any loans from Brazilian companies to foreign companies is difficult. If such a loan bears interest rates less than market, the loan would probably not be approved.
3. No, the loan cannot be considered an additional equity investment by P.

Subsidiary in Brazil

The transaction as defined can not be made in Brazil. To allow future remittances of principal from S to P the money P loans to S must be loaned under a written contract with a minimum term of eight years and a frozen period of 30 months. Zero interest rate is allowed. Loan contract must be registered with the Central Bank.

C. Intangibles

Assumed Facts

P and S are manufacturers located in different countries. P performs research and development which has led to P's ownership of certain intangibles consisting of patents, trademarks and know-how. P makes available to S exclusive right to use in S's country all of P's intangibles. P does not charge S for the use of P's intangibles.

Parent in Brazil

1.14. As mentioned earlier, no allocations of P's income or expenses would likely be made. However, if there was a bona fide cost sharing agreement that was approved by exchange authorities it would, of course, be followed for tax purposes.

Subsidiary in Brazil

No allocation to S will be allowed and S will not be allowed to make any payments to P.

D. SERVICES

Assumed Facts

P is a large multinational concern which wholly owns foreign subsidiary S. Both P and S are engaged in manufacturing and sales activities. P's headquarters division performs general management services for P's multi-national operations including services which directly relate to S. The services performed for S include periodic visits by P's executives to review S's operations, financial analysis of S's future requirements, engineering services in connection with S's manufacturing activities and marketing services in connection with S's sales activities. P does not charge S for such service.

Parent in Brazil

No allocations will be made.

Subsidiary in Brazil

No allocations to or payments by S will be allowed.

E. LOAN GUARANTEES AND RENTALS

Assumed Facts

P is a multinational company whose main business is manufacturing and selling. P plans to establish foreign sales subsidiary S located in country S. P capitalizes S with $500,000 and guarantees a loan to S of $500,000 obtained from an independent bank. Land and a warehouse which P owns in country S will be used as a site for S's operations. P plans to make this land and warehouse available to S at a fee of $1 per year for 99 years.

Parent in Brazil

1. No income will be allocated to P. As a matter of fact, any income or any loss from P's investment in S abroad will not be taxable or deductible in Brazil.

P will probably not be allowed, however, to deduct depreciation for the warehouse.

2. P could not be treated as having made an additional equity investment in S.

Subsidiary in Brazil

No allocation to S or payments by S will be permitted.

PART III. TAX TREATIES

A. Yes, most of the tax treaties into which Brazil has entered contain a provision allowing allocation of income and expenses between related parties.

B. Theoretically, these treaty provisions modify previous answers. The Brazilian general tax code (article 98) states that tax treaties revoke or modify the existing internal tax law and should be considered by future tax laws.

This, however, is only a general principle that, in practice, is not enforced by the tax authorities.

C. There are no provisions for invoking these treaty provisions.

D. There are no provisions for applying to competent authority.

E. Double taxation must result where the competent authority of one country will not enter negotiations.

F. There are no provisions to appeal a settlement made between two competent authorities.

G. No conforming adjustments or payments will be allowed without exchange authorities' approval.

H. The experience in Brazil with settling cross-broder tax disputes has obviously been poor in the light of the currency situation in Brazil. It is important to anticipate problems in advance and seek approval from exchange authorities before payments are made.

PART IV. SPECIAL SITUATIONS

A. Brazil would not apply its laws differently:
1. if either of the related companies does not have any gross income;
2. If either of the related companies has an operating loss for the year;
3. Where the tax rates of the countries involved are substantially equal;
4. Where the tax rates in the two countries are substantially different.

Canada

Ronald W. Larter/Wm. R. Lawlor

PART I. GENERAL RULES

A. 1. Arm's Length and Reasonableness Tests

The general rules regarding allocation of income and expenses in Canada are contained in section 69 of the Income Tax Act (Canada) ('the Income Tax Act'). Section 69 is generally a one-sided section (ie only the party who has *understated* his Canadian tax will be affected), designed to prevent non-residents from charging excessive amounts to Canadian taxpayers. The primary sections dealing with international transactions are as follows:

Section 69(2)

'Where a taxpayer has paid or agreed to pay to a non-resident person with whom he was not dealing at arm's length as price, rental, royalty or other payment for or for the use or reproduction of any property or as consideration for the carriage of goods or passengers, or other services, an amount greater than the amount (in this subsection referred to as the "reasonable amount") which would have been reasonable in the circumstances if the non-resident and the taxpayer had been dealing at arm's length, the reasonable amount shall, for the purpose of computing the taxpayer's income under this Part, be deemed to have been the amount that was paid or payable therefor.'

Consequently subsection 69(2) operates to decrease the price paid by a Canadian taxpayer where the actual price paid was in excess of a reasonable amount. If the Canadian taxpayer had paid an amount less than a reasonable amount, there may be no correlative adjustment provided for in the Canadian income tax system, and consequently, this is a 'one-sided' provision.

Section 69(3)

'Where a non-resident person has neither paid or agreed to pay to a taxpayer with whom he was not dealing at arm's length as price, rental, royalty or other payment for or for the use of reproduction of any property, or as consideration for the carriage of goods or passengers or for other services, the amount that would have been reasonable in the circumstances if the non-resident person and taxpayer had been dealing at arm's length, that amount shall, for the purposes of computing the taxpayer's income under this Part, be deemed to have been received or receivable by the taxpayer therefor.'

As with the previous section, this is a tax avoidance measure and does not apply if the non-resident person had paid an amount greater than their market value.

Other portions of section 69 apply similar principals in a domestic context. Other general provisions in the Canadian tax system could be relevant to the allocation of income and expense. For instance:

a. No deductions are allowed in respect of any outlays or expenses except to the extent that the outlays or expenses are reasonable in the circumstances.
b. Where a corporation resident in Canada loans money to a non-resident and the loan remains outstanding for one year or longer without interest at a reasonable rate, interest will be imputed at a prescribed rate. This rate, which was 10 per cent in the third quarter of 1985, is changed quarterly and set about one percentage point below a commercial bank's prime lending rate. However, a Canadian corporation may loan money interest-free to a controlled foreign subsidiary (where more than 50 per cent of the voting stock is owned) as long as the loan is to be used in the subsidiary's business for the purpose of gaining or producing income.
c. Where a Canadian company loans money to a non-resident shareholder or non-resident sister company at rates below the prescribed rate in (b), the shortfall is a benefit received by the non-resident which attracts Canadian withholding tax. Also, the principal of such loans can be regarded as dividends where they remain outstanding over two year-ends.
d. No deductions are allowed except to the extent that the outlay or expense was made for the purpose of producing income.
e. Benefits conferred on shareholders or other non-arm's length parties may be included in computing income of those persons, or be subject to withholding taxes where those persons reside outside Canada.

2. As referred to above, the standard generally used between non-residents and resident taxpayers is whether or not amounts are 'reasonable in the circumstances'. The Canadian tax authorities often equate reasonable in the circumstances to be the same term as fair market value. However, they acknowledge the two terms can be different, for example, when a parent is

trying to establish a new or expanded foreign market and temporarily sells to a foreign subsidiary at less than fair market value. Canada does not have any other specific rules governing transfer of goods, services, know-how, etc. However, a draft Information Circular on which Revenue Canada has been working for a couple of years, will generally have Canada follow OECD guidelines. Generally, Canada will follow the principles outlined in the 1979 OECD Committee report on fiscal affairs – 'Transfer Pricing and Multinational Enterprises'. Consequently, any particular transaction will generally be viewed on its own merits as if the two parties were dealing with each other at arm's length. In determining an arm's length price, the following methods outlined in the OECD report are considered to be appropriate to Canada.

Comparable Uncontrolled Price Method

Canadian tax authorities will generally look to the corporation's dealings with unrelated parties in order to determine the price at which comparable goods, services, etc, are transferred. In cases where there are no dealings with unrelated parties, recourse will then generally be had to transactions between third parties for comparable goods, services, etc. It is often difficult to find comparable uncontrolled prices, for one would have to find transactions with unrelated parties that did not differ significantly, from the related party transaction under review, in terms of nature of product, same or similar market, credit terms, and many other factors which can affect price.

Resale Price Method

If it is too difficult to determine relevant prices under the comparable uncontrolled price method, then resort is generally had to the resale price method or the cost plus method described below. Generally speaking, the resale price method will begin with a price at which a product which has been purchased from a related seller is resold to an independent third party. The unrelated third party selling price is then reduced by an appropriate mark-up representing a reasonable amount to cover costs and a reasonable profit to the vendor. The profit mark-up will be determined utilizing various factors and its magnitude generally determined from the value of functions and risks undertaken by the person reselling the product. The resale price method is generally utilized when the vendor of the product to the third party provides a minimal amount of work with respect to the product being sold, ie the resale price method is more useful in a wholesale operation than a situation whereby raw material is purchased and substantial manufacturing or other operations are performed with respect to the product being sold.

Cost Plus Method

This method is generally useful in cases where the purchaser will add substantial value to the goods before reselling them. In applying the cost plus method, the seller of the product (to the third party) will generally determine his cost by looking to his related supplier's cost and adding thereto a reasonable mark-up. In turn, the related supplier will review all of his costs and determine his selling price by adding to all his costs a reasonable profit margin. The magnitude of the profit margin will generally be determined by looking at the normal profit margin each obtains in similar circumstances when dealing with arm's length parties. Failing that, they may look at norms in relevant industries.

In determining appropriate charges for services, patents, know-how etc, generally speaking the Canadian tax authorities will attempt to find an arm's length price. The factors which will govern this arm's length price will vary greatly with the circumstances involved.

Any Other Reasonable Method

Where none of the previous methods seem clearly applicable, Canada will accept any other reasonable allocation of profit on the transaction given the relative importance of the functions performed by each party to the transaction.

3. Other than the general arm's length test there are no safe haven rules provided for under the Canadian tax sytem. There is, however, the prescribed rate referred to earlier, used for the imputation of interest on certain loans and the measuring of benefits subject to Canadian withholding on certain loans.
4. There are situations where different rules will apply between domestic taxpayers vs transactions between residents and non-residents. For instance:

   Subsection 69(2) and 69(3) referred to above will not apply with respect to domestic taxpayers. A substantially similar rule, subsection 69(1), applies to domestic taxpayers, but 69(1) seems to apply only where a taxpayer has either acquired or disposed of any property and, consequently, may not have applications to services, rentals, royalties, etc. Where a non-resident is involved in the transaction, these fair market value rules clearly apply also to services, rentals, royalties, etc.

   Other rules in the Income Tax Act may, however, apply. For instance, in computing Canadian income, no deductions will be allowed unless amounts are reasonable in the circumstances or, again, no deductions may be allowed except to the extent that the outlay or expense was made for the purpose of gaining or producing income. These rules do have limitations, however. For instance, where services are provided to a related domestic taxpayer there is no requirement to charge for services as long as the company providing the services can still maintain that all of its expenses are reasonable and have been incurred for the purpose of gaining or producing its income. This may be the case where, for instance, outlays or expenditures would be incurred anyhow, regardless of whether or not a related party also benefited (eg advertising).

Where loans are made between related taxpayers there is no similar provision to provide for imputation of interest income as with non-residents. There is, however, the limiting factor that any interest cost associated with interest-free loans to other taxpayers would not be deductible by the lender since the lender would have borrowed money and incurred interest charges for a non-income producing purpose.

It should also be noted that section 69(1), which primarily deals with domestic taxpayers, states that property shall have been acquired or disposed of at fair market value whereas the similar provisions dealing with non-residents only provide that amounts will have to be 'reasonable in the circumstances'. There may be differences between fair market value and reasonable in the circumstances; however, Canadian tax authorities generally interpret the two provisions as being the same.

Again, the provision dealing with non-arm's length taxpayers is a one-sided approach and does not statutorily provide for a correlative adjustment to the other non-arm's length party. As a general rule however, the Canadian tax authorities will make correlative adjustments between the related parties. There may also be some authority for making a correlative adjustment (see *Allfine Bowlerama Limited* v. *MNR* – 72 DTC 1502). In this case, it was stated that there is a general presumption in law against taxing the same income dollars twice and double taxation could only exist where it is equitable and the language of the taxing statute is clear and unequivocable.

B. Non-Arm's Length Persons

The Canadian anti-avoidance rules generally apply to persons who do not deal with each other at arm's length. Whether two or more parties are dealing with each other at arm's length is primarily a question of fact. In determining whether a transaction is at arm's length, regard will be had to

a. the existence of a common mind which directs the bargaining for both parties to a transaction,
b. whether parties to a transaction act in concert without having separate interests, and
c. whether there is de facto common control which affects the bargaining positions of the parties.

One factor which is of prime importance in determining arm's length is whether or not the parties have separate economic interests which would lead to hard bargaining between the parties in the particular transaction.

In addition to questions of fact, 'related persons' are deemed not to deal with each other at arm's length for Canadian tax purposes. Related persons are generally defined as:

a. individuals connected by blood relationships, marriage or adoption
b. a corporation and a person who controls the corporation, or a person who is a member of a related group which controls the corporation;
c. any two corporations,
    i. if they are controlled by the same person or group of persons
    ii. if each of the corporations is controlled by one person and the person who controls one of the corporations is related to the person who controls the other
    iii. if one of the corporations is controlled by one person and that person is related to any member of a related group which controls the other corporation
    iv. if one of the corporations is controlled by one person and that person is related to each member of an unrelated group that controls the other corporation
    v. if any member of a related group that controls one of the corporations is related to each member of an unrelated group that controls the other
    vi. if each member of an unrelated group that controls one of the corporations is related to at least one member of an unrelated group that controls the other corporation.

Other rules are provided which may, in some cases, expand the meaning of related persons. For instance, a person who has a right under a contract in equity or otherwise, either immediately or in the future and either absolutely or contingently, to acquire shares in a corporation, or to control the voting rights of shares in a corporation, shall be deemed to be in the same position as if he owned the shares. This provision generally applies in the case of options to acquire shares. The meaning of control for Canadian tax purposes generally means the ownership of enough shares which carry voting rights to elect the majority of the board of directors. In general terms, this means owning more than 50 per cent of voting rights of the corporation.

C. Transaction Basis

In Canada, the principal approach in making adjustments between related parties or parties who do not deal with each other at arm's length is on a transaction basis rather than a net income basis.

D. Statute of Limitations

Generally speaking, the Canadian statute of limitation is three years from the date of an original notice of assessment in respect of a particular taxation year. The three year period was four years prior to 1983. The Income Tax Act provides for making an original assessment which generally is done on an annual basis about midway through the year following the transaction year. The statute of limitation will run for three years from the assessment date. Adjustments can only be made beyond that date by the Canadian tax authorities (not the taxpayer) and only where –

a. the taxpayer has made any misrepresentation attributable to neglect, carelessness or wilful default, or has committed any fraud in filing or in supplying any information, or
b. where the taxpayer has filed a waiver within the three-year limitation period referred to above in respect of any item for that year, and such waiver has not been revoked. In other words, a taxpayer can waive his three-year limitation with respect to any item of income or deduction of a year. This would generally be useful in providing beneficial correlative adjustments beyond the three year limitation. The Canadian taxpayer might be anticipating such adjustments perhaps as a result of reassessments in another country. Taxpayers may retract a waiver upon giving tax authorities six months' notice, or
c. where a loss is suffered in any of the three succeeding tax years, part of the loss can be carried back to the particular year. Generally, business losses can be carried back three years and forward seven years.

E. Correlative Adjustments

As referred to above, Canada is not statutorily bound in its Income Tax Act to make correlative adjustments with respect to the income of Canadian taxpayers. Sections 69(2) and 69(3) are one-sided and do not require an offsetting adjustment where a Canadian taxpayer pays less than fair market value for goods, services, or other amounts. There are, however, a number of Court decisions which may have a bearing on Canada's acceptance of correlative adjustments (see cases of Lily Cups and Aluminum Company of Canada referred to below. In addition, the case of Allfine Bowlerama referred to above may be of some assistance.).

Correlative adjustments are also contemplated (although not insisted upon) in virtually all of Canada's Income Tax Treaties where, because of a particular adjustment in a foreign country, a lack of any correlative adjustment would lead to double taxation. In Canada, new treaties generally follow the provisions contained in the OECD Draft Tax Convention with respect to competent authority provisions. Revenue Canada, however, has modified its competent authority procedures with respect to interest. Revenue Canada states that it will not allow to a Canadian corporation a deduction in respect of interest on interest-free loans or advances made to it, notwithstanding that the non-arm's length lender may have interest imputed with the result that double taxation could result. This procedure is effective for taxation years beginning on or after September 1st, 1974. In addition, a more recent Revenue Canada position would negate any competent authority provisions between Canada and the United States in respect of the disallowance of interest arising as a result of either countries' application of its 'thin capitalization' rules.

The Canadian tax authorities will generally require amounts which are allocated to Canada from abroad to be deducted only in the years to which they relate, if they allow them at all. Resort will most often have to be made to the competent authority provisions of the particular tax treaty with the foreign country. Without a tax treaty, it is likely that Revenue Canada would take the position that the allocable amounts are not deductible as they do not relate to the current year and the relevant year may be statute barred, or that they are not deductible because there was no legal obligation to pay the expense.

A position might be taken, however, that a charge from a related company is deductible in the year that the charge was incurred. This position has been sustained in two Canadian tax decisions – *Aluminum Company of Canada Ltd and Lily Cups Ltd* v. *MNR*. In both of these cases, due to action of foreign authorities, amounts were charged to the Canadian operation. For instance, in the Lily Cups Ltd decision, a United States parent charged its Canadian subsidiary with a management fee in one year which related to services provided in that year and prior years. It was upheld that the charge was properly deductible in the year that the parent actually charged the amount, even though the services related to previous years. It would appear that this decision was based upon a number of factors which included: the fact that the parent company always had a right and never gave up its right, to charge for services which were provided; the services were actually rendered; the Canadian corporation obtained an identifiable benefit from such services and, consequently, the expenditure was incurred to earn its income. In other words, if it could be sustained that an arm's length party, from a practical business standpoint, would accept the charge then perhaps it would be deductible in the year charged, even though the services were provided in prior years.

Although the facts are somewhat different in the case of the *Aluminum Company of Canada Ltd* v. *The Queen*, it was held that the amount in question was properly deductible since it related to an income earning process and the payment was made as a matter of commercial morality. In other words, the payment was made from a practical business point of view to preserve the company's image as a good corporate citizen and because the company desired a continuance of friendly relations with a foreign country. Again, it would appear that, if an arm's length party would have accepted such a charge as a matter of business reality, then perhaps it would be deductible in the year incurred.

F. Adjustments in Foreign Countries

1. The Canadian tax system does not allow for filing of income tax returns on a consolidated basis and, consequently, an adjustment to a company located outside of the country would not have an immediate impact on the

income or loss of the Canadian taxpayer, barring any allowance of any correlative adjustments as referred to above.

2. As a general rule, dividends from a Canadian company's foreign affiliate (generally a foreign company where the Canadian company has a 10 per cent or more equity interest) are unaffected by adjustments made to that non-resident company. For instance, dividends received by a Canadian corporation from a foreign affiliate which carries on an *active business* in a country with which Canada has a *tax treaty* would generally be exempt from tax in Canada as long as the dividend is paid from the active business income of that foreign corporation. In addition, there would be no allowance of any foreign tax credits with respect to that exempt dividend income. Therefore, if the foreign tax authorities increase or decrease the foreign company's income, the only effect would be on the cash available to pay a dividend to the Canadian corporation.

   Where a dividend is received from a foreign affiliate which carries on an active business in a *non-treaty country*, then Canada would only tax the resultant dividend to the extent that the foreign tax is less than the applicable Canadian tax. As long as the foreign country's effective tax rate is equal to or greater than Canada's, then the resultant dividend when received by Canada will generally not be subject to taxation.

3. In Canada the payment of allocated amounts is generally not required. However, where non-residents have charged the Canadian operation with amounts in excess of an arm's length price, Canada will impose a withholding tax on the excess as an 'appropriation of property' or dividend unless the non-resident agrees to pay the difference to the Canadian taxpayer.

G. Adjustments Made on Transaction Year Normally

As a general rule, if correlative adjustments are allowed as a matter of administrative practice, Canada adopts the position that the adjustment may be made to the tax year in which the underlying transactions took place. This would also be true where adjustments are made under the competent authority provisions of the various income tax treaties. This will have significance in cases where Canada's statute of limitations has expired. For instance, Canada takes the position that it will not allow any adjustments either under its own administrative practices or under provisions of a tax treaty if such adjustments cannot be made within its three-year statute of limitations. Canada takes the position that it is barred by the statute from making any adjustment to the particular year, unless misrepresentation or fraud exists or the taxpayer has filed a waiver in respect of that year as referred to above. None of Canada's tax treaties, except the new treaty with the US, give the Canadian tax authorities any directive or permission to ignore the time limitations in the Canadian Income Tax Act. There may, however, be instances where the underlying adjustment could take place in the year that a charge is made by the non-resident corporation. For instance, if the particular circumstances fit within the principles outlined above in the case of *Lily Cups* v. *The Queen*, then a charge might be deductible.

H. How Adjustments Initiated

Depending upon the specific circumstances, the Canadian tax authorities will listen to any request by the particular taxpayer to make a correlative adjustment. The tax authorities are not bound to do so and, consequently, whether or not they adhere to such a taxpayer's request depends upon the circumstances. It has been the practice of Revenue Canada to allow a correlative adjustment in certain cases involving an allocation of administrative expenses or services between related parties which would be necessary to correctly reflect the income of the Canadian taxpayer. Generally, however, these cases have involved situations where the competent authority provisions of the particular tax convention would otherwise come into play to generally allow the correlative adjustment.

The Canadian tax authorities are not bound to accept a correlative adjustment when a change is initiated in another country. In cases where the statute of limitations is about to expire and there is a danger of adjustments being initiated in a foreign country, it would be prudent to file a waiver under the Canadian tax system to keep the particular year open to allow for offsetting adjustments under the competent authority provisions.

PART II. SPECIFIC EXAMPLES

A. Sale of Goods

Assumed Facts

Assume P is a manufacturer which sells finished products to S which is located in a different country. P sells these products to S at cost. P also sells these products to unrelated parties at cost plus 10 per cent mark-on. Both S and the unrelated parties incur the same selling and promotional expense and both resell P's products at the same price per unit.

Parent in Canada

1. Under subsection 69(3), it is likely that income will be allocated to P with respect to its sales to S. Under the comparable uncontrolled price method as referred to above, it would appear that S has paid an amount less than the amount which would have been reasonable in the circumstances, since P makes sales to arm's length parties at cost plus a 10 per cent mark-up.

2. As above, the factors that would be considered would be the sale of like goods in uncontrolled circumstances. Generally speaking, for the price of goods to be comparable it would be necessary to look at prices of goods sold on markets which are economically comparable. In this case, S resells at the same price to outsiders as do P's unrelated customers and both S and P's unrelated customers incur the same selling and promotional expenses. Consequently, it should be held that these are truly comparable goods sold in uncontrolled market situations.
3. If there were no sales to independent third parties, then regard may be had to other factors to determine what a fair price would be. Regard would be had to the resale price method or cost plus method to determine a reasonable profit in the particular situation.

If S incurred greater selling or promotional expenses or resold products at lower prices so as to establish a market, Revenue Canada would generally resist any price which is lower than the cost plus 10 per cent mark-up referred to above. However, if it could be asserted that an arm's length party would also have sold it at a lower price in similar circumstances, ie to penetrate the market, then Revenue Canada would generally accept the lower prices. In establishing a reasonable price if there were no sales to independent parties etc., there may be some justification to lower the price from the cost plus 10 per cent mark-on but regard would have to be had to the particular set of circumstances.

Subsidiary in Canada

1. The Canadian tax authorities would not be bound by any provisions of the Income Tax Act to accept the charge from P. Regard would generally have to be had to the competent authority provisions of the tax convention, in which case Canada would make an independent determination of an arm's length price.
2. As referred to above, generally, recourse would have to be had to the competent authority provisions of the double taxation convention. Depending on the circumstances, as a matter of administrative practice the Canadian tax authorities may allow the deduction from S's taxable income. In addition, in light of the decisions of *Lily Cups* v. *MNR* and *Aluminum Company of Canada* v. *The Queen*, there is at least limited legal support for a reasonable charge being acceptable in the Canadian subsidiary.
3. If the Canadian tax authorities have allowed the foreign adjustment as a bona fide deduction in Canada under the competent authority provisions, as a matter of administrative practice or otherwise, then it is unlikely that the payment of the allocated amount will be subject to withholding tax. However, if no such correlative adjustment were allowed in Canada any payment of the allocated amount would be treated as an appropriation (dividend) subject to withholding tax.

B. Loans and Advances

Assumed Facts

P and S are manufacturers located in different countries. P loans to S money on open account without interest so that S can expand its operations. P is not engaged in the business of lending money.

Parent in Canada

1. Since S is a subsidiary controlled corporation (where P owns more than 50 per cent of all of its voting shares) and since S will be utilizing the borrowed money in its business, interest will not be imputed to P.
2. The answer would not be different if the loan was evidenced by a non-interest bearing note with a fixed maturity date.
3. Assuming that the loan is legally a loan, then it would not be regarded as an additional equity investment by P in S. When the loan is repaid it would be regarded as a tax-free return of capital for Canadian tax purposes.

Subsidiary in Canada

1. The characterization of the transaction by the foreign parent's country will not have a bearing on the Canadian characterization of the transaction.
2. For Canadian tax purposes, assuming it is legally a loan, the amount will not be treated as additional equity investment whether or not there was any specific interest charge, note in existence, or fixed maturity date.
3. In Canada, there would be no specific allocation of interest since Canada is not paying an amount in excess of a reasonable amount for the funds. If the foreign parent allocates interest to Canada, as a matter of administrative practice (and under its practice with respect to the competent authority provisions of the treaties), Canada would not allow a deduction for any allocated interest. To deduct interest in Canada there must be a binding, legal, prospective agreement to pay the interest.
4. Since Canada would not allow any deduction in respect of interest allocated by P in respect of the loan there would be no tax deduction in Canada. In addition, Canada would in all likelihood assess withholding tax in respect of any amount paid to P in respect of the adjustment initiated in the foreign country.
5. As stated above, it is unlikely that Canada would treat the loan as additional equity investment unless the circumstances were such that there was not legally a debtor/creditor relationship between the parties. If, however, the transaction was characterized as a contribution to capital (ie gift to Canadian subsidiary without it issuing more shares to P) then any amount repaid in respect of the contribution would be subject to withholding tax as a dividend distribution.

Thin Capitalization

In Canada if P had loaned money to S with interest (whether at a rate greater or lower than fair market value) regard would have to be had to Canada's 'thin capitalization' rules. Generally speaking, Canada would disallow a portion of the subsidiary's interest expense if the greatest amount (during the year in question) of S's *interest bearing* debts to its parent, or other related non-resident shareholders, exceeded three times the 'equity' of S. Generally speaking, the equity would be equal to the retained earnings of S at the commencement of the year, its contributed surplus at the commencement of the year (to the extent that it was contributed by P or other related non-resident shareholders) and the paid up capital (share capital) of subsidiary S but only that portion attributable to shares owned currently by P or other related non-resident shareholders. In determining whether a company is thinly capitalized, only the interest bearing debt outstanding to P would be taken into consideration. Regard would not be had to any non-interest bearing debt nor to any debts owing to arm's length parties. Revenue Canada will not entertain any competent authority interest allocations with respect to disallowances of interest under its thin capitalization rules with respect to the United States.

C. Intangibles

Assumed Facts

P and S are manufacturers located in different countries. P performs research and development which has led to P's ownership of certain intangibles consisting of patents, trademarks and know-how. P makes available to S exclusive right to use in S's country all of P's intangibles. P does not charge S for the use of P's intangibles.

Parent in Canada

1. Canada will require an allocation of income to P. Prior to amendments on May 9, 1985, it was quite arguable that no allocation of income to P was required if P was allowing S to use the patents, etc., free of charge. Subsection 69(3) did not previously impute income to P unless S had agreed to pay some amount, and that amount was unreasonably low. P would not be regarded as contributing the intangibles to the capital of S.

2. The income imputed to P would normally be a reasonable periodic royalty. However, if P had granted to S a perpetual right to use the intangibles in S's country, then Revenue Canada may argue that P has disposed of part of its patent, etc., and deem P to have received a reasonable price therefor. P would be taxed on its gain from the partial disposition.

It would not make any difference if S's country does not allow payments for the use of intangibles or if S's country allows payments but does not allow a deduction for tax purposes. Revenue Canada may also attempt to impute an annual benefit to the non-resident if no charge was made by P. This benefit would be subject to withholding tax.

3. Depending upon the circumstances, it may not be possible to allocate a portion of the research and development costs incurred by P to S. If the R & D costs were incurred for the purpose of gaining or producing P's income and would be incurred whether or not S used the intangibles then no part of such R & D costs would have to be allocated to S. Where S had undertaken to bear some costs, Canada could clearly disallow some costs to P.

4. If P and S entered into a *bona fide* cost sharing arrangement with respect to the research and development costs which resulted in S's exclusive use of the intangibles then it would appear that no basis would be available for Canada's right to attribute any transfer of property to S or require any income allocation, since P and S would have entered into an arm's length cost sharing arrangement. The contract should then govern.

Subsidiary in Canada

1. The Canadian tax authorities will not accept an allocation from P's country. As stated above, the acceptance of an allocation may be made as a matter of administrative practice by the Revenue authorities of Canada where they feel that the charge is reasonable in the circumstances. However, it is likely that as a matter of course they would not accept the charge but resort would have to be had by S or P to the competent authority provisions provided for under a double taxation agreement with Canada. If no such agreement exists, then there is no assurance that Canada will accept the allocation from P's country. Even if an allocation were to be accepted Canada would make a separate determination of the magnitude of the amount. Regard would also have to be had to the case of Lily Cups and the Aluminium Company of Canada as referred to above.

2. If the adjustment in P was accepted as a charge in Canada (see above) then its deductibility depends upon the nature of the charge. A charge for current use whether lump sum or otherwise is deductible. A charge for use over a specified number of years is deductible over that period. However, if the charge was for the acquisition of the property, then it would not be currently deductible. All or, in some cases, half the cost of this property would be depreciable over time.

3. It is likely that, if Canada accepts the royalty charge, they would require a withholding tax in respect of the amount so charged unless the payment was for the outright purchase of rights to use the patent, trademark, etc.

D. Services

Assumed Facts

P is a large multinational concern which wholly owns foreign subsidiary S. Both P and S are engaged in manufacturing and sales activities. P's headquarters division performs general management services for P's multi-national operations including services which directly relate to S. The services performed for S include period visits by P's executives to review S's operations, financial analysis of S's future requirements, engineering services in connection with S's manufacturing activities and marketing services in connection with S's sales activities. P does not charge S for such service.

Parent in Canada

1. After the May 9, 1985 amendments, Canada will clearly require a reasonable allocation of income to P. Previously, Canada could make no allocation where the services were provided free of charge. However, Canada always could disallow some of the costs to P if they did not relate to earning P's own income.

Where P incurs mere stewardship expenses relating to simply monitoring or protecting its investment in S, then such costs would not be disallowed to P and no income would be imputed to P. Where P incurs expenses which are of direct benefit to S, then P will be deemed to have received a reasonable price for such services.

2. While the reasonable price imputed to P should include a modest profit margin, not just cost recovery, we suspect that Canadian tax authorities will be happy to get cost recovery in most cases.

Subsidiary in Canada

1. As in the previous case with intangibles and other allocations, Canada would not be bound to accept the foreign adjustment and regard would have to be had to the competent authority provisions provided for under the various tax treaties. The tax authorities may, however, accept a charge based on the Lily Cups and Aluminum Company of Canada cases. However, resistance to any allocation would be expected.

2. Payment by S to P would not ordinarily be subject to withholding tax in Canada if the amounts were merely a recovery of P's cost incurred for the benefit of S. To the extent that any of the charges related to a profit factor by P, then this amount would normally be subject to withholding tax.

Pursuant to the new Canada–United States tax treaty, management fees are regarded as business profits. Thus, reasonable management fees earned by a US parent from a Canadian subsidiary will no longer be subject to Canadian profits tax (unless the US parent has a permanent establishment in Canada) and would not be subject to Canadian withholding tax either, even if the fee included a reasonable profit element. Care must be taken to ensure the fee is not really a royalty, which would attract a 10 per cent Canadian withholding tax.

E. Loan Guarantees and Rentals

Assumed Facts

P is a multinational company whose main business is manufacturing and selling. P plans to establish foreign sales subsidiary S in country S. P capitalizes S with $500,000 and guarantees a loan to S of $500,000 obtained from an independent bank. Land and a warehouse which P owns in country S will be used as a site for S's operations. P plans to make this land and warehouse available to S at a fee of $1 per year for 99 years.

Parent in Canada

1. It is unlikely that Canada could allocate any amount in respect of P's guarantee of the loan to S. However, Canada could allocate a reasonable rental to P for S's use of P's land and warehouse. The amount of the rental would be based upon the arm's length rental fee.
2. Canada would not treat the transactions as additional equity investment in S.

Subsidiary in Canada

1. As in the other cases above, it is unlikely that Canada would accept the characterization of the transaction by P's country but would make a separate determination and would resist any charge to the Canadian subsidiary by P's revenue authorities. Regard would have to be had to the competent authority provisions under the applicable tax treaties.
2. Canadian tax authorities would not be likely to accept an adjustment in S with respect to guarantee fees, as that would be regarded as interest which requires a prospective legal obligation to be deductible. They may, however, accept an annual rental charge or depreciation on the fair market value of the buildings depending on the circumstances.
3. If income were to be allocated to P and the Canadian tax authorities would accept a charge, subsequent payment of the allocated amounts would be subject to a withholding tax absent any treaty provisions to the contrary. If Canadian tax authorities did not accept the charge, a withholding tax would clearly apply as in the case of a dividend.

PART III. TAX TREATIES

A. Most tax treaties that Canada has entered into contain a mutual agreement procedure.

B. As referred to above, the allocation of income/expense by a non-resident country would generally only be deductible or properly allocable to Canada under the competent authority provisions contained in the various tax conventions. In ascertaining the magnitude of the settlements concerning the allocations of income and expenses, the Canadian tax authorities will apply an arm's length approach to the quantum of deductions and to their allocability. As referred to above Canada has taken a stance with respect to some of its older conventions (not *requiring* a mutual agreement) disallowing allocations of interest expense charged by foreign countries to Canadian enterprises.

C. To invoke the competent authority provisions, Canada follows the 1977 OECD model convention and consequently requires the resident person to make application to the contracting state of which he is a resident. The tax authorities will not automatically invoke this provision.

D. Most of Canada's competent authority provisions require that the taxpayer submit his application for competent authority consideration in writing. In cases where no specific mention is made in the tax convention the Canadian tax authorities generally require a letter to be sent to the competent authorities. Canada, in most of its treaties, must simply endeavour to resolve the case by mutual agreement with the competent authority of the other state. It would appear that, under the various tax treaties which Canada has entered into (with few exceptions), the competent authorities are not duty bound to come to an agreement but rather are duty bound to endeavour to resolve the situation.

E. As above, if there is a failure to reach an agreement between the competent authorities of the two treaty countries, regard would have to be had to domestic law. If there are no provisions for alleviation, then double taxation would result.

F. A taxpayer cannot appeal a settlement made between the two competent authorities.

G. Where agreement is reached as to the correct allocation, confirming adjustments and payments will be allowed with the exception that withholding taxes may be eligible in respect of items otherwise subject to such taxes.

H. Canada's experience has been such that, as a general rule, competent authority provisions have been successful and agreement has ordinarily been reached. The length of competent authority negotiations depend upon the particular circumstances but, fair to say, it is a rather lengthy procedure which could extend beyond one year.

PART IV. SPECIAL SITUATIONS

A. The normal allocation rules described earlier are not modified or applied differently in any of the following situations –

1. If either of the related companies does not have any gross income;
2. If either of the related companies has an operating loss for the year;
3. Where the tax rates of the countries involved are substantially equal;
4. Where the tax rate of the country to which the income is to be allocated is substantially lower than the rate of tax in the country where the income was originally reported.

B. The Canadian tax authorities have undertaken a number of special audit programmes in the past dealing with special industries in order to ferret out any allocation problems between Canadian taxpayers and non-residents. These are undertaken normally along the lines of industry wide audits where Revenue Canada has reason to believe that reallocations could be made. In addition, Canada has entered into a programme with the United States for a joint audit approach in respect of large multinational organizations and is in the process of entering into similar joint audit approaches with other countries.

It is fair to say that particular attention is made by Canadian tax authorities where non-residents are involved in lower or 'tax haven' countries. In those situations, the Canadian tax authorities will pay special attention to the transactions between the related parties.

PART V. OTHER CONSIDERATIONS

Canadian tax authorities are becoming much more sophisticated and effective in the area of related-party, cross-border transactions. Several of the larger Canadian tax offices have staff specializing in this area and a few new audit techniques have also increased their effectiveness. Industry-wide audit approaches see them review all major players in an industry so that they can collect good comparable data to use against other taxpayers. Their large-file audit programme now sees them comprehensively review the transfer pricing, etc., policies of an entire organization, rather than trying to look only at one company or one division in a related group. Doing simultaneous audits, with U.S. and other foreign tax authorities, on the same organization is making it much easier for Canadian authorities to get answers to thorny questions and not run the risk of the organization giving conflicting answers to different tax authorities. It is hoped that Canadian tax authorities will soon spell out some comprehensive guidelines for acceptable practice in this area.

Denmark

Esther Schmith/Peter Nordahl

PART I. GENERAL RULES

A. In general, both income and expenses should be allocated on an arm's length basis. Expenses incurred in generating income are, generally, tax allowable costs. As a corollary, normally only the expenses incurred in generating a given source of income are allowed against that income.

1. The allocation should be made so as to reflect the related income and expenditure, not just to counter tax avoidance.
2. The general criteria is that the allocation should be made on an arm's length basis.
3. No safe havens are provided for.
4. In general, it makes no difference whether or not one company is non-resident. However, S.12. of the Company Taxes Act provides that where transactions between a Danish subsidiary and its foreign parent are not on an arm's length basis, the tax authorities may apply arm's length criteria when arriving at taxable income.

B. The question of when the above adjustments can be made has not been fully tested in our courts. Generally, a group relationship exists either by virtue of the size of shareholding or by the exercise of effective influence or control.

C. Principally a transactions basis is used to make adjustments but other criteria can be used as a rule of thumb approximation.

D. Adjustments to income are allowed for 5 years after the year of assessment. However, there could be difficulties where this requires adjustment to the statutory accounts, even though in Denmark there is no legal requirement for unity between legal and fiscal accounts. For example, it may prove difficult to claim additional management fees or interest charges which a foreign parent company feels the Danish subsidiary should absorb, if the Danish company did not book those expenses in its statutory accounts for the financial year in question.

E. If Denmark increases the taxable income of a Danish parent company, this company is allowed to receive a payment to give effect to this adjustment without further Danish tax on the receipt. Where no payments are made, however, Denmark would make no adjustment to normal tax on, say, future dividends from the foreign subsidiary.

F. 1. Where a consolidated taxation basis is applied, the taxable income of the group should be calculated according to Danish tax rules without regard to adjustments made by other fiscal authorities.
2. There is no effect on dividends but credit for foreign taxes is allowed where joint taxation principles (F.1) are being applied, thereby compensating for the effect of non-correlative adjustments.
3. There are no requirements for the payment of reallocated amounts but foreign exchange regulations may after that in certain circumstances.

A Danish parent company can elect, but is never forced, to be taxed on a consolidated basis with its foreign subsidiaries. Once the Danish parent company ceases to consolidate the results of a particular subsidiary, it normally cannot start again. To be eligible for consolidation, the Danish parent (or other corporations eligible for consolidation therewith) must own 100 per cent of the shares of the foreign subsidiary or at least own the maximum shares permitted by that foreign country. Where the consolidation approach is chosen, Denmark would grant credit for the foreign taxes paid and would ensure that subsequent dividends from consolidated profits do not bear tax in Denmark a second time.

G. Adjustments are made in the year of the underlying transactions.

H. Normally the Danish taxpayer can only request an adjustment to a cross-border transaction in response to an adjustment made by foreign tax authorities. There are no special procedures when applying for adjustments and the points raised in D above need to be considered.

PART II. SPECIFIC EXAMPLES

A. Sale of Goods

Assumed Facts

Assume P is a manufacturer which sells finished products to S which is located in a different country. P sells these products to S at cost. P also sells these products to unrelated parties at cost plus 10 per cent mark-on. Both S and the unrelated parties incur the same selling and promotional expense and both resell P's products at the same price per unit.

Parent in Denmark

1. Yes, an allocation of income to P would be made.
2. The allocation would be made according to the 'volume of trade'. The 10 per cent markup on sales to third parties may be used as a guide to arrive at a transfer price to S, but if a lower percentage would still see P make a profit on sales to S, then a lower percentage might be used.
3. The allocation of income would be made even though there are no comparable third party sales. Comparability merely provides a measure of the margin. Allowance could be made in certain circumstances where S undertook to bear promotional costs as it could if these costs arose through trade with third parties.

Subsidiary in Denmark

1. For fiscal purposes no adjustment to P's income will be reflected in S's income taxable in Denmark unless it is passed through the books of account, whereupon it will be assessed according to Danish fiscal rules without particular regard to overseas fiscal rules.
2. S can only deduct allocations made in Denmark complying with Danish fiscal rules. See 1 above. Retroactive adjustments would be accepted if proper documentation is presented and the adjustment arises from recalculation of allocation rates or actual expenditures.

Retroactive adjustments would not be accepted if they represent charges which the subsidiary has no legal commitment to pay.
3. If not adjusted through the books the amount would become a dividend subject to withholding tax.

B. Loans and Advances

Assumed Facts

P and S are manufacturers located in different countries. P loans S money on open account without interest so that S can expand its operations. P is not engaged in the business of lending money.

Parent in Denmark

1. It is possible to make interest-free loans without imputed interest provided the transaction is necessary for the advancement of the subsidiary. However, arbitrating of money through a subsidiary could give rise to an imputation of income at market rates.
2. The existence of a non-interest-bearing note would not change the results.

3. The loan would not be regarded by Denmark as an equity investment by P in S.

Subsidiary in Denmark

1./2./3./5. Imputed income of overseas parent companies are not allowable costs in Denmark but the laws of the country governing the contract can affect the interpretation of the terms of the contract for taxation and exchange control purposes. However, the terms of the contract notwithstanding, nothing can change a loan to a Danish subsidiary into equity in that company unless the rules for increasing capital in Denmark are complied with.
4. Generally, normal Danish commercial criteria will prevail. It is possible to conceive of a subsidiary paying excessive interest rates consistent with those in the country of residence of its parent. However, if these rates significantly exceeded Danish commercial rates there is a risk that the excess interest would be deemed a dividend and so disallowed against income and subjected to withholding tax.

C. Intangibles

Assumed Facts

P and S are manufacturers located in different countries. P performs research and development which has led to P's ownership of certain intangibles consisting of patents, trademarks and know-how. P makes available to S exclusive right to use in S's country all of P's intangibles. P does not charge S for the use of P's intangible.

Parent in Denmark

1. In accordance with the arm's length concept, income must be allocated to P for S's exclusive rights to use the intangibles.
2. Allocation can be in the form of either annual royalties or a lump sum payment. The allocation will be required regardless of whether country S allows the deduction or permits the payment.
3. A portion of P's current R & D costs would normally be allocated to S. If P made no charge to S, then a portion of the costs would simply be non-deductible to P.
4. P could allocate R & D costs to S based on a bona fide cost-sharing arrangement and the tax authorities would normally insist that such a cost-sharing agreement be followed.

Subsidiary in Denmark

1. Fiscal allocations made overseas would not necessarily be fiscally enforceable against subsidiaries resident in Denmark. An independent determination would be made in Denmark.
2. Without any actual charge to S no deduction would be allowed in Denmark but, where a charge between the two companies is made, the cost would be dealt with for tax purposes in the form in which it was incurred. An annual royalty charge would be deductible. A lump sum charge is depreciated for tax purposes at a 10 per cent per annum straight line rate or over the number of years in question.

The same rules apply to purchase of patents, trademarks, etc.
3. No requirement of withholding tax exists for dividends. If other types of payments are considered to be hidden dividend distributions, these amounts will, of course, be considered taxable income, taxable at the 30 per cent rate. Special claims for payment would then be presented to the shareholder.

D. SERVICES

Assumed Facts

P is a large multinational concern which wholly owns foreign subsidiary S. Both P and S are engaged in manufacturing and sales activities. P's headquarters division performs general management services for P's multi-national operations including services which directly relate to S. The services performed for S include periodic visits by P's executives to review S's operations, financial analysis of S's future requirements, engineering services in connection with S's manufacturing activities and marketing services in connection with S's sales activities. P does not charge S for such service.

Parent in Denmark

1. Expenses which directly and exclusively benefit S must be allocated to S. Otherwise P may not deduct the expenses. Stewardship expenses normally do not have to be allocated to S.
2. Normally only direct costs need be recovered by P from S.

Subsidiary in Denmark

1. In this context again imputed income of overseas parent companies does not affect the fiscal income of subsidiaries resident in Denmark. However, the allowability of management charges made through the books can be reviewed by the tax authorities in Denmark and disallowed if deemed unreasonable under Danish tax rules. To be acceptable, management charges must only include costs relative to the subsidiary or subsidiaries and, where covering a number of subsidiaries, be apportioned on a fair basis without bias to any subsidiary or group of subsidiaries.

2. No Danish withholding tax would be levied on payments from S to P for services, even if the amount was not accepted as a reduction of S's taxable profit.

E. Loan Guarantees and Rentals

Assumed Facts

P is a multinational company whose main business is manufacturing and selling. P plans to establish foreign sales subsidiary S located in country S. P capitalizes S with $500,000 and guarantees a loan to S of $500,000 obtained from an independent bank. Land and a warehouse which P owns in country S will be used as a site for S's operation. P plans to make this land and warehouse available to S at a fee of $1 per year for 99 years.

Parent in Denmark

1. Where a tax allowance is claimed for an asset, a matching imputed income may be raised by the tax authorities. Thus, in this case the guarantee will not give rise to imputed income but the nominal lease may attract an imputed commercial rental income.

2. P would not be regarded as having made an equity investment in S.

Subsidiary in Denmark

1. No imputed income in P will automatically affect the nature of transaction for tax purposes in Denmark. Denmark would look for contractual obligations and generally contracts are interpreted under the laws of the country governing the contract.

2. It is likely that P will be taxed in Denmark on the ownership of the property (even though P is a tax resident overseas). There is no automatic right of offset in S for Danish tax purposes. In such circumstances, the owner is best advised to make a charge to the user.

3. No withholding tax will apply to payments of rentals or guarantee fees out of Denmark. P's net profit from rental of land and warehouse is taxable in Denmark but no withholding tax applies. P's assessment would be based on market value rental income.

PART III. TAX TREATIES

A. In the more recent treaties there has been a trend towards the inclusion of mutual agreement procedures – for instance, the treaty with the United Kingdom dated November 11, 1980, and the new treaty with the USA signed in 1983.

B. The existence of a treaty does not override the domestic rules in Denmark's tax laws when looking at reallocation of revenues or expenses. So far, Denmark has had no practical experience with this question.

C. The Danish taxpayer would have to invoke the treaty provisions by making a request to Danish tax authorities.

D. Application should be made via the tax return. No guidelines are available other than formal fiscal rules for claims, allowances, etc.

E. A Danish interpretation would be applied in Denmark, so double taxation could result if the two countries tax authorities do not agree on a matter. However, there is a provision in Danish tax law for unilateral tax relief.

F. In Denmark one can always appeal to the Danish courts, but one would be appealing the interpretation of Danish tax laws not the negotiated settlement between the two competent authorities.

G. In general, when Danish tax authorities agree to adjustments, they will allow conforming payments without further tax consequences.

H. Experience with mutual agreement procedures has been extremely limited.

PART IV. SPECIAL SITUATIONS

A. Danish tax laws will not be applied differently to cross-border transactions because the tax rates in the two countries are: substantially the same, substantially different, or if one of the companies has no gross or net income in the years in question.

B. There are no special type of transactions or special industries which get unique attention for Danish tax purposes. However, transactions with tax haven companies are given special attention.

Finland

Ake Ammondt

BACKGROUND NOTES

CORPORATE TAXATION

1. In Finland, income tax is levied for the State, the municipalities and for the Church. The basis for the determination of the income tax is the taxpayer's taxable income. The income tax legislation is based on the principle of separate assessment of taxpayers; consequently, group taxation is not permitted.
2. For tax purposes, companies are classified as residents, non-residents and exempt companies. Resident companies are those which are registered in Finland or have their centre of management there. Subsidiaries of foreign companies are treated as resident Finnish taxpayers in the same manner as any Finnish company. A resident company is subject to national income tax, municipal income tax and Church tax, which are levied on worldwide income. Relief from double taxation is provided by both unilateral and treaty provisions. A non-resident company, even when it has a permanent establishment in Finland, is liable to pay tax in Finland only on income derived from Finland.
3. The present rate of the national income tax is 43 per cent. If annual profits are less than FIM 250,000, the tax rate is reduced proportionately. The municipal tax rate varies between 14 per cent and 19 per cent, depending on the municipality. The Church tax varies between 1 per cent and 2 per cent. Individual taxpayers are taxed in national income according to a progressive scale. If the income declared by a corporation is less than income declared by corporations in the same trade and under similar conditions, municipal and Church taxes may be assessed on an income arbitrarily fixed by the tax authorities, except for the first five years of operation.
4. The taxable profit of companies and other business enterprises, which is computed in accordance with the provisions of the Taxation of Business and Professional Income Act, consists of taxable income less deductible expenses as defined by that Act. With a few minor exceptions, the provisions of the Act apply equally to the computation of national, municipal and Church taxes.

As a general rule, deductions are allowed for all expenses incurred by the business within the tax year for the purpose of earning, securing or maintaining the company's income. In addition to deductions from net income for normal business expenses, there are several special tax regulations aimed at providing investment incentives to business and to help combat economic fluctuations.

5. Resident companies are no longer subject to the national net worth tax. However, a non-resident company having a permanent establishment in Finland is subject to net worth tax with respect to property belonging to the permanent establishment. The rate of the net worth tax on the property of non-resident corporations located in Finland is currently 1 per cent.

6. Dividends received by a foreign corporation from a Finnish corporation are deemed to be taxable income in Finland. The tax is determined on the basis of the 'Source Tax' Act. The source tax is 25 per cent of the gross amount of the dividends. For royalties, the rate is 30 per cent. The withholding tax rate for interest is normally zero in accordance with provisions in the income and wealth tax law. The 30 per cent rate on interest applies only exceptionally, eg in cases of permanent loans in lieu of contribution of capital. Provisions in tax treaties grant relief to the above rates. However, interest on bonds, debentures and similar instalments, on bank accounts, foreign trade credits and trade loans, are not subject to tax in Finland.

7. Unilateral relief from double taxation is granted in accordance with the provisions in the Tax Credit Law in force since June 1, 1981. The relief does not apply if double taxation is avoided or reduced by a tax treaty in force between Finland and the source country.

The relief is given in the form of a tax credit. Finally assessed or withheld foreign national taxes on income and property may be credited against the Finnish national income and net worth tax respectively, but the credit may not exceed the Finnish tax attributable proportionately to the foreign income and net worth.

Finland has tax treaties with 36 countries. The treaties, except for a few of the oldest ones and the treaty with the Soviet Union, are based on the OECD model taxation treaty. Each tax treaty should be consulted, as there are often exceptions to general rules.

Partnerships

8. Partnerships are not taxed as separate units but the income and capital are considered to pass to the individual partners and are assessed on them whether distributed or not. However, a general partnership or limited partnership carrying on business and registered in the Trade Register is taxed as separate units. The rate of tax is the same as for individuals. Losses of general partnerships and limited partnerships may not be deducted from other income of the partners, except on liquidation of unregistered general and limited partnerships.

Branches

9. A branch of a foreign corporation, whether engaged in selling or manufacturing, would constitute a permanent establishment in Finland. The amount of taxable income declared in the annual tax return is based on profit shown in the income statement according to the books. Adjustments for tax purposes are basically the same as those required for corporations. The tax rates on national income are the same as those required for corporations. Branches are subject to net worth taxes but cannot make dividend deductions available to corporations. Branch profit remittances are not subject to withholding taxes.

Income Determination

10. The tax year is the calendar year but, if the accounting period is not a calendar year, that accounting period ending during the calendar year is considered a company's tax year.
11. The taxable income is the profit shown by the audited annual income statement adjusted as accepted or required by the tax law.
12. If the business income declared by the company is less than the average income declared by other taxpayers in the same trade and under similar conditions, the income for local income tax purposes may be arbitrarily fixed by the tax authorities. This cannot, however, be done for the first five years of a new company's business. The arbitrary income assessments are normally based on a certain percentage of turnover.
13. Capital gains arising from the sale of real property or of shares forming part of the taxpayer's capital assets are exempt from tax if the real property has been acquired at least ten years earlier or, in the case of shares, five years earlier. Losses are deductible without time limits as regards shares and buildings, but loss on sale of land is deductible only if the property sold has been in the possession of the owner for less than ten years.
14. Dividends received by a resident company from another resident company are normally exempt from national income tax, irrespective of the degree of share ownership, unless the shares are held by banks, insurance companies and dealers in securities as inventory or portfolio investments. Subject to certain exceptions, the exemption is not granted to holding and investment companies unless they redistribute at least 80 per cent of the dividends to their own shareholders.
15. Dividends received by a resident company from foreign sources may either be exempt under double taxation treaties or a credit may be obtainable for the foreign taxes paid.
16. All interest income derived from assets belonging to the business, as well as royalties and service fees received from Finnish sources, are taxable income.

Deductible Business Expenses

17. As a general rule, expenses are deductible when they are incurred by the business within the tax year for the purpose of earning, securing or maintaining the company's income.

Depreciation of Intangible Assets

18. The acquisition cost of patents and other intangible rights such as copyrights, trademarks, etc., must be written off using the straight-line method over ten years or such shorter period of economic use as the taxpayer regards as realistic.
19. Expenses such as goodwill, leasehold improvements, advertising campaigns, etc., which produce or maintain income during three or more fiscal years, are similarly written off on a straight-line basis over a maximum of ten years.

Other Deductions

20. Interest expense is generally a deductible cost. In cases where the interest is paid between affiliated companies, the interest charge must correspond to that of an arm's length transaction. When a holding company is not engaged in business activities, the annual deductible amount is limited to FIM 10,000. Interest paid to a parent company abroad is not deductible if the loan from the parent company is of a permanent nature.
21. Royalties and service fees are deductible. In the case of royalties and service fees paid between related companies, the fee must correspond to that of an arm's length transaction.

Non-Deductible Expenses Include the Following:

22.
1. Expenses not necessary for earning income.
2. Expenses incurred in connection with the acquisition of tax-free income; however, any excess of such expenses over tax-free income actually earned is deductible.
3. All taxes on income and net worth, and additional charges and penalties for non-payment of taxes or for inadequate tax returns.
4. Excessive salaries or other types of compensation paid to a shareholder or a member of his family.

Group Relief

23. Groups of affiliated companies are not consolidated for tax purposes. Losses of one company may not be offset against profits of another.

24. Group contribution between resident companies is often but not always deductible for payer company. This is normally the case when the resident affiliates have business relationships and business transactions between themselves or one company's operations are for the benefit of the group.
25. However, if the group contribution is given to an affiliated company to secure its operations, which are unrelated to the operations of the group, the contribution is more of a capital nature and, as such, is not taxable income/deductible expenses.

PART I. GENERAL RULES

A. The following two paragraphs of the Taxation Act cover a large area of the topic:

Section 56
'Where a circumstance or measure has been given such juridical form, which does not correspond to the real nature or purpose of this matter, the taxation shall be executed as if the correct form had been used. Where purchase money, other compensation or time of performance in a contract of purchase or other contract has been defined or other step taken obviously to avoid taxes, the tax board has the right to estimate the taxable income and property.'

Section 73
'Where a taxpayer who carries on business in the country with anyone who financially participates in his enterprise or has influence on its management or in whose enterprise he himself financially participates or on whose management he has influence, has sold goods at a lower price or bought goods from him at a higher price than the current price, or else has agreed with him on financial terms which differ from those which would be made between independent enterprises, and should the income for this reason be less than it would have otherwise been, and the one to whom the income has been transferred is not taxable here, the amount shall be accrued by the person to whom it would have risen if the abovementioned steps had not been taken.'

If it is obvious that taxation should be carried out in the way referred to in the first paragraph, the Tax Board shall carefully consider all facts that might be of guidance by judging the case and give the taxpayer an opportunity to present a detailed statement of the facts.

1. The adjustments of cross-border transactions are made mainly to prevent tax avoidance.
2. Arm's length rates are the dominating principle in the Finnish legislation.
3. Management fees and interest are specifically provided for. No safe havens are provided for.
4. The same principles apply to transactions between domestic taxpayers and cross-border transactions.

B. Adjustments can be made when one party –
a. financially participates in the other, or
b. has an influence on the management of the other.
See Section 73 cited above.

C. Adjustments are made on a transactions basis.

D. There is no statute of limitations for this type of adjustment.

E. When Finland initiates an adjustment, no correlative adjustment is made for Finnish tax purposes to income or tax of the foreign party to the transaction.

F. 1. Consolidated reporting between Finnish and foreign entities is not allowed.
2. If a foreign country makes a change in the income or tax owing by a subsidiary in that country, this does not affect the foreign tax credit rules in Finland when dividends are later paid from the subsidiary to the Finnish parent.
3. When adjustments are made to cross-border transactions, Finland does not require the reallocated amounts to be paid to or from Finland.

G. Generally, the adjustments are made to the years in which the transaction took place.

H. Yes, a Finnish taxpayer can initiate an adjustment by making a request to Finnish tax authorities.

PART II. SPECIFIC EXAMPLES

A. Sale of Goods

Assumed Facts

Assume P is a manufacturer which sells finished products to S which is located in a different country. P sells these products to S at cost. P also sells these products to unrelated parties at cost plus 10 per cent mark-on. Both S and the unrelated parties incur the same selling and promotional expense and both resell P's products at the same price per unit.

Parent in Finland

1. Yes, an allocation of income to P would be made.
2. Income is adjusted to correspond to the situation where two unrelated

parties would have agreed on the price. Note, however, that a 10 per cent difference is unlikely to alarm the tax authorities.

3. a. If there were no sales to independent third parties, an adjustment would still be made if it could be shown that the transfer price was less than open market prices.

b. If S incurs greater selling or promotional expenses than unrelated parties, then

i. IF unrelated parties are situated in S's country, the lower price to S could hardly be justified;

ii. IF unrelated parties are situated elsewhere it depends on the market situation in S's country. The price to S would be adjusted if unrelated parties is S's country would pay more than the cost price without sacrificing P's long-term interests in that country.

c. If a lower price is charged so as to establish a market in S, this is acceptable if the marketing situation differs from other countries where the price is +10 per cent. P's long-term profitability is decisive.

Subsidiary in Finland

1. The determination of S's income will be made independently.
2. The adjusted price must be claimed by P and proven by S to be the market price, then S can be granted a deduction.
3. A Finnish withholding tax could apply if S makes payments to P and the price adjustment cannot be proven to reflect the actual market conditions.

B. Loans and Advances

Assumed Facts

P and S are manufacturers located in different countries. P loans S money on open account without interest so that S can expand its operations. P is not engaged in the business of lending money.

Parent in Finland

1. Yes, P's income would be adjusted to correspond to the market rate in Finland.
2. No, the existence of a non-interest-bearing note would not change the results.
3. It is possible that the loan might be regarded as an equity investment by P and S and, if so, there would be no Finnish tax consequences on repayment of the loan.

Subsidiary in Finland

1. A separate determination of S's income would be made by Finland.
2. The transaction would probably be characterized as an additional equity investment if no maturity date fixed.
3. In principle, the Finnish tax authorities would accept a retroactive charge. For instance, if a charge is made for 1983 and a corrected income statement, balance sheet and tax return is filed by the end of October, 1984, it would be accepted. If, however, a charge for 1982 were made in summer, 1984, the allocation rules would cause difficulties. A charge for any one year is not deductible in any subsequent year and the year end statements for any particular year cannot be corrected after October of the following year.
4. If the interest charged exceeds the market rate (in P's country), the extra interest is treated as a dividend and would normally be subject to withholding tax.
5. No Finnish tax consequences result from a repayment of the loan even if Finnish tax authorities had regarded it as additional equity investment in S. If the transaction is characterized by Finland as additional capital investment, the interest will be taxable income for P and not deductible by S. The payment would also be subject to the Finnish withholding tax on dividends.

C. Intangibles

Assumed Facts

P and S are manufacturers located in different countries. P performs research and development which has led to P's ownership of certain intangibles consisting of patents, trademarks and know-how. P makes available to S exclusive right to use in S's country all of P's intangibles. P does not charge S for the use of P's intangible.

Parent in Finland

1./2. Normally no allocation of income to P is made here.
3. Yes, a portion of the R and D costs could be allocated to S.
4. No, the existence of an R and D cost sharing agreement would not have much impact, if P did not in fact charge S for the R and D.

Subsidiary in Finland

1. Finland would make a separate determination of S's income (the need for it arises only if P actually charges S for the intangibles).

2. If Finland accepted the charges to S, they would be deductible as follows:

a. Lump sum payment – the intangibles must be clearly specified. The expense is deductible only insofar as it corresponds to the 'market price' of the intangible and the benefit which S can derive from it. The cost should be allocated to the years of the economical life on the intangibles. Maximum ten years.
b. Annual royalty – currently deductible.
c. Reduction of P's expense – currently deductible but the expense should directly concern S (eg the expense is incurred on behalf of S and by S's own initiative).

3. Yes, Finland would levy a withholding tax on payments to P for the use of intangibles.

D. Services

Assumed Facts

P is a large multinational concern which wholly owns foreign subsidiary S. Both P and S are engaged in manufacturing and sales activities. P's headquarters division performs general management services for P's multi-national operations including services which directly relate to S. The services performed for S include periodic visits by P's executives to review S's operations, financial analysis of S's future requirements, engineering services in connection with S's manufacturing activities and marketing services in connection with S's sales activities. P does not charge S for such service.

Parent in Finland

1./2. Normally, no allocation of income to P would be made.

Subsidiary in Finland

1. Finland would make a separate determination of S's income. The expense must –

a. be clearly specified;
b. directly concern S;
c. clearly contribute to the business of S;
d. be proportional to the real needs of S.

2. No withholding tax would be levied by Finland on a payment by S to P for services. (See Background Notes)

E. Loan Guarantees and Rentals

Assumed Facts

P is a multinational company whose main business is manufacturing and selling. P plans to establish foreign sales subsidiary S located in country S. P capitalizes S with $500,000 and guarantees a loan to S of $500,000 obtained from an independent bank. Land and a warehouse which P owns in country S will be used as a site for S's operations. P plans to make this land and warehouse available to S at a fee of $1 per year for 99 years.

Parent in Finland

1. No allocation of income to P would be made for the guarantee, but would be made for S's use of P's land and warehouse. The amount of allocation would be determined according to market rates.
2. Finland would not regard P as having made an equity investment in S.

Subsidiary in Finland

1. Finland would make a separate determination of S's income.
2. Such expenses actually charged to S would be deductible up to market rates.
3. No, Finland would not levy a withholding tax on either guarantee fees or rentals paid from S to P. In this case, however, P would be subject to Finnish profits tax on rentals but not on guarantee fees.

PART III. TAX TREATIES

A. Yes, Finland's treaties have mutual agreement provisions. Finland has treaties with 37 countries.

B. Yes, the treaty provisions aim at avoiding double taxation of incomes. The agreements concluded in recent years comply in general with principles laid down by the OECD in its Model Agreement. Treaties often lower withholding tax rates on dividends and royalties.

C. Treaty protection will not be invoked unless a Finnish taxpayer requests Finnish tax authorities to do so.

D. There are no set procedures to trigger the mutual agreement provisions but, generally, the Finnish taxpayer would apply as is called for under the OECD Model Agreement.

E. Double taxation will result from a failure of tax authorities to reach mutual agreement.

F. Theoretically, the taxpayer can appeal a settlement of two competent authorities to The International Court, but this has never occurred.

G. When agreement is reached between competent authorities then conforming adjustment and payments will be allowed without any further tax consequences.

H. Settlement has usually been reached between Finnish and other competent tax authorities.

PART IV. SPECIAL SITUATIONS

A. Expenses are difficult to justify in any company that has no gross income. Other than that, the Finnish tax rules would not be applied differently in cross-border transactions just because the tax rates in the two countries were substantially the same or substantially different.

B. Transactions closely examined:
- management fees
- service, R&D, marketing fees, etc.
- transfer pricing
- royalties
- interest

Generally, foreign-owned subsidiaries in Finland are closely examined so as to see if any of the items mentioned above contain hidden dividend payments.

France

Jean Marc Tirard

PART I. GENERAL RULES

Legal Basis

A. The relevant provisions dealing with intercompany transactions are contained in Article 57 and Article 238 A of the General Tax Code (C.G.I.).

a. Article 57 CGI provides that, in assessing the income tax due from enterprises which are controlled by or which control enterprises established outside of France, any profits indirectly transferred to the latter, whether by an increase or reduction in purchase or sale prices or by any other means, shall be added back to the results shown in the accounts. The same applies to enterprises which are controlled by an enterprise or a group of enterprises which also control enterprises situated outside France. Tax authorities are allowed to presume control when an advantage is accorded to an enterprise located in a low tax country as defined for Article 238 A purposes.

b. Article 238 A generally provides that payments of interest, royalties or service fees to a person resident in a foreign country, where such recipient is exempt from tax or taxed at an appreciably lower rate than would apply in France, are deductible only if it can be shown that the expenses correspond to actual transactions and are not abnormal or exaggerated.

An 'appreciably lower rate' has been defined by a note issued on June 26, 1975 by the French Tax Administration as existing when the recipient incurs a tax rate which is at least one-third less than the French corporate tax rate. Hence, a rate of 33.33 per cent or less is 'appreciably lower' (50 per cent × 66.67 per cent).

The presumption that certain payments made to persons located in tax haven countries are not bona fide expenses has been extended to deposits made in a bank account located in such countries by Article 90 I of the 1982 Financial Law.

A. 1. Although tax avoidance is not a requirement for an allocation it should be noted that Article 238A is especially aimed at preventing abuse of tax haven countries as a means of tax avoidance.

2. French tax authorities are empowered to adjust prices between related companies organized in different countries to reflect arm's length charges.
3. The Tax Code does not provide 'safe haven' rules to be used in determining an arm's length transfer price.

   Over the years, the Tax Administration has issued notes (circulaires) on the implementation of Article 57. The latest one was issued on May 4, 1973. These instructions are generally not very specific, unlike the U.S. and German rules.
4. The above provisions apply only when one of the entities involved is foreign. Other cases must be dealt with under the general provisions of the law relating to the deductibility of business expenses.

What is a Related Person for Purposes of Making Allocation?

B. Article 57 CGI refers to the concept of common control rather than to the concept of related parties but without defining control.

The tax authorities interpret it to include both legal control and control in fact.

There is deemed to be legal control when the foreign company holds a majority of the capital or shareholder votes of the French company, or where the foreign company (directly or through intermediaries) exercises functions in the French company carrying the power to make decisions.

Intermediaries include, inter alia, intermediary companies themselves under control of the foreign company, managers, directors and members of their respective families, and any person who owns an interest in the capital of any of the undertakings concerned.

Even if legal control cannot be shown to exist, there can be 'de facto' control; this may be contractual in origin or may flow from the business relationships between the two companies.

When transactions are carried out with enterprises or individuals located in tax havens, it is not necessary for the tax authorities to establish the existence of control in either direction between payer and payee. (See A.1)

Basis for Making Adjustments

C. The principal approach in making adjustments is a transaction basis. It is only where specific data is not available for making adjustments that the taxable profits are determined by comparison with similar enterprises (net income basis). In practice, this second approach is rarely used.

Statute of Limitation

D. The general statute of limitation is four years after the end of the taxable year, and is applicable to the making of allocations.

E. When France initiates an adjustment to, say, a French parent company no special adjustments are made for subsequent dividends (or related foreign tax credits) coming back from the foreign subsidiary.

F. If an adjustment is made to, say, a foreign subsidiary, such adjustments have no effect in France.
1. No consolidation is permitted between the French and foreign company.
2. No special adjustments are made for foreign tax credit claims in France.
3. France does not insist that the reallocated income is paid to or out of France.

G. Adjustments are only made to the tax years in which the underlying transactions took place.

H. A taxpayer cannot initiate an adjustment. If there is an applicable tax treaty which provides for competent authority consideration, however, the taxpayer may request it.

PART II. SPECIFIC EXAMPLES

A. Sale of Goods

Assumed Facts

Assume P is a manufacturer which sells finished products to S which is located in a different country. P sells these products to S at cost. P also sells these products to unrelated parties at cost plus 10 per cent mark-on. Both S and the unrelated parties incur the same selling and promotional expense and both resell P's products at the same price per unit.

Parent in France

1. Income may be allocated to P by French tax authorities.
2. In the note of May 4, 1973, the tax authorities indicated that the tax inspectors should refer to the prices at which the foreign manufacturer generally sells products to independent companies in evaluating the price charged to French affiliates for these same products. The same rule applies for pricing of goods sold by a French company to foreign affiliates. Consequently, in this specific example, the 10 per cent mark-on would probably be allocated to P.
3. a. No sales to independent parties
In theory, even if there were no sales to independent parties, the tax authorities would not accept zero profit margin on sales to the subsidiary company since unrelated parties normally sell products at a profit.

However, the tax authorities would have to prove the basis for the adjustment. When comparable uncontrolled prices do not exist, experience shows that the methods most commonly considered are the cost-plus and resale price methods.

b. S incurs greater expenses

In the abovementioned note, tax inspectors are recommended not to apply Article 57 in respect of sales which, for commercial reasons (eg to establish a market), have been made to subsidiaries at prices near to cost.

Furthermore, the Supreme Court (Conseil d'Etat) has decided that a parent company may charge preferential prices to a subsidiary which has some difficulty in carrying on the business.

Subsidiary in France

1. France will make an independent determination.
2. Under internal law there is no procedure for a French taxpayer to request an allocation.
3. France will treat the payment of the allocated amount to P as a dividend, subject to French withholding tax (except if agreed to under competent authority procedures).

B. Loans and Advances

Assumed Facts

P and S are manufacturers located in different countries. P loans S money on open account without interest so that S can expand its operations. P is not engaged in the business of lending money.

Parent in France

1. The 1973 note provides that where a loan is made to a foreign related company without interest or at a reduced rate of interest, grounds exist for including in income an amount to reflect a normal charge.

Each case is to be reviewed individually but the amount charged could be based on the mean of interest charged by the Banque de France or on rates used by the company on loans contracted by it.

Several court decisions have stated that an interest-free loan made to a financially troubled foreign subsidiary was not subject to Article 57 because the French parent was protecting its ownership. If no income is imputed to the French parent, the related interest expense of the French parent is not denied as a deduction.

2. The amount of interest allocated would be unaffected by the existence of a non-interest bearing note with a fixed maturity date.
3. No, France would not regard the transaction as an equity investment by P.

Subsidiary in France

1. France will make an independent determination.
2. The transaction would be characterized as a loan and not as an additional equity investment.
3. S would not be permitted any deduction.
4. France would treat the payment of the allocated amount to P as a dividend subject to French withholding tax.
5. The transaction would not be characterized as an additional equity investment.

C. Intangibles

Assumed Facts

P and S are manufacturers located in different countries. P performs research and development which has led to P's ownership of certain intangibles consisting of patents, trademarks and know-how. P makes available to S the exclusive right to use in S's country all of P's intangibles. P does not charge S for the use of P's intangibles.

Parent in France

1. Income will be allocated to P. P will not be treated as contributing the intangible to the capital of S.
2. The allocation will be in the form of annual royalties and will be computed on an arm's length basis. Theoretically, whether or not S's country allows a tax deduction for payments for the use of intangibles is not relevant to the determination of whether there should be an allocation.
3. Yes, a portion of P's expenses could be allocated to S as an alternative.
4. A bona fide cost sharing arrangement with respect to the research and development costs is an acceptable alternative to 2. Such an arrangement is not advisable, however, as royalties benefit from capital gains tax treatment (subject to corporate tax at the rate of 15 per cent), whereas reimbursement of costs is treated as ordinary income (subject to corporate tax at the rate of 50 per cent).

Subsidiary in France

1. France will make an independent determination.
2. There is no procedure for a French taxpayer to request an allocation.
3. France will treat the payment of the allocated amount to P as a dividend, subject to French withholding tax.

D. SERVICES

Assumed Facts

P is a large multinational concern which wholly owns foreign subsidiary S. Both P and S are engaged in manufacturing and sales activities. P's headquarters division performs general management services for P's multi-national operations including services which directly relate to S. The services performed for S include periodic visits by P's executives to review S's operations, financial analysis of S's future requirements, engineering services in connection with S's manufacturing activities and marketing services in connection with S's sales activities. P does not charge S for such service.

Parent in France

1. Theoretically, an imputed charge could be included in P's taxable income. Such an adjustment, however, is unlikely for general management, periodic reviews and financial analysis.
2. The test to be adopted is the arm's length price which, in the absence of comparable sales to third parties, can only be established by a build-up of costs both direct and indirect. The outcome would be the result of negotiation and it may be expected that any profit margin imputed would be minimal.

Subsidiary in France

1. France will not accept that P's country's allocation affects S's taxable income. If P's country makes an allocation to P, the only way to resolve future problems will be for P and S to enter into a service agreement describing the services rendered and the method of calculating the fee (allocation). From that date S may deduct the payments to P, subject to production of evidences.
2. France will treat the payment of the allocated amount to P as a dividend subject to French withholding tax.

E. Loan Guarantees and Rentals

Assumed Facts

P is a multinational company whose main business is manufacturing and selling. P plans to establish foreign sales subsidiary S located in country S. P capitalizes S with $500,000, and guarantees a loan to S of $500,000 obtained from an independent bank. Land and a warehouse which P owns in country S will be used as a site for S's operations. P plans to make this land and warehouse available to S at a fee of $1 per year for 99 years.

Parent in France

1. Income will be allocated to P for both the loan guarantee and the use of the property at arm's length rate and rental.
2. No.

Subsidiary in France

1. France will make a separate determination.
2. There is no procedure for a French taxpayer to request an allocation and it is unlikely that French tax authorities would make an allocation which would reduce the income of a French taxpayer.
3. Assuming the payment is not accepted by French tax authorities as service fee or rental, the payment could be considered as a dividend subject to French withholding tax.

PART III. TAX TREATIES

A. Yes, France has mutual agreement procedures in her tax treaties.

B. No, the existence of treaties really does not alter the French tax burden. Authorities apply domestic law.

C. Usually the procedure is initiated by the taxpayer. However, the tax authorities occasionally undertake to do this.

D. Guidelines as to procedures to be followed when filing an application for competent authority procedures do not exist. The application has to be filed with the Director of the International Relations Services, in the Service of Tax Legislation.

E. If no settlement is reached, the taxpayer may still submit his claim in the usual way.

F. No. Furthermore, the tax authorities are free to refuse to initiate the procedure.

G. Adjustments and payments would be allowed without further tax consequences when two competent authorities reach an agreement.

H. In the past ten years, about 150 claims have been brought before this authority, most of them successful. In our experience, it is a lengthy procedure (several years).

PART IV. SPECIAL SITUATIONS

A. 1./2. In theory, tax law should not be applied differently to cross-border transactions just because the French company is showing a loss or reporting no gross income. However, experience indicates that the French tax authorities may be reluctant to accept allocations of expenses to a French company from a non-resident affiliate where the French company is already incurring a loss or producing no gross income.

3. No.
4. No. However, it may adversely influence the thinking and investigation process of the French tax authorities. Moreover, in such a situation, the tax authorities do not bear the burden of proof (see I A(a)).

B. The French tax authorities closely scrutinize management fees to determine if they correspond to real services rendered.

Experience indicates that problems can be minimized by:

a. issuing separate invoices or debit notes showing the details and nature of services rendered.
b. providing, where possible, written documentation such as agreements, letters, memoranda, etc., as evidence of the assistance rendered to the French company.

PART V. OTHER CONSIDERATIONS

In addition to the rules on allocations mentioned above, the French tax law contains provisions (Article 209 B of the General Tax Code) which bear certain resemblances to the subpart F provisions of the U.S. internal revenue code.

In essence, Article 209 B states that, whenever an enterprise which is subject to French corporate tax, owns, directly or indirectly, 25 per cent or more of the shares of another corporation domiciled in a foreign state having a so-called 'privileged tax system' – as defined by Article 238 A cited above – the foreign corporation's profits are subject to the French corporate tax to the extent of the French enterprise's interest in those profits by virtue of its shareholding.

The Article taxes these profits separately and allows a credit in France for those taxes paid on this income to the foreign country (the French tax law does not generally provide for foreign tax credits). This tax treatment can only be avoided when the French company can demonstrate that:

- the foreign profits in question result from bona fida industrial or commercial operations in the deemed tax haven country which do not have, as their primary reason for being, the accumulation of profits on that country;
- the majority of its transactions are with unrelated third parties in the foreign country in question.

Germany (West)

Helmut Becker

PART I. GENERAL RULES

A. Legal Basis

The legal basis for allocation of income and expenses between related companies is found in Article 8(3) of the Corporation Tax Law (Koerperschaftsteuergesetz) and Section 31 of the Corporation Tax Regulations (Koerperschaftsteuerrichtlinien) relating thereto, Article 1 of the Foreign Tax Affairs Law (Aussensteuergesetz) as well as numerous rulings of the Supreme Tax Court (Bundesfinanzhof) and district tax courts (Finanzgericht); it is supplemented by the provisions of tax treaties, most of which follow the OECD model treaty.

Article 8(3) Corporation Tax Law merely states that hidden distributions of income do not reduce taxable income. Section 31 of the Corporation Tax Regulations summarizes the interpretation of a hidden distribution of income as found in many supreme tax court rulings to be a benefit granted by a company to its individual or corporate shareholder, or a person related to the shareholder, outside the normal statutory profit distribution but brought about because of the shareholder relationship, which an orderly and conscientious manager would not have granted to a non-shareholder under comparable circumstances.

Article 1(1) of the Foreign Tax Affairs Law (AStG) states that, where the income of a taxpayer resulting from his business relationship with a related person is reduced because the taxpayer has, within his business relationship extending to a foreign country, agreed on terms and conditions which deviate from those which unrelated third parties would have agreed upon under the same or similar circumstances, then his income shall, notwithstanding other provisions, be so determined as such income that would have been earned under terms and conditions agreed upon between unrelated third parties.

Most of the German double taxation treaties contain provisions similar to Article 9, paragraph 1, of the OECD model convention. In essence, these provisions authorize the adjustment of the profits of an enterprise if it has engaged in commercial or financial activities with an affiliate on a basis other than that which would exist between independent enterprises.

A further basic rule to be observed is the concept of hidden contribution of capital. Article 8(1) Corporation Tax Law provides that income shall be determined in accordance with the provisions of the Income Tax Law. Article 4(1) of the Income Tax Law defines income as the difference between opening and ending net assets, increased by drawings and reduced by contributions made by the taxpayer during the financial year.

Where a corporation is concerned, Section 36(a) of the Corporation Tax Regulations in conformity with supreme tax court rulings defines a hidden capital contribution as the transfer, by a shareholder or related person to the company, of contributable benefits which a non-shareholder acting like an orderly and conscientious businessman would not have granted to the company. For example, where a foreign parent transferred to a German GmbH, a machine worth 100,000 DM and received consideration of only 5,000 DM, there is a hidden contribution of 95,000 DM. Permission to use or utilize an asset, eg patent, does not qualify as a contributable benefit. The same is true for the benefit arising from non-interest or low-interest loans granted by a shareholder; however, if the shareholder himself had to pay interest on direct refinancing of his loan to the company the interest expense can qualify as a hidden contribution of capital.

Last but not least, the general rules of the Fiscal Rule (Abgabenordnung) as to economic ownership of an asset, taxability in spite of violation of law or morality, sham transactions and abuse of contractual possibilities under the Civil Code, apply and may overrule the allocation rules.

The above rules appear to be conflicting but their applicability to taxpayers varies.

The Corporation tax law deals only with hidden distributions of income by corporations, both within Germany and across the border.

The foreign tax affairs law deals with all kinds of related or affiliated taxpayers, ie individuals, partnerships, corporations, and restricts itself to cross-border transactions.

The double taxation treaties relate to certain countries only and limit somewhat the taxation rights Germany would normally have under the provisions of the corporation tax law and foreign tax affairs law.

The tax authorities claim that, where corporations are concerned, the provisions of the corporation tax law and case law developed on hidden distributions of income should be applied. This means that the somewhat more favourable treatment under the foreign tax affairs law of compensating disadvantages for a related person or entity with advantages granted by the related taxpayer under the same business relation in the three following years (provided an offsetting arrangement is documented at the end of the first year) is not available to corporations. Here, case law requires offsetting advantages in the same accounting period under the same agreement or in direct connection with the non-arm's length transaction, eg product price high, freight charge low.

1. Adjustments under the above rules are made to clearly reflect income and prevent avoidance of taxation in Germany. Since the introduction of the

corporation tax imputation system, ie credit for the corporation tax paid on income distributed (including hidden distributions) against the corporate or individual German income tax of the shareholder, the avoidance aspect has declined in importance where German shareholders are concerned. In practice the emphasis on enforcing these rules is, therefore, in cross-border affiliation cases and on German shareholders with tax exempt status, eg municipalities, labor unions, etc.

2. The standard used for determining adjustments is the arm's length rule described above. This rule is general in nature and must be interpreted on the basis of tax regulations, tax court rulings, possibly the OECD guidelines and commentaries.

3. There are not presently any safe haven rules on the allocation of income and expenses between related companies.

   However, the corporation tax regulations contain examples of hidden distributions of income as follows:
   - excessive remuneration for manager who is also a shareholder
   - non-interest or low-interest loan of company to a shareholder
   - loan granted to shareholder although inability to repay is known
   - excessive interest rate paid to shareholder for loan granted by him
   - supply to or purchase from the company of goods or assets at unusual prices or special discounts or rebates
   - sale of shares by a shareholder to the company at inflated price or vice versa at reduced price
   - the company takes over debts or other obligations from, as well as guarantees for, a shareholder
   - the company waives rights which it has against a shareholder
   - a third party receives payment for services rendered to both the company and a shareholder entirely at the expense of the company
   - a company provides services for its controlling shareholder without a clear and precise prospective agreement.

All examples cited are based on supreme tax court rulings.

The regulations to the Foreign Tax Affairs Law do not contain any guidance for acceptable inter-company pricing methods.

In order to ensure uniform treatment of comparable facts and circumstances, the German tax administration developed an internal manual for tax treatment of cross-border transactions which was not available to the public other than on a photocopying 'black market'. On February 23, 1983, the German tax authorities issued 'Administrative Principles for Examination of Income Allocation Between Internationally Related Entities' which is an attempt to transform the OECD guidelines into a national regulation.

It is the declared intention of the German tax administration to have, as much as possible, consistency with similar provisions in the guidelines of other EEC and OECD countries.

Many of the provisions contained in the draft guideline are being challenged by the various industrial and professional pressure groups.

The following is a brief analysis of the more important provisions of the guideline:

a. Formal Requirements

If charges from related persons are claimed, these are deductible only if clear and precise, legally binding agreements have been concluded on a prospective basis.

b. General Considerations

Business transactions between related entities shall be governed by the arm's length principle, ie the actions of an orderly and conscientious manager within the conditions of free competition viz-a-viz a third party shall serve as a basis for review of the arm's length character of the transaction. The function of the taxpayer shall be properly remunerated; subsidiaries without a function or with insignificant functions shall not be remunerated or only on the basis of cost-plus.

c. Standard Pricing Methods

1. The Comparable Uncontrolled Price Method
   - by external comparison, ie comparison with public quotations, prices ruling in a particular branch of business, or prices actually contracted between independent third parties;
   - by internal comparison, ie comparison with market prices contracted by the taxpayer or affiliated entities with unrelated parties.
2. The Resale Price Method
   Under this approach, the transfer price is developed by deducting from the selling price to third parties a normal rebate allowing for the functions and risks of the re-seller. This could also be called the functional rebate method.
3. The Cost-Plus Method
   This method provides for determination of the transfer price on the basis of costs of the manufacturer (or provider of services) calculated under the same method employed for costing of sales to third parties, and increased by a profit mark-up usual in the enterprise or the branch of business.
4. Internal and External Operations Comparison
   This compares overall results of operations which the taxpayer or related entities (internal comparison) or unrelated third parties (external comparison) have achieved.

   A sequence of application of methods is not identified. However, a combination of more than one method and emphasis on the method based on the most reliable information is encouraged. Application of the resale price method for a manufacturer of semi-finished goods is excluded.

Uniform group pricing methods may be accepted if the system permits adequate differentiation for varying facts and circumstances, can be examined easily and completely, and are reviewed and adjusted to changing conditions currently.

In cases where none of the above methods can reasonably be applied or documented, it is permissable to agree on an appropriate allocation of total income from the transaction between the related entities involved (net income basis).

d. Important Specific Provision of the Guideline

1. A separate charge for patents, know-how or other intangibles incorporated in a product purchased from parent or affiliated entities will be disallowed.
2. If government controlled prices and other restrictions exist, these can be taken into account.
3. Services usually connected with a purchase of goods and deemed covered by the purchase price cannot be charged for separately, eg warranty, maintenance or concessional repairs.
4. It is assumed that product advertising may be a function attributable to both the manufacturer of the product and the reseller. If the reseller is to bear advertising expenses, that must be allowed for noticeably in the transfer prices or by special agreement.
5. The cost of introduction of a product on a market is usually borne by the reseller only to the extent that a reasonable profit remains to him. Having the reseller bear a major part of market introduction expenses is permissable if contractual rebates are increased sufficiently to enable short-term recovery of these expenses by the reseller. Alternatively, the takeover of these expenses by the manufacturer can be reflected in a correspondingly reduced gross profit margin granted to the reseller.

   Exceptional market penetration costs, like price cutting to increase or maintain a market share on a highly competitive market, are to be borne by the manufacturer.
6. Start-up losses arising on formation, expansion or major reorganization of the company and not caused by 4 and 5 are accepted inasmuch as future profitability is likely to permit recovery.
7. Interest rates shall be those at which banks would provide loans under comparable facts and conditions; for medium and long-term loans, it is considered normal to have an interest rate adjustment provision to periodically reflect changes of the money market conditions. Currency loans shall be at rates including the cost of sheltering against exchange

risks. Lower interest rates obtainable on other money markets must be taken into account.

8. Where charges for services rendered by parent or affiliated companies or headquarter organizations are concerned, these can either be on a cost-plus or market price basis for individual identified and quantified services or an allocation of cost only basis.

   The allocation of costs only method requires that: charges be limited to costs for service areas actually needed and used by the taxpayer, the taxpayer must have the right to request such services, application of a fair allocation method considering the actual current or expected utilization of these services, deduction of other income achieved by the service centre against allocated costs, and takeover by the centre of costs of services rendered by the taxpayer for the benefit of the service centre or its participants on a corresponding basis. These rules also apply for research centres.

   Services not deductible by a subsidiary company but to be borne by the parent company include:
   - the so-called group support including use of group name or entrepreneurial decision making
   - shareholders' meetings and audit in the interest of the parent company
   - production and investment planning and control
   - control, supervision, coordination and planning within the group
9. Whether a shareholder's loan represents a substitute for equity shall be governed by Supreme Tax Court rulings (if repayment not seriously expected, circumstances demand equity contribution) and the abuse rules.
10. Guarantee commissions can only be charged if there is a saving of interest expense and if they likewise would have been charged to an unrelated business associate (distributor).
11. Licence fees for patents, know-how or other intangibles can be charged at arm's length rates (comparable uncontrolled licence fee rates) applied to a reasonable base (sales, quantity, lump sum). If comparable rates are not available, the charge must leave a reasonable operating profit from manufacture and sale of the licensed product in Germany.

The guideline clarifies that the German subsidiary must submit all information necessary to examine transfer prices or cost allocations, including information on affiliated entities, and should include provisions to this effect in contracts with affiliated entities. A transitional rule provides that, if enterprises change their intercompany transfer price or cost allocation arrangements to the principles laid down in the guideline within a three-year period, this will not adversely influence the tax auditor's review of the past.

B. Related Persons

Article 1(2) of the Foreign Tax Affairs Law defines a related person as follows:

1. The person holds directly or indirectly a participation of at least one-fourth in the taxpayer's capital (major participation) or if the person is able to exert, directly or indirectly, a controlling influence upon the taxpayer or vice-versa, if the taxpayer holds a major participation in the capital of the person or is able to exert, directly or indirectly, a controlling influence upon such person, or
2. A third party holds major participations both in the capital of the person and of the taxpayer or is able to exert, directly or indirectly, a controlling influence on both of them, or
3. The person or the taxpayer are able, in agreeing on the terms and conditions of a business relationship, to exert influences on the taxpayer or on the person based on facts beyond such business relationship or if one of them is personally interested in the other party's earning of such income.

Court rulings on hidden distributions had developed similar rules. A participation of less than 25 per cent does not normally permit the assumption of non-arm's length dealing except where several shareholders have identical interests. For holdings between 25 per cent and 50 per cent, the influence of the shareholder relation shall be examined and, for majority holdings, it is deemed to exist.

C. Basis for Making Adjustments

The adjustment of taxable income for intercompany transactions shall be made on an individual transaction or group of similar transactions basis. Profitability of a company or the lack of profitability only serves as an indication for the possible non-arm's length nature of transactions, eg, to compare royalties paid to parent or affiliated company with residual profit of the company from licensed transactions. If due to information withheld or not provided by the taxpayer the basis of taxation must be estimated then, in the absence of other suitable criteria, such estimation shall be based on the criteria of, a return on the capital invested in the enterprise, or of a gross profit which on the basis of experience and usage can be expected under normal circumstances (Article 1(3) Foreign Affairs Law).

D. Statute of Limitation

The normal statutes of limitation apply to the making of allocations. These provide for a four-year period of limitation, starting with the end of the year during which the tax return was filed which contains the income or expense to be reallocated. There are various rules governing interruption and deferral of the period of limitation. In the case of tax evasion, the period of limitation is extended to ten years. Competent authority procedures under tax treaties usually overrule the statute of limitation.

E. Correlative Adjustments

Where foreign tax authorities adjust the income of a foreign company which is related to a German company, then the German company can apply for a correlative adjustment under the competent authority procedure contained in German tax treaties. Where non-treaty countries are concerned the German tax authorities, in accordance with Section 1.15.1 of the Regulations to the Foreign Tax Affairs Law, provide the taxpayer with official confirmation as to the adjustments intended to enable him to apply for correlative adjustment.

A legally enforceable entitlement of the taxpayer to obtain a correlative adjustment from the other state or in Germany does not exist, however.

F. Effect of Adjustment

Two groups of cases must be distinguished when analyzing the effect of an adjustment made:

a. a German parent company with a foreign subsidiary;
b. a foreign parent company with a German subsidiary.

a. If the German parent grants a contributable benefit to its foreign subsidiary, eg transfer price of products is artificially low, the adjustment determined by the German tax authorities is added to the cost of the investment in the foreign subsidiary as a hidden contribution of capital. Ordinary taxable income of the German parent company is increased. The taxpayer may then attempt to obtain a corresponding adjustment in the other country under treaty provisions or with a confirmation by the German tax authorities.

A consolidation of the German parent and the foreign subsidiary company's taxable income is not permissible under German tax law. Only dividends received from the foreign subsidiary represent taxable income with foreign tax credit or tax exempt income if received from most treaty countries. In exceptional cases, a write-down of the increased book value of the investment in the foreign subsidiary may be obtainable.

Although hidden distributions of income or hidden contributions of capital cannot normally be converted into open adjustments of current business transactions with retroactive force, it is occasionally possible to obtain such retroactive adjustment if the adjustments proposed are very significant or if competent authorities of the two states agree on this treatment.

If the foreign state demands the upward adjustment of profits of a foreign subsidiary, the German tax authorities may agree to a correlative adjustment in which case taxable income of the German parent company is reduced while the additional income of the foreign subsidiary, if distributed as a dividend, may be exempt from German tax under treaty or brings along an increased foreign tax credit.

If, however, the German tax authorities are not willing to grant a correlative adjustment, double taxation may well arise. If competent authority procedures are not available or are unsuccessful, the German parent company could then possibly write-down in a tax deductible manner its investment in the foreign subsidiary, if the additional foreign taxes payable reduce the equity in the foreign subsidiary below the cost of the investment.

b. If a German subsidiary carries out a hidden distribution of income to its foreign parent or affiliate as defined earlier, the tax effect on the German subsidiary of this adjustment can vary substantially depending on the profitability or otherwise, as well as on the retention or distribution habits of the German subsidiary.

A hidden distribution of income is deemed made out of retained earnings existing at the end of the year. If fully taxed retained earnings exist, then the hidden distribution of income will carry the same tax burden as an open dividend distribution. If no, or inadequate, retained earnings or a deficit exists at the end of the year, a so-called distribution burden of 56.25 per cent (36 per cent of grossed-up hidden distribution) has to be accrued.

This can, together with the municipal income tax and withholding tax on dividends, lead to a total tax burden on the hidden distribution of income in excess of 80 per cent. If a current year loss exists, the adjustment would reduce this tax loss while at the same time the distribution burden of 56.25 per cent and the withholding tax of 25 per cent (or lower treaty rate) is payable in the absence of income!

Special rules apply if tax exempt income or pre-1977 income had been retained or if contributions of capital other than capital stock were made.

If the foreign parent company has granted contributable benefits to the German subsidiary, a subsequent correlative adjustment may be agreed to in competent authority procedures under tax treaties. This would result in a reduction of taxable income to the German subsidiary with correspondingly lower corporation tax burdens if not already distributed as dividends to the foreign parent.

G. Year of Adjustment

Adjustments are made to the tax years in which the underlying transaction took place. If a taxpayer voluntarily, or due to contractual or statutory tax clauses, or as a result of the provision of company law prohibiting repayment of capital stock, carries out a retroactive adjustment of income, the German tax authorities treat the adjustment first as a hidden distribution of income and the subsequent repayment by the shareholder as a contribution of additional capital. This treatment is in line with the basic principle of German taxation expecting clear prospective agreements with affiliated entities and prohibiting retroactive arrangements between shareholder and company.

H. Limitation of Adjustment under Allocation Rules

The taxpayer can, where years covered by assessments are concerned, initiate adjustment by filing a request for competent authority procedures under tax treaty. The request should normally be initiated with the tax authorities in the country of residence of the parent company because only there the double taxation effect can be demonstrated. In practice, the request for competent authority procedures usually follows an adjustment made or proposed by tax auditors of the German or foreign company.

PART II. SPECIFIC EXAMPLES

A. Sale of Goods

Assumed Facts

Assume P is a manufacturer which sells finished products to S which is located in a different country. P sells these products to S at cost. P also sells these products to unrelated parties at cost plus 10 per cent mark-on. Both S and the unrelated parties incur the same selling and promotional expense and both resell P's products at the same price per unit.

German Parent Company

1. Yes, Germany would allocate income to P.
2. Under the dealing-at-arm's-length-provisions the comparable third party sales price should also apply for sales to S.
3. Yes and no: If no sales to independent partiers occur, the profit margin realized by S would have to be reviewed to determine whether P had to sell at cost in order to permit S to make a normal profit commensurate with the marketing functions fulfilled by S. It is a standard allocation rule that the cost of market penetration efforts like price-cutting, advertising campaigns etc., should be borne by the manufacturer P because P has the primary interest in selling its products to the foreign market.

German Subsidiary Company

1. German tax authorities will not automatically accept allocations of foreign parent company's country but will make an independent determination of the value of the benefit contributed.
2. Foreign initiated adjustments are accepted only if competent authority procedures come to the conclusion that the adjustment is agreeable. Internal German tax law does not permit retroactive adjustment.
3. Should S choose to make payment of extra income allocated to P by P's tax authorities, the payment is treated as a hidden distribution of income except if agreed to under competent authority procedures.

B. Loans and Advances

Assumed Facts

P and S are manufacturers located in different countries. P loans S money on open account without interest so that S can expand its operations. P is not engaged in the business of lending money.

German Parent Company

1. The rules described earlier would normally require interest income allocation. The exception to the rule, ie parent company has no interest expense attributable to the non-interest bearing loan to S, is not in practice applied by the tax authorities where a foreign subsidiary is concerned. The interest rate should be the market lending rate for the currency involved or the German mark rate plus cost of sheltering exposure.
2. No: the existence of a non-interest bearing note to evidence the debt would not prevent the income allocation to P.
3. No: repayment of loan has no income effect.

German Subsidiary Company

1. German allocation rules do not require an interest charge by the shareholder, do not consider interest a contributable benefit and do not permit retroactive charge of interest. If competent authority procedures are invoked, German tax authorities will make separate determination.
2. Transaction will be characterized as a loan in any event.
3. No, see 1. above. The interest rate should under German allocation rules be the market borrowing rate for the currency and duration agreed. If agreement is put in place, then reasonable interest will be allowed on a prospective basis.
4. Not applicable as competent authority agreement is required. Otherwise, excess payment is treated as a hidden distribution of income.
5. Not applicable, see above. If German subsidiary without agreement of tax authorities retroactively pays interest it is treated as a hidden distribution of income. If paid with agreement no withholding tax is payable on interest for loans not secured by mortgage or not in bond form.

C. Intangibles

Assumed Facts

P and S are manufacturers located in different countries. P performs research and development which has led to P's ownership of certain intangibles consisting of patents, trademarks and know-how. P makes available to S exclusive right to use in S's country all of P's intangibles. P does not charge S for the use of P's intangibles.

German Parent Company

1. Yes, if S is given ownership of intangibles a contribution to capital of S can be assumed giving rise to income at the discounted value of hypothetical future net arm's-length royalty payments of S.
2. See 1. above. Treatment by tax authorities of country of S does not influence German taxability. (Exception: Brazilian subsidiary pays royalty; this is treated as a hidden distribution, ie a dividend received from S).
3. Yes, a portion of the R&D costs could be allocated to S as an alternative to 1. and 2.
4. Yes, a bona fide cost-sharing agreement is an acceptable alternative to 1. and 2.

German Subsidiary Company

1. The use of intangibles is not a contributable benefit. If competent authority procedures are invoked, German tax authorities will make a separate determination.
2. The German subsidiary will not be allowed a deduction for the income imputed to P except if competent authority procedures are successful. Determination will be by third party comparison or by analysis of fairness of cost sharing methods employed.
3. Yes and no: If S makes payments to P in line with competent authority agreement a withholding tax may be payable depending on the provisions of the respective tax treaty, eg USA none, Canada 15 per cent. If payment is made in excess of agreed amount it is treated as a hidden distribution of income (dividend).

D. Services

Assumed Facts

P is a large multinational concern which wholly owns foreign subsidiary S. Both P and S are engaged in manufacturing and sales activities. P's headquarters division performs general management services for P's multi-national operations including services which directly relate to S. The services performed for S include periodic visits by P's executives to review S's operations, financial analysis of S's future requirements, engineering services in connection with S's manufacturing activities and marketing services in connection with S's sales activities. P does not charge S for such service.

German Parent Company

1. Yes, income will be allocated to P for services which relate to assistance with day-to-day business transactions like engineering services, marketing services.

No income will be allocated for services which relate to supervision, control and coordination of subsidiary's activities or other shareholding related activities (stewardship).

The service charge for administrative services is usually computed on a cost basis (including indirect costs) not to exceed third party prices. Where engineering services, not covered by a licence agreement, or other technical services are concerned a cost-plus allocation is made if a cost sharing approach does not appear appropriate under the circumstances.

2. See 1. above. Joint facilities in central location would require cost-sharing approach, whereas special individual services would require cost-plus or fee approach.

German Subsidiary Company

1. No, a reduction in income of S for the imputed income in P is not made automatically because retroactive charges are generally disallowed. However, competent authority procedures may lead to a corresponding adjustment. German tax authorities will make a separate determination, based on rules described under 1. and 2. above. Germany will not accept allocations for stewardship functions, but may accept allocations regarding engineering or marketing costs if they are fairly allocated and substantiated.

2. No, German withholding tax will apply if a charge for services is paid in accordance with competent authority agreement. Otherwise treated as hidden distribution of income (dividend).

E. Loan Guarantees and Rentals

Assumed Facts

P is a multinational company whose main business is manufacturing and selling. P plans to establish foreign sales subsidiary S located in country S. P capitalizes S with $500,000 and guarantees a loan to S of $500,000 obtained from an independent bank. Land and a warehouse which P owns in country S will be used as a site for S's operations. P plans to make this land and warehouse available to S at a fee of $1 per year for 99 years.

German Parent Company

1. No income will be allocated to P for guaranteeing the bank loan. Income would normally be allocated for the use by S of P's real estate. If, however, the distributorship agreement clearly provided for free use of office and warehouse space in return for a correspondingly reduced discount/rebate on P's products purchased, this offsetting agreement would be acceptable if prospectively concluded.
2. Treatment as additional equity investment is likely in that a 99-year lease at $1 is equal to economic ownership of the building, the useful life of which is 50 years for tax purposes. This would lead to recognition of gain for the difference between book value and fair market value at the date of contribution. The fair market value of the building is debited to the investment account. No further consequences on a current basis.

German Subsidiary Company

1. German tax authorities will make their own separate determination.
2. Under the general rules analyzed above the shareholder is not obliged to charge the company for the use of an asset. A retroactive charge in later years is disallowed. Only competent authority procedures could lead to a correlative charge at market rates or deemed contribution to capital and a depreciation charge.
3. If income allocation is agreed to by competent authorities (or prospectively by tax authorities), the rental income or gain on contribution will be assessed to German corporate income tax. Rental income from German real property is liable to corporation tax at the rate of 50 per cent of net rental income (gross less depreciation, connected interest, land tax) on an annual assessment basis.

PART III. TAX TREATIES

A. Yes, Germany has mutual agreement procedures in its treaties.

B. The competent authorities or mutual agreement procedures have already been referred to in the answer to the case studies in Part II. The German tax authorities in negotiation with other treaty countries would analyze whether the adjustments proposed would be in conformity with German tax law if they had been agreed on prospectively, ie whether disallowance is based on form or substance of the adjustment. They also take into account whether the German taxes payable mean a special hardship on the taxpayer, eg a distribution burden is assessed in loss years. Where both form and substance under German tax law would not permit a correlative adjustment, and a hardship case is not given or was brought about through carelessness of the taxpayer, an agreement by the

German competent authorities to an adjustment proposed by the other country is not likely.

C. Competent authority procedures for an individual tax case must be invoked by the taxpayer. It is standard procedure that the application is first directed to the tax authorities of the parent company's country, and that correspondingly the subsidiary applies in its country through copy of the application filed by the parent company.

D. Guidelines do not exist for procedures to be followed when filing application for competent authority procedures. The application is usually channelled via the tax office to the state and federal ministries of finance.

E. If the competent authorities of the two treaty countries fail to reach a settlement there is no legal remedy or appeal possible. If the parent company is German it may be possible to obtain some unilateral relief, eg by writing down the investment as indicated earlier.

F. There is no right of appeal on the result of competent authority procedures. A draft guideline prepared by the EEC on compulsory arbitration will probably take a long time to finalize and approve.

G. Yes and no: There may be consequences where net assets tax and trade tax on capital is concerned, eg a receivable raised against a subsidiary increases taxable net assets. Alternatively, if a German subsidiary made hidden distributions of income and a receivable is now raised for this, the German tax authorities usually accrue interest on this receivable. If this is not removed by competent authorities then this indirect effect on income remains, if not correspondingly adjusted in the parent company's country.

H. Not much is known in public about the outcome of competent authority procedures. If the case is complex, it may take several years before a mutual agreement is reached. In general, it can be said that the German tax authorities are not willing to concede any points in competent authority procedures if a tax audit had previously settled many issues in a compromise and the taxpayer now desires a correlative adjustment just for one or certain of the ingredients of the compromise.

On the other hand, if the German taxpayer does not agree to a compromise in the closing conference on the tax audit but reserves all rights of appeal including competent authorities, the tax authorities will maximize their findings in view of the pending litigation. It may well be advantageous, therefore, to forego competent authority procedures in the interest of an early solution even if the other state (like the USA) insists on keeping all rights of appeal open.

PART IV. SPECIAL SITUATIONS

The normal allocation rules described earlier are not modified or applied differently in the following situations.

A. 1. If either of the related companies have no gross income.
   2. If either of the related companies has an operating loss for the year.
   3. Where the tax rates in the different countries are substantially equal.
   4. Where income is to be allocated to a low tax rate country. However, this may adversely influence the thinking and investigation process of the German tax authorities.

B. In addition to the rules on allocation mentioned above, the Foreign Tax Affairs Law contains provisions for current taxation in Germany of base company income which are very similar to the US sub-part F rules. If these provisions do not lead to current taxation, the tax authorities investigate much more closely the individual business transactions with the foreign subsidiary. The fiscal code provides for an increased obligation of the taxpayer to provide information on transactions involving foreign affiliates. This rule is often used where foreign multinational groups have base companies, ie international marketing organizations, service pools (eg European headquarters), etc., and the substance of transactions with these companies appears to be doubtful.

PART V. OTHER CONSIDERATIONS

As a result of changes in the political situation and in order to increase tax revenues, one can notice a gradual tightening of the attitude of the German tax authorities towards cross-border transactions of multinational groups as well as individual German investors abroad. In 1964, a 'tax oasis report' was prepared by the German government outlining the revenue impact of certain tax reducing arrangements of foreign activities of taxpayers. Following this the Foreign Tax Affairs Law was drafted and became effective in 1972. A special Federal Tax Office (*Bundesamt fur Finanzen*) with central functions for foreign and cross-border tax matters was created, which also performed training functions for tax auditors and coordination functions through internal guidelines.

The German government is proposing to introduce a thin capitalization rule which may treat interest charged on shareholder's loans if outside a 1:1 debt:equity ratio as hidden distributions of income. If this law change is enacted, the volume of competent authority applications may increase significantly primarily because the debt:equity relation proposed is much lower than that applicable in other countries which also have a thin capitalization concept. No noticeable progress has been made, but tax offices now try to bring practical cases of thin capitalization before the Supreme Tax Court in order to upset previous Supreme Tax Court rulings, leaving almost total freedom to the shareholder on how he wishes to finance his company.

Hong Kong

Marshall H. Byres/Alexander Mak

PART I. GENERAL RULES

A. The Hong Kong Inland Revenue Ordinance does not provide for allocation of income or expenses between related entities. However, it does have provisions intended to counter the types of abuses at which the allocation provisions of other jurisdications are aimed. Before explaining these provisions, it must be stressed that they are rarely invoked. Because of the low tax rate in Hong Kong, it is quite likely that more income is artificially diverted to Hong Kong than from it. Probably as a result of this and the overriding laissez-faire attitude of the government to business, the local tax authorities generally respect the form of business transactions, are very reluctant to invoke the anti-avoidance measures, and have had only limited success when they have invoked them.

B. Keeping in mind that it is rarely invoked, Section 20 of the Inland Revenue Ordinance is the prime weapon of Hong Kong tax authorities to counter the diversion of taxable profits to related entities out of Hong Kong's tax jurisdiction. Under Section 20 (reproduced in Appendix) if a non-resident person carries on business with a closely connected resident person in such a manner that the profits of the resident which would ordinarily be expected to arise in Hong Kong are reduced, then the profits of the non-resident will be deemed to arise in Hong Kong. Two persons are 'closely connected' if 'the Commissioner in his discretion' considers that they are substantially identical or that the ultimate controlling interest of each is owned by the same person or persons.

C. It should be noted that Section 20 does not allocate income or expenses to arrive at an arm's length result but deems the entire profit of the non-resident which is involved in the related party transaction to arise and, therefore, be taxable in Hong Kong. This is done on a transactional rather than a net income basis, ie the non-resident's net income is not apportioned but all of the income from the related party transactions is deemed to arise from doing business in Hong Kong. The resident entity's tax status is not changed, but the non-resident entity is subject to tax. That tax is levied on the resident entity as agent of the non-resident.

D. No standards are given for invocation of Section 20, no safe havens are provided for, and no transactions are singled out for coverage. Section 20 does not apply to transactions between resident entities. However, the terms 'resident' and 'non-resident' are not defined. In general the Revenue has six years from the end of the year of assessment to raise an additional assessment. If fraud or wilful evasion is involved, the statute of limitations is increased to 10 years.

Hong Kong Revenue also has authority to disregard, under Section 61 (reproduced at the Appendix), any transaction it regards as artificial or fictitious or any disposition that is not in fact given effect to. As with Section 20, this section is only invoked in cases of extreme abuse.

Under Section 16 (partially reproduced in the Appendix) business expenses are only allowed as deductions to the extent they are incurred in the production of chargeable profits. The Revenue is more likely to invoke this general principle to disallow all or a portion of expenses than to invoke Section 20 or Section 61. In many cases, this can be seen as having the same effect as an allocation of expenses. No safe havens or guidelines are given for Section 16.

There has recently been a significant change of attitude towards tax avoidance schemes in the Courts of the United Kingdom. In particular, the House of Lords decided, in the case of *Furniss* v. *Dawson*, that any 'pre-ordained series of transactions into which there are inserted steps that have no commercial purpose apart from the avoidance of a liability to tax should, as a matter of principle, be looked through'.

Since the Hong Kong Inland Revenue tends to follow and apply Court decisions in the United Kingdom, the decision in *Furniss* v. *Dawson* may have application in Hong Kong, but the extent of the application is still uncertain. The ultimate court of appeal on Hong Kong tax disputes is the Privy Council of the UK's House of Lords so that, in theory at least, the decision does have potential ramifications in Hong Kong.

E./F. Hong Kong tax law has no provision for correlative adjustment due to allocations made by other tax jurisdictions. A tax assessment can be corrected under Section 70(A) (reproduced in the Appendix) if it can be established that the tax charged was excessive due to an error or omission in the return, but allocation by a foreign tax jurisdiction would not generally be held to indicate an error in the original return. Such a claim might have weight, however, if there was a provision in an original contract which provided for changes to reflect subsequent tax jurisdiction allocations. The statute of limitations for an amendment under Section 70(A) is the later of six years from the end of the year of assessment, or six months after the service of the notice of assessment.

Many of the ancillary problems of an allocation are not problems in Hong Kong because of the relative simplicity of Hong Kong tax law. There are no provisions for consolidated tax returns or group relief under Hong Kong tax law. Hong Kong does not tax dividend income and does not grant foreign tax credits. There is also no withholding tax on dividends paid from Hong Kong. Consequently, if payment of a foreign jurisdiction's allocated amount is made from a Hong Kong subsidiary to a foreign parent, the question of whether such payment will be subject to dividend withholding does not arise.

G. Any adjustments which Hong Kong authorities might make would be to the underlying transaction year.

H. Hong Kong tax authorities do not care about allocations unless income of Hong Kong subsidiaries is understated. In many cases, Hong Kong authorities will make changes only prospectively as they put much reliance on what was included in original financial statements filed.

PART II. SPECIFIC EXAMPLES

A. Sale of Goods

Assumed Facts

Assume P is a manufacturer which sells finished products to S which is located in a different country. P sells these products to S at cost. P also sells these products to unrelated parties at cost plus 10 per cent mark-on. Both S and the unrelated parties incur the same selling and promotional expense and both resell P's products at the same price per unit.

Parent in Hong Kong

1. If a Hong Kong parent sells goods to a foreign subsidiary for less than an arm's length price, the Hong Kong Revenue will not allocate income to the parent.
2. Under Section 20 the Revenue could deem the income of the subsidiary to derive from a business carried on in Hong Kong through the parent acting as agent of the subsidiary. If Section 20 were invoked all of the subsidiary's income from those transactions would be taxable in Hong Kong and the tax would be assessed on the parent as agent of the subsidiary. It is unlikely that Section 20 would be invoked unless the transfer price was clearly abusive.
3. Arguments as to selling and promotional expenses or establishing a market might be taken into consideration along with all the other facts and circumstances to determine if 'less than the ordinary profits which might be expected' were subject to tax in the colony.

Subsidiary in Hong Kong

1. If the tax jurisdiction of the foreign parent of a Hong Kong subsidiary allocated income from the subsidiary to the parent, the Hong Kong Revenue would not generally accept that allocation as being a basis to reduce its tax assessment.
2. It may be possible to reduce the Hong Kong assessment under a Section 70(A) claim that the original assessment was based on an error in the transfer price if the original transfer price was made under an agreement that was conditional on acceptance by the foreign revenue; but even this is doubtful.
3. Payment of the allocated amount to the foreign parent would not give rise to any withholding tax.

B. Loans and Advances

Assumed Facts

P and S are manufacturers located in different countries. P loans S money on open account without interest so that S can expand its operations. P is not engaged in the business of lending money.

Parent in Hong Kong

1. Until recently, the interest income of a non-financial institution was only taxable to the Hong Kong parent if the funds were made available in Hong Kong. Legislation has, however, been introduced which seeks to assess to Profits Tax, interest earned outside Hong Kong but arising through or from the carrying on of a business in Hong Kong.

In view of this legislation, and having regard to the UK decision in *Furniss* v. *Dawson*, it is probable that if an interest-free loan is made to a subsidiary outside of Hong Kong, the Revenue might regard any dividends received from this subsidiary as, in their true nature, interest in respect of the loan given. However, no such practice has yet evolved although a statement is presently (October, 1984) awaited.

If interest is payable on the loan, even at less than an arm's length rate, the Revenue would not normally allocate additional interest to the Hong Kong parent. However, if the Hong Kong parent company were to buy capital stock of a foreign tax haven subsidiary who invested the funds, subsequent dividends from the subsidiary going back to Hong Kong should not be taxable in Hong Kong.
2. It would make no difference if the loan were evidenced by a non-interest-bearing note with a fixed maturity date.
3. The loan could not be considered as an additional equity interest but even if

if it were, as Hong Kong does not tax dividend income, repayment would have no tax consequences.

Subsidiary in Hong Kong

1./2. The Hong Kong Revenue would not generally regard an allocation of interest by a foreign jurisdiction as sufficient basis for a Section 70(A) amendment.
3. If a Hong Kong subsidiary were the borrower and the interest rate was excessive, Revenue might disallow a portion of the interest as not being incurred in the production of chargeable profits. There are no safe haven or other guidelines to determine what might be considered an excessive interest rate by the Inland Revenue Department.
4./5. Whereas payment of interest to an overseas parent might require withholding of 15 per cent, if Revenue did not recognize payment of the allocated amount as an increase in interest expense of the subsidiary, there would generally be no increase in interest subject to withholding tax as there is no withholding tax on dividends or royalties leaving Hong Kong. Also, there is no withholding on interest if the loan was arranged outside of Hong Kong; there is otherwise a 15 per cent withholding on interest.

C. INTANGIBLES

Assumed Facts

P and S are manufacturers located in different countries. P performs research and development which has led to P's ownership of certain intangibles consisting of patents, trademarks and know-how. P makes available to S exclusive right to use in S's country all of P's intangibles. P does not charge S for the use of P's intangibles.

Parent in Hong Kong

The Revenue would not allocate royalty income to a Hong Kong parent from its overseas subsidiary. The Revenue might disallow all or a portion of the parent's expenses as not being incurred in the production of profits assessable to tax. This would most likely be done if it were obvious that the parent was not using the intangibles to produce profits assessable in Hong Kong.

Subsidiary in Hong Kong

Royalties paid for the use of intangibles in Hong Kong are deductible if incurred in the production of profits chargeable to tax. If Revenue considered a royalty payment to be excessive, it might disallow a portion of the expense as not being incurred in the production of chargeable profits. Revenue would not generally accept a foreign jurisdiction's allocation of royalty to be sufficient to justify a Section 70(A) error claim. There is a de-facto withholding tax on royalties of 1.85 per cent (profits tax rate of 18.5 per cent times an assumed profit element in the payment of 10 per cent) which would apply if Revenue accepted the Section 70(A) claim to allow an increase in the subsidiary's royalty expense. In the more likely case that the Section 70(A) claim was not allowed, payment of the allocated amount would not give rise to any withholding tax.

D. Services

Assumed Facts

P is a large multinational concern which wholly owns foreign subsidiary S. Both P and S are engaged in manufacturing and sales activities. P's headquarters division performs general management services for P's multi-national operations including services which directly relate to S. The services performed for S include periodic visits by P's executives to review S's operations, financial analysis of S's future requirements, engineering services in connection with S's manufacturing activities and marketing services in connection with S's sales activities. P does not charge S for such service.

Parent in Hong Kong

If a Hong Kong parent performs services for an overseas subsidiary Revenue would generally accept whatever fee the parent charged the subsidiary but might be expected to question the expenses of the parent. If no fee is charged by the parent then all or a portion of the applicable expenses of the parent would be disallowed under Section 16 as not having been incurred in the production of assessable profits.

Subsidiary in Hong Kong

If a Hong Kong subsidiary pays a foreign parent an abusively high fee for management services, Revenue might disallow a portion of the subsidiary's expense as not being incurred in the production of chargeable profits. The Hong Kong Revenue would not generally accept an allocation of management fees by the foreign jurisdiction as being sufficient basis for a Section 70(A) amendment to the Hong Kong return. There is no Hong Kong withholding tax on management fees, so acceptance or rejection of the Section 70(A) claim would not give rise to withholding tax on payment of the allocated amount.

E. Loan Guarantees and Rentals

Assumed Facts

P is a multinational company whose main business is manufacturing and selling. P plans to establish foreign sales subsidiary S located in country S. P capitalizes S with $500,000 and guarantees a loan to S of $500,000 obtained from an independent bank. Land and a warehouse which P owns in country S will be used as a site for S's operations. P plans to make this land and warehouse available to S at a fee of $1 per year for 99 years.

Parent in Hong Kong

No income would be allocated to a Hong Kong parent for its guarantee of a foreign subsidiary's debt or for the use by the foreign subsidiary of real property in the foreign country. Even if payments were received for the use of real property outside of Hong Kong they would not be taxable.

There would be no tax consequences to treating the transaction as an equity investment.

Subsidiary in Hong Kong

The Hong Kong Revenue would not recognize the allocation of income by a foreign jurisdiction to the parent of a Hong Kong subsidiary with regards to the property or the guarantee. Hong Kong would not make an allocation but would recognize a formal arrangement made by the two parties. There would be no withholding tax on payment of the allocated amounts.

PART III. TAX TREATIES

Hong Kong has not entered into any tax treaties with other countries. Hong Kong tax authorities have little or no dealings with their counterparts in other countries.

APPENDIX

Applicable Inland Revenue Ordinance Sections

16. 1. In ascertaining the profits in respect of which a person is chargeable to tax under this Part for any year of assessment, there shall be deducted all outgoings and expenses to the extent to which they are incurred during the basis period for that year of assessment by such person in the production of

profits in respect of which he is chargeable to tax under this Part for any period, including – . . . .

20. 1. For the purposes of this section –

a. a person is closely connected with another person where the Commissioner in his discretion considers that such persons are substantially identical or that the ultimate controlling interest of each is owned or deemed under this section to be owned by the same person or persons;

b. the controlling interest of a company shall be deemed to be owned by the beneficial owners of its shares, whether held directly or through nominees, and shares in one company held by or on behalf of another company shall be deemed to be held by the shareholders of the last-mentioned company.

2. Where a non-resident person carries on business with a resident person with whom he is closely connected and the course of such business is so arranged that it produces to the resident person either no profits which arise in or derive from the Colony or less than the ordinary profits which might be expected to arise in or derive from the Colony, the business done by the non-resident person in pursuance of his connection with the resident person shall be deemed to be carried on in the Colony, and such non-resident person shall be assessable and chargeable with tax in respect of his profits from such business in the name of the resident person as if the resident person were his agent, and all the provisions of this Ordinance shall apply accordingly.

6. Where an assessor is of the opinion that any transaction which reduces or would reduce the amount of tax payable by any person is artificial or fictitious or that any disposition is not in fact given effect to, he may disregard any such transaction or disposition and the person concerned shall be assessable accordingly.

70A. 1. Notwithstanding the provisions of Section 70 if, upon application made within 6 years after the end of a year of assessment or within 6 months after the date on which the relative notice of assessment was served, whichever is the later, it is established to the satisfaction of an assessor that the tax charged for that year of assessment is excessive by reason of an error or omission in any return or statement submitted in respect thereof, or by reason of any arithmetical error or omission in the calculation of the amount of the assessable income or profits assessed or in the amount of the tax charged, the assessor shall correct such assessment:

Provided that under this section no correction shall be made to any assessment in respect of an error or omission in any return or statement submitted in respect thereof as to the basis on which the liability to tax ought to have been computed where the return or statement was in fact made on the basis of or in accordance with the practice generally prevailing at the time when the return or statement was made.

Ireland

Dermot P. Clarke

INTRODUCTION

It should be stated at the outset that there is no all-embracing piece of legislation in the Irish tax code dealing with the allocation of income and expenses between related companies. It is also true to say that this area has generally not been critical as far as the Irish Revenue authorities are concerned because, since 1949, it has been government policy to promote industrial development here and one of the major features of this policy has been the existence of a low/nil tax rate for qualifying (generally manufacturing) companies. In this respect, Ireland has attracted significant foreign investment under the Export Sales Relief legislation which provided full relief for a period of fifteen years and tapering relief for the following five years. Export Sales Relief does not apply to companies commencing operations after January 1, 1981 but it will continue to apply until 1990 in respect of trades qualifying before that date. Currently, manufacturing companies which do not qualify for Export Sales Relief can avail of the new 10 per cent rate of Corporation Tax. Again, qualifying activities are, in general, manufacturing type activities and the 10 per cent rate applies to profits generated from the sale of goods whether or not they are exported. The 10 per cent rate will apply until the year 2000. As a result of these reliefs, it will be appreciated that the allocation of income and expenses to an Irish entity is likely to be such that profits are maximised here and, consequently, the Revenue's interest in this area is perhaps less than one would find in other jurisdictions.

Having said this, however, it is the case that legislative provisions in relation to the allocation of income and expenses have been introduced over the years to deal with specific circumstances. It should also be remembered that, where transactions fall outside these circumstances, there are some general tax provisions which might be invoked to restrict allocations between companies. It is the specific and general tax law provisions which will be referred to in this paper and these are outlined in the 'General Rules' section below. Before looking at these, however, it is worth mentioning that there may be non-tax constraints to be considered. For example:

a. Audit Requirements

Under the Companies Act 1963, every company is required to appoint independent auditors to report to the shareholders. The auditor reports as to whether proper books of account have been maintained by the company and whether the accounts show a 'true and fair view' of the company's results. Therefore, where there are material intercompany transactions, a 'true and fair view' of the company's results may necessitate disclosure of those transactions unless they are dealt with on a reasonable commercial basis.

b. Exchange Control Requirements
The Irish Exchange Control regulations basically operate to restrict outward movements of funds and to ensure that funds accruing to Irish residents from external sources are not withheld from the country's external reserves. Although commercial transactions are not generally restricted they are supervised to avoid unapproved capital outflows. In theory, therefore, 'extreme' transactions involving the allocation of income and expenses might come under Exchange Control scrutiny.

In summary, therefore, one needs to bear in mind that specific Irish legislation in this area is not as developed as may be the case in other countries, and many of the answers will refer to Revenue practice as opposed to the effect of particular statutory provisions.

PART I. GENERAL RULES

As previously outlined, there are:
a. specific provisions, and
b. general tax law provisions
which may be used by the Revenue Authorities to make allocations of income and expenses between related parties.

Specific Provisions

1. Section 62 Corporation Tax Act 1976

This applies where a company (the buyer) claiming Export Sales Relief buys from a company (the seller) which it controls, or the seller controls it, or both companies are under common control. In such cases, if the price charged is less than would have been expected if they were independent parties dealing at arm's length, then the income of the buyer will be computed as if the price was on an arms length basis.

2. Section 44 Finance Act 1980

Where a company is claiming the 10 per cent rate of the Corporation Tax and it either buys from or sells to a person which controls it, or it controls the other person (being a company or a partnership) or some persons controls both the buyer and seller, and the price of the transaction is less than would be expected if they were independent parties dealing at arm's length, then the income or losses of the buyer and the seller shall be computed for any purpose of the Tax Acts as if the price in the transaction was what it would have been on an arm's length basis.

3. Sections 202 to 204 Income Tax Act 1967

Section 202 applies where a non-resident person carries on business with a resident person and it appears to the Inspector that, owing to the close connection between the two and to the substantial control exercised by the non-resident over the resident, the business done by the resident as a result of the connection produces either no or less than ordinary profits to the resident person than might be expected to arise, then the non-resident will be assessed tax as if the resident person were an agent of the non-resident.

Section 203 applies where it appears to the Revenue that the true amount of the profits or gains of a non-resident person, chargeable in the name of a resident person, cannot be readily ascertained, then the non-resident may be charged on a percentage of the turnover of the business done by the non-resident through or with the resident person in whose name he is chargeable.

Section 204 states that, where a non-resident is chargeable in the name of any branch, agent, factor, etc., in respect of profits arising from the sale of goods produced outside Ireland by the non-resident, the person in whose name the non-resident is chargeable may apply to have the assessment to tax made on the basis of profits which might reasonably be expected to have been earned by a merchant or retailer who had bought direct from the producer.

4. Miscellaneous Specific Legislation

There are other specific areas in Irish legislation where market value may be imposed on a particular transaction. For example, in computing Capital Gains Tax liabilities or capital allowances (depreciation allowances) available on fixed assets, etc., there are rules interposing market value to non-arm's length transactions. Since this paper concentrates on allocation of income and expenses in 'trading' situations, any of the miscellaneous specific legislation will only be referred to if it is of relevance to a particular question asked.

It is clear from the above that specific legislation is of limited application. Moving on then to general tax law (and related Revenue practice) it will be seen that, in theory, this could be applied in a broad range of situations.

General Tax Law

1. Section 61 Income Tax Act 1967

This section provides that only expenses which are laid out or expended wholly and exclusively for the purposes of trade are deductible in computing taxable profits. This point is expanded on in that it is stated that any loss connected with or arising out of the trade is disallowable.

2. Tax Cases

The basic principles of Irish tax law are similar to those in the United Kingdom and, therefore, decisions in the UK Courts are regarded as 'persuasive' for Irish tax purposes.

With regard to the allocation of income and expenses, one of the most significant cases is *Sharkey* v. *Werhner* (36 TC 275) which was concerned with the transfer of horses from the taxpayer's stud farm business for private use in his racing activities. It was held that the transfer of the horses from the taxable stud farm business should be regarded as having been made at market value for tax purposes.

It has been Revenue practice in Ireland not to follow this decision although, in recent years, there seems to be a slight change of attitude and Revenue have indicated that they will not necessarily disregard the *Sharkey* v. *Werhner* decision or the more recent decisions in the UK Courts which are of relevance in this area. With regard to these later decisions, the following are notable:

a. *Petrotim Securities Limited* v. *Ayres* (41 TC 389)
   This case concerned a share dealing company which sold shares at a loss (deliberately) to its parent company. A claim for loss relief was disallowed on the grounds that the loss was not made in the course of the trade and furthermore that the sale should be treated as having been made at market value on the date of transfer.
b. *Ridge Securities* v. *C.I.R.* (44 TC 373)
   A share dealing company sold War Loan in the open market shortly after it had purchased it at under value from a fellow subsidiary. It was held, following the principles laid down in *Sharkey* v. *Werhner*, that the acquisition of the War Loan should be brought into the computation at its market value (with the consequence that there was no profit).

There are also a significant number of tax cases on the question of whether an expense charged is deductible under the basic rule in Section 61, ie wholly and exclusively for the purposes of the trade. In this respect, there are a number of cases which specifically deal with situations where non-arm's length transactions were involved, eg *Marshal Richards Machinery Company Limited* v. *Jewitt* (36 TC 511); *Littlewoods Mail Order Stores Limited* v. *McGregor* (45 TC 519). This latter case involved the payment of an increased rent in order to enable a subsidiary to obtain a freehold interest in property for a reduced consideration. The increased rent was arranged by surrendering the old lease and granting a new lease for a lesser term. The increase in rent was disallowed in computing the taxable profits of the payer on the basis that it was a payment for a capital asset and, consequently, not a trading expense.

With regard to the four specific questions under Section A:

A. 1. In theory, adjustments could be made to either prevent tax avoidance or to clearly reflect income. In practice, such adjustments are only made to prevent avoidance of Irish tax.

2. As indicated in the general outline, market value/arm's length rates are likely to form the basis on which adjustments are made.

3. Under general law no specific transactions are covered. Transactions specifically covered in legislation are identified above. Safe havens are not provided for in allocating income and expenses between related parties. However, there is a specific legislation covering transactions with companies claiming an incentive rate of tax in Ireland.

4. While general law can be applied to transactions between resident and non-resident taxpayers alike, specific legislation can also be applied to certain transactions with non-residents as outlined in the commentary above.

B. Under general principles, allocations could effectively be made whether the parties are related or not. The question is unlikely to arise, however, where they are not related. Where specific legislation applies, the question of whether two companies are related will generally be determined by establishing whether they are under common control. 'Control' is defined in Section 158, Corporation Tax Act 1976, as the power of any person to secure, by means of the holding of shares, or the possession of voting power or by virtue of any powers conferred by the Articles of Association or other document regulating the company, that the affairs of the company are conducted in accordance with the wishes of that person.

C. The principal approach in making adjustments is a transaction basis, ie arm's length principles. It is also true that a form of net income basis might be used – for example, the legislation covering transactions between a resident and non-resident specifically states that a percentage of turnover may form the basis of charge where the true amount of profits cannot be readily ascertained. The general principle applied here may also be used in practice in certain cases where a non-resident company is trading through a branch in Ireland (not necessarily with a connected resident person) but it is difficult to determine exactly what profits arise in Ireland from the activities of that non-resident. In certain circumstances, the Revenue will agree to determine Irish profits as a percentage of the expenses attributable to the Irish branch activities.

D. Under the 'discovery' provisions an Inspector can raise an additional assessment within ten years of the end of an accounting period if he discovers that profits have not been assessed, or an assessment is insufficient, or relief given is excessive. Where fraud or neglect is involved there is no time limit on raising additional assessments.

E. Where an adjustment is made in the country of the foreign related party there is no provision in Irish law whereby correlative adjustments can be claimed in Ireland. Obviously, of course, if Irish profits are under-assessed, the discovery provisions above could be invoked to 'adjust' those profits. In practice if an adjustment would operate to reduce Irish profits it may be possible to obtain effective correlative adjustments depending on the facts of the case – and this area is discussed further below.

F. When an adjustment is made to a non-Irish resident company there is no automatic correlative adjustment for Irish tax purposes.

1. The non-resident company is not taxed on a consolidated basis with Irish resident companies.
2. Foreign tax credits attaching to dividends can be affected if an adjustment is made in the foreign country. There are no statutory provisions in Irish law whereby correlative adjustments are deemed to be made for the purposes of computing Irish tax on subsequent dividends from the related non-resident companies. In other words, there could be an effective double charge to tax on the same profits. For example, although profits will not generally be allocated to an Irish parent company, if this did not happen such profits could be taxed a second time in Ireland when they are subsequently paid out to the parent company as dividends in subsequent years. Similarly, foreign tax credits are not automatically adjusted following an adjustment made in a foreign country and the normal Irish tax rules would apply in computing the credits. Therefore, depending on the circumstances of the case, an excess foreign tax credit position could occur in Ireland in a situation where that would not have been the case if no adjustment had been made overseas.
3. Payment of allocated amounts is not required. However, it may be desirable to make correlative adjustments in the books and accounts of both companies since, unless this is done, it will generally not be possible for the adjustment to become effective for Irish tax purposes.

G. Where adjustments are made in Ireland they will be made by Revenue to the profits of the accounting period in which the underlying transaction took place. In practice they may, however, treat an adjustment as a current year item to avoid opening prior years which have been settled. The taxpayer, of course, would have to be agreeable to this procedure.

H. As far as the taxpayer is concerned, he cannot simply initiate an adjustment as such unless there has been an 'error or mistake'. In this respect a change in the basis of intercompany pricing would not generally be regarded as falling within the error mistake provisions. On the other hand, as outlined previously, the taxpayer can to some extent initiate an adjustment in the period in which the adjustment is made in the accounts. Clearly, however, if a tax deduction is sought for the adjustment it will have to be justifiable under general principles, ie wholly and exclusively for the purposes of the trade, etc.

PART II. SPECIFIC EXAMPLES

A. Sale of Goods

Assumed Facts

Assume P is a manufacturer which sells finished products to S which is located in a different country. P sells these products to S at cost. P also sells these products to unrelated parties at cost plus 10 per cent mark-on. Both S and the unrelated parties incur the same selling and promotional expense and both resell P's products at the same price per unit.

Parent in Ireland

1. The transaction is of no real interest to the Irish Revenue where Export Sales Relief applies. In theory, Revenue could invoke the specific arm's length pricing legislation where the 10 per cent rate of Corporation Tax is claimed by P and, similarly, the specific legislation applicable to residents dealing with 'connected' non-residents might be applied. Moreover, general law principles which have been developed in tax cases on arm's length pricing could be used to substantiate a case that income should be allocated to P.

In summary, therefore, an adjustment is unlikely to be made since Revenue have not in practice relied on the arm's length pricing tax cases. Also, specific provisions outlined are unlikely to be used because, for example, where the 10 per cent rate is claimed, any adjustment is unlikely to yield significant extra tax.

2. If an allocation was made it would be on an arm's length pricing basis which in itself would take into account the price charged to unrelated parties, the volume of business with S, marketing conditions in S's country, etc.

3. All the circumstances mentioned would be relevant in determining the arm's length price.

Subsidiary in Ireland

1./2. Ignoring the effects of tax treaties, the Irish Revenue would not accept the allocation determined in P's country. Again, an effective adjustment might be achieved in Ireland by charging it in the accounts of the then current year or future years.

3. A payment of the allocated amount would not be regarded as a dividend if it is accepted as a transaction in the course of the trade. If it was not so regarded and treated as an effective dividend, ie transfer of assets for inadequate consideration, there would be no tax deduction available for the payment.

Withholding tax would not apply since there is no such tax on payment of dividends from Ireland. However, one should also review the impact of Advance Corporation Tax which has been recently introduced in Ireland, and works similarly to that in the United Kingdom.

B. Loans and Advances

Assumed Facts

P and S are manufacturers located in different countries. P loans S money on open account without interest so that S can expand its operations. P is not engaged in the business of lending money.

Parent in Ireland

1. Interest free loans are frequently made in Ireland without tax penalty. There is no specific legislation by which interest income would be allocated to P. There is a general provision which it is felt could perhaps be invoked but Revenue have not sought to use it in practice. This provision is Section 41(4) Finance Act 1974, which provides that where a person agrees to forego income arising from property (without selling or transferring it) then he is chargeable to tax on the amount of income foregone. It is arguable that this provision could not be applied anyway in that income is not necessarily foregone.

Ireland would also not deny P a deduction for interest on its borrowings which related to a low interest loan to S, as long as S used those funds in its trade.

It should be noted that Exchange Control Authorities may, however, insist on interest being charged but this is only likely to apply where the loan is being made by a company which is ultimately controlled by persons regarded as resident in Ireland for Exchange Control purposes.

2. The existence of a non-interest bearing note would not affect the results.

3. The loan would not be considered as additional equity investment for tax purposes.

Subsidiary in Ireland

1. The characterization of the transaction in P's country will not be accepted in Ireland for S.

2. The Irish tax authorities will look at the legal form and, therefore, if it is a non-interest-bearing loan it will be treated as such.
3. Interest will not be voluntarily allocated or imputed to S where none was provided for in earlier agreements entered into by S.
4. However, if S pays the amount allocated by P's country, the legislation relating to payment of interest will have to be considered. Briefly:
  a. since the loan is for trading purposes (and presumably the allocation is based on commercial rates, etc.) the interest paid will be allowed in full;
  b. such allowance will not apply if S is a 75 per cent subsidiary of P since the interest will be deemed a distribution (dividend). This is subject to a limited number of tax treaties which negate this deeming provision.
  It should be noted that, in spring of 1983, Ireland introduced an Advance Corporation Tax on payment of dividends similar to that in the UK. This is not a withholding tax *per se* but a non-refundable payment on account of the payor company's profits tax liabilities.
5. The transaction would not be regarded as an equity investment in S.

C. Intangibles

Assumed Facts

P and S are manufacturers located in different countries. P performs research and development which has led to P's ownership of certain intangibles consisting of patents, trademarks and know-how. P makes available to S exclusive right to use in S's country all of P's intangibles. P does not charge S for the use of P's intangibles.

Notes: It should be noted that under Irish tax law the treatment of income from patents, trademarks and know-how is not uniform. There is specific legislation dealing with patents and, very briefly:
a. income from 'qualifying' patents (work leading to the invention is carried out in Ireland) is exempt from tax in the hands of an Irish resident;
b. capital sums derived from the sale of (non-exempt) patent right are charged as income (provisions for spreading the charge apply);
c. under the general tax provisions dealing with annual payments, patent royalties are specifically excluded as deductions in computing income. Instead, they are allowable under the somewhat more restrictive 'charge' provisions as deductions from total profits.
d. there are specific capital allowance provisions granting a deduction by way of an annual writing down allowance for capital expenditure on the purchase of patent rights.

With regard to expenditure on know-how and trademarks, if such expenditure qualifies as a trading expense it will be deductible in computing profits. There are specific provisions allowing a deduction in computing trading profits for know-how payments which otherwise might be regarded as capital payments.

Parent in Ireland

1./2. There is no specific legislation by which the Revenue authorities would allocate income to P. It is also unlikely that income could be imputed on intangibles under general law where such income does not *arise* as such. As a matter of practice, Revenue do not currently seek to allocate such income.
3. Research and development costs incurred by P would not be allocated to S as such but the Irish Revenue could perhaps seek to disallow some of the expenses on the grounds that they were not incurred wholly and exclusively for the purposes of P's trade. The success of such a contention would depend on the facts of the case.
4. If there was a *bona fide* cost sharing arrangement, the possibility of a disallowance of P's share of the costs would be less likely.

Subsidiary in Ireland

1./3. As previously explained the Irish Revenue will not accept correlative adjustments. If payment is made in the form of an annual royalty it would, subject to double tax treaty provisions, be subject to withholding tax. This is subject to the principle that the royalty is not deemed to be a distribution since, if it was, withholding tax would not apply. The deemed distribution provisions could, of course, also be applied to a lump sum or other payment, in which case a tax deduction would not be available. Whether a lump sum or other payment would be deductible in computing profits will be determined on the facts of the case (ie whether wholly and exclusively incurred for the purposes of the trade/qualifying for writing down allowances if capital expenditure).

D. SERVICES

Assumed Facts

P is a large multinational concern which wholly owns foreign subsidiary S. Both P and S are engaged in manufacturing and sales activities. P's headquarters division performs general management services for P's multi-national operations, including services which directly relate to S. The services performed for S include periodic visits by P's executives to review S's operations, financial analysis of S's future requirements, engineering services in connection with S's manufacturing activities and marketing services in connection with S's sales activities. P does not charge S for such service.

Parent in Ireland

1./2. As with intangibles, it is unlikely that Revenue could allocate income to P but, as in that case, they could seek to disallow some of the headquarter's division expenses on the grounds that they are not laid out wholly and exclusively for the purposes of P's trade. The fact that no income from management services is received by P could be a significant factor supporting a contention that the expenses should be disallowed. On the other hand, it should be remembered that the fact that there is no income is not conclusive – the tax treatment will depend on the facts of the case. For example, in a 1982 UK tax case – *Robinson (Inspector of Taxes)* v. *Scott Bader Company Limited* – it was held that the salary paid to an employee of a UK parent company, who was seconded to a French subsidiary to act as manager, was incurred for the purposes of the taxpayer company (the UK parent) in that, among other things, it was shown that without the French company supplying basic products to a major customer, sales of specialist products by the taxpayer to that customer would have been lost.

Subsidiary in Ireland

1. An allocation of income to P will not in itself affect S's Irish tax position. If S subsequently pays for the services, a deduction will be allowed in the period when payment is made, provided, of course, it is wholly and exclusively for the purposes of S's trade.
2. Payments by S to P in respect of services will not be subject to withholding tax in Ireland.

E. Loan Guarantees and Rentals

Assumed Facts

P is a multinational company whose main business is manufacturing and selling. P plans to establish foreign sales subsidiary S located in country S. P capitalizes S with $500,000 and guarantees a loan to S of $500,000 obtained from an independent bank. Land and a warehouse which P owns in country S will be used as a site for S's operations. P plans to make this land and warehouse available to S at a fee of $1 per year for 99 years.

Parent in Ireland

1. Income will not be allocated to P in respect of the guarantee of the loan or S's use of the land and warehouse.
2. P would not be treated as having made an additional equity investment in S.

Subsidiary in Ireland

1./2. The characterization of the transaction by P's country will not be accepted in Ireland.
3. A payment of rent would be subject to withholding tax but a payment in respect of the loan guarantee would not.

PART III. TAX TREATIES

A. The tax treaties which Ireland has entered into include provisions for re-allocation of profits between companies under common control. Although most of these treaties incorporate the standard OECD Model Treaty provision on mutual agreement procedures, the few older treaties (eg the Irish/US Treaty) do not include this provision, although they have provision with regard to exchange of information. The Irish/US Treaty is presently being renegotiated and it is anticipated that it will follow very closely the existing US/UK Treaty.

B. The Irish tax authorities would only give effect to a solution reached under a treaty if it is in accordance with local tax law in Ireland.

C. As indicated, the Irish Revenue will apply Irish tax principles in negotiating a settlement under the treaty provision. Normally, the Irish Revenue would not initiate action regarding protection under the treaty and it would be up to the taxpayer to invoke the mutual agreement procedure.

D. The taxpayer should submit a claim under the mutual agreement procedure in his country of residence. There are no guidelines defining when such claims should be submitted.

E./F. In either a situation where the competent authorities fail to reach agreement or the taxpayer does not accept a settlement made between them, he can still invoke the normal appeal procedures operative in Ireland, as long as the assessment for the year in question has not already been determined.

G. Repayments or other adjustments made in order to conform with the allocation determined by the two competent authorities can be made without further tax consequences.

H. In our experience, competent authority provisions in this area are not often invoked. Settlement would generally be reached but it is likely that in some cases negotiations could last for some time before the matter would be finalized.

PART IV. SPECIAL SITUATIONS

A. The normal allocation rules outlined previously, ie arm's length basis, would not necessarily be modified in the special situations identified although, of course, these situations may be relevant as one of the factors to consider in assessing the arm's length nature of a transaction. In practice, the Irish authorities are likely to take account of differing tax rates between countries, simply because these are factors in themselves which can be indicative of tax avoidance.

B. As indicated in Part I, specific legislative anti-avoidance measures exist for companies which qualify for Export Sales Relief and the 10 per cent rate of Corporation Tax. Clearly, these provisions are more likely to be invoked where there are related party transactions between two Irish resident taxpayers and profits are being moved from a company chargeable at the standard rate of Corporation Tax (ie 50 per cent) to a tax relieved company. As stated at the beginning of this paper, transactions between Irish resident tax relieved companies and foreign related companies will not generally be scrutinized since profits are likely to be maximized in Ireland, anyway.

Italy

Fabio Greco/Michael Neale

PART I. GENERAL RULES

PREAMBLE

The relevant provisions dealing with intercompany transactions are set out in Presidential Decree (DPR) 597 of September 29, 1973, which includes the following:

> Art.53 states that revenues include:
> 'the difference between the normal value of goods and services and the consideration received for transfers and services rendered to companies which do not have either the registered or administrative seat of the main corporate purpose in Italy and control directly or indirectly the entity or that are controlled by the same company that controls the entity.'
> In addition, Art.56, sub-paragraph 2, provides that:
> 'the cost of acquisition of goods transferred and services rendered by the abovementioned companies is reduced by any excess over the normal value.'
> The same provision applies to goods transferred and services rendered by those companies not having either their registered office or administrative base or their main corporate activity located in Italy, on behalf of which the Italian entity carries on activities of selling and placing raw materials or goods, or of manufacturing or processing products.

In addition to these basic regulations, the tax authorities have recognized the need to provide interpretative guidance that takes adequately into consideration the experiences acquired by other countries and the guidelines of the various international bodies and, in particular, of the Organization for Economic Co-operation and Development (OECD). In its report of May 16, 1979 on this argument, the latter recommended that tax authorities of the participating countries adopt the open market principle in examining and adjusting transfer prices.

Accordingly, the Italian authorities (Ministry of Finance) issued to its dependent staff an interpretative 'Instruction No.9/2267 of September 22, 1980' dealing with the question of 'transfer prices in the determination of taxable income of foreign-controlled companies'. This Instruction was openly published with a view to providing guidance to relevant 'user' entities. The standard underlying this instruction, and derived from the legislation that it is designed to clarify, reflects the concept of 'normal value'.

The circular, in fact, elaborates the position in the following terms:

> 'In the Italian tax system, the concept of normal value is defined, for income tax purposes, by Art.9, DPR 597 of September 29, 1973, as follows:
> 'Normal value shall mean the price of the consideration generally applied for goods and services of the same or a similar kind, in a free market and at the same commercial stage, at the moment and in the place in which the consideration and the proceeds are considered earned and the charges and expenses are considered incurred for the purposes of determining income or, if necessary, at the moment and in the place that are closer. In order to compute the normal value, reference should be made whenever possible to the price lists and tariffs of the company which has supplied the goods and services and, in the absence of these to the indeces and the price lists of Chambers of Commerce, to professional fees and to the Stock Exchange listings, taking into account normal discounts. The concept of normal value, thus defined by law, already includes the principles of an open market price, recommended by the OECD for calculating the transfer price: that is, the price that would have been fixed for similar transactions by independent companies.'

This is clearly analogous to the arm's length principle embodied in the legislation of other industrialized countries. The instructions subsequently discuss in considerable detail alternative approaches to establishing or calculating this 'normal value'.

Notwithstanding these relatively clear statements of principle with respect to the definition and interpretation of tax legislation, the practical difficulties in applying such principles (negatively influenced by such factors as the lack of a solid tradition of tax administration, and evident qualitative and quantitative staff deficiencies) have resulted in significant accumulating arrears in the determination and settlement of corporate and individual tax liabilities. Recourse has been made regularly to the periodic blanket settlement of open liabilities by the introduction of amnesty provisions, leading to settlements on a mathematically calculated forfeitary basis which effectively pay no attention to the individual circumstances of the entity concerned.

This had led therefore to a position where, in practical terms, tax paying entities may elect to run the risk of not respecting the precise provisions of the law as defined above, in the expectation of benefiting from eventual amnesty provisions (which result inevitably from the backlog pressures suffered by the tax administration). It is largely because of this environment and the slowness of the juridical process, that there is a lack of defined practice and precedent which could give an authoritative interpretational basis for the relevant legislation. Advance rulings are, in effect, impossible to obtain and individual circumstances tend to be determining.

A powerful disincentive against abuse of this somewhat unregulated situation is, however, provided by the extremely onerous provisions of the exchange control provisions aimed at disciplining the controlling foreign investment and transactions, with a particular view towards punishing illegal profit transfers abroad and the (presumed) accumulation of unreported capital abroad. The penal provisions of this legislation (including imprisonment of all those party to such transactions whether in an initiatory or supporting role) constitute a significant deterrent and a strong inducement, especially to international corporations (potentially vulnerable to, and therefore less able to resist exposure), to conform to the requirements of Italian legislation and relevant interpretations and instructions.

A. 1. The 'normal value', equivalent to the arm's length rate, is the required basis for establishing allocations of income between related companies. This is a basic principle to be applied, and is not particularly aimed at any particular abuses (eg transactions with tax haven countries).

2. The authorities are empowered to adjust prices between related companies in different countries to reflect arm's length charges, for the purpose of determining taxable income only. Such adjustments have no effect on the official ('civil') statements prepared for local statutory shareholder approval and filing purposes.

3. The principles described in the preamble are very wide ranging and there are no 'safe haven' provisions or concessions.

4. The above provisions are defined in such a way as to relate specifically only to circumstances where there is a cross-border transaction and a foreign parent condition. The arm's length principle allied to the fundamental concepts of accrual (matching of expense and revenue) and the direct relevance of costs to the generation of matching revenues, effectively lead to the application of the above described related party principles to situations involving related domestic taxpayers and transactions and to operations, involving Italian parents and foreign controlled entities.

B. The scope of the provisions under consideration, as described in the preamble above, is restricted to goods transferred and to services rendered:
- between a foreign company and an Italian entity directly controlled by it;
- between a foreign company and an Italian entity indirectly controlled by it through another foreign company;
- between a foreign company and an Italian entity both controlled by a third foreign company.

Therefore, the legislator formally intended the law to exclude all those transactions in which an Italian corporation controls in any way the foreign entity. In other words, the law as such excludes those transactions that take place between an Italian controlling company and a foreign entity directly or indirectly controlled by the Italian company, and those transactions between a foreign company and an Italian company that are both controlled by an Italian company.

This, taken alone, would seem to suggest that, in theory, an Italian parent selling its products to a foreign subsidiary at less than cost for no valid reason, would not be subject to adjustment. In practical terms, it is unlikely that this situation (and it is to be noted that, until fairly recent years, there were comparatively few Italian international parent holding companies) would be accepted, but the exchange control regulations in force would act as a significant disincentive to the application of evidently non-arm's length criteria.

It is important to recognize that the fiscal concept of 'control' essential to the application of the related party concept is much wider than the strict legal definition laid down in Art.2359 of the Civil Code (just as the types of business subject to related party considerations extend beyond narrowly-defined corporate enterprises, and take in foreign partnerships, foreign branches, foreign sole traders and other foreign permanent establishments). Experience has suggested that changes in transfer prices may reflect the influence of one enterprise over the managerial decisions of another, and this goes beyond the contractual or shareholder relationship and may reflect simply economic considerations. It therefore follows that the concept of 'control' should be extended to cover all situations involving potential or actual economic influence with reference to the circumstances in questions, and may include:

a. The exclusive right to sell the products manufactured by the other company;
b. the impossibility for the company to operate without the capital, products and technical co-operation of the other company (a case which includes joint ventures);
c. the right of nominating the members of the board of directors or of the company's management;
d. common members of the board of directors;
e. family relationships between the parties;
f. the granting of large credits or prevailing financial dependence;
g. the participation of companies in centralized purchasing or selling;
h. the participation of companies in cartels or consortia, especially if their purpose is to fix prices;
i. control of sources of supply or restriction of sales markets;
j. the holding of contracts that constitute a monopoly position;
k. in general, all situations in which, potentially or actually, an influence over management decisions is exercised.

C. The preferred approach is the transactions basis where three principle methods are suggested:
1. comparable price;
2. resale price;
3. cost plus.

Only if such methods are not capable of application is recourse made to alternative methods which may, in the last resort, fall back on net income criteria.

D. The authorities have 5 years in which to challenge the reported taxable income. Failure to make any corrective assessment (which would trigger an appeals process exempt from the statute of limitations, subject to any overriding settlement options available to the company under subsequent amnesty legislation) will lead to automatic acceptance of the tax returns, as filed. The subsequent disclosure of apparently flagrant criminal activity (serious exchange control offences would certainly be classified as such) are sufficient, however, to override statutory limitation conventions and re-open 'lapsed' years.

E. Italian law gives recognition to the principle of the juridical-fiscal autonomy of the individual enterprise. Only where an international tax treaty provides for close co-operation and co-ordination with a foreign tax authority giving rise to the concept of fiscal unity and a fair sharing of global profits, would reciprocity be recognized when imposing profit adjustments. As of the present time, no existing tax treaties include such clauses, and foreign transfer-pricing adjustments would not be accepted as valid adjustments to Italian taxable income.

F. If an adjustment would be made to a foreign subsidiary or parent, there would be no recognition given to compensatory adjustments in Italy unless formally documented and falling within acceptable Italian transfer pricing criteria (though in practical terms it would be impossible to recognize such adjustments if not given accounting status in the period of related costs or revenues):
1. no consolidation is permitted between Italian and foreign entities;
2. dividends from foreign entities or foreign tax credits would not be influences;
3. there would be no requirement for cash settlement of any tax adjustments affecting transactions with foreign entities.

G. Adjustments would be made to the years in which the underlying transactions took place.

H. It is not open to an Italian taxpayer to initiate an adjustment under the allocation rules – he is held to be responsible for preparing proper underlying financial statements in the first instance, and there are no provisions for filing corrected returns (without attracting possible fines, penalties and interest charges for improper filings).

PART II. SPECIFIC EXAMPLES

A. Sale of Goods

Assumed Facts

Assume P is a manufacturer which sells finished products to S which is located in a different country. P sells these products to S at cost. P also sells these products to unrelated parties at cost plus 10 per cent mark-on. Both S and the unrelated parties incur the same selling and promotional expense and both resell P's products at the same price per unit.

Parent in Italy

Although legislation does not make specific reference to transfer pricing criteria where an Italian parent is involved, it is likely that inter-company pricing principles as previously described would be extended to such situations, particularly where material amounts are involved:

a. Income could be allocated to P by the tax authorities.
b. In the simple example quoted, a 10 per cent mark-up might well be made since the circumstances lead themselves to the application of the recommended principle involving determination of the normal value (open market price) through reference to the 'internal comparison' (ie between an enterprise of the group and an independent third party).
c. Alternatives in descending order of preference (ie where circumstances are less clear-cut and documentable, and where more arbitrary approaches may be necessary), include:
   - external comparison (transactions between totally independent entities);
   - resale price method;
   - cost-plus method.

   The above methods would involve specific considerations of elements requiring adjustment to arrive at strict comparability (eg if S incurs greater selling or promotional expense). This would not preclude the authorities, where consideration of underlying costs is necessary, from using cost methods completely different from those adopted by the entity.

In extreme cases, where the above methods may not be appropriate or applicable, recourse might even be made to:
- the allocation of global profits;
- comparability of profits;
- return on capital invested;

– gross margins of the relevant economic sector.

There is no provision for special pricing concessions being extendable selectively to subsidiaries only (ie not made available to independent third parties). Where the 'internal comparison' requirement is respected, it is likely that loss-provoking market-establishing pricing policies could be defended.

Subsidiary in Italy

1. The allocation of income from S to P determined in P's country would certainly not be accepted automatically in Italy. An independent determination might or might not be made in Italy, depending on circumstances (humour of tax office, materiality, apparent differences in comparability, etc.).
2. There is no provision under Italian legislation for such an allocation to be deducted from local taxable income.
3. Existing exchange regulations render it extremely unlikely that payment could ever be made, unless recorded (and documented and successfully defended) as a price adjustment in the period of the original transaction. Such a hypothetical payment would not be treated as a dividend subject to withholding.

B. LOANS AND ADVANCES

Assumed Facts

P and S are manufacturers located in different countries. P loans to S money on open account without interest so that S can expand its operations. P is not engaged in the business of lending money.

Parent Company in Italy

1. Again, by extension, it is likely that even where there is no provision made in the applicable tax treaty, interest income would be imputed where a loan is made to a foreign related subsidiary without interest or, at a rate lower than the 'open market' or 'normal' rate on the lender's market (or the rate on the market where such loan funds may have been borrowed). It is likely that the imputed rate would approximate the Bank of Italy's discount rate. It would, therefore, be difficult for an Italian lending entity to satisfactorily justify an interest-free loan (always assuming that a correcting assessment is raised).
2. The answer would be no different if the loan was evidenced by a non-interest bearing note with a fixed maturity date.
3. There is no legislative basis for an interest-free loan to a foreign subsidiary to be treated by the tax authorities as additional equity investment. This matter

would tend to be settled by reference to the exchange control treatment/ classification of the original loan transaction.

Subsidiary in Italy

1. Italy would make an independent determination. The tax authorities would tend to take an interest-free loan at its face value and might be expected to resist imputed interest if the loan agreement is documented or initially stated to be interest-free.
2. The transaction would always be characterized as a loan unless official application was made to convert the loan to equity status. Loans evidenced by a non-interest bearing note with a fixed maturity note would not create any change.
3. No tax-deductible interest could or would be allocated.
4. It is difficult to envisage that a payment of interest allocated to the foreign parent by its tax authority would ever be permitted, given the present restrictions imposed on banks under current exchange control regulations.
5. The transaction would not be characterized as an additional equity investment.

C. INTANGIBLES

Assumed Facts

P and S are manufacturers located in different countries. P performs research and development which has led to P's ownership of certain intangibles consisting of patents, trademarks and know-how. P makes available to S exclusive right to use in S's country all of P's intangibles. P does not charge S for the use of P's intangibles.

Parent in Italy

1. Again, by extension of the underlying principles described in the preamble it is possible that revenues deriving from a foreign subsidiary may be challenged as to whether they give a normal return measured in accordance with the base principles (comparability, resale, and cost-plus but with special weight added for technical and judicial considerations) that would be considered in, for example, challenging a charge for equivalent services rendered by a foreign related entity. In this event, income would be allocated, but P would not be treated as contributing the intangible to the capital of S.
2. Such income would probably be allocated in the form of royalties. By referring to the principles applicable to Italian entities paying royalties to foreign related parties, an approach could be made to express the royalty in

terms of a percentage of the relevant sales of the beneficiary entities (on a scale from 2 per cent, up to say 7 per cent depending on degree of high technological content in relation to the cost of the 'intangible asset' or on an arm's length basis if this could be reasonably determined. Deductibility of royalties as such or of a royalty allocation in S's country would not be a relevant consideration.
3. R and D costs incurred by P could be allocated to S but this approach should have been adopted in the year when S became a beneficiary of P's expenditure in those areas. Such arrangements should be documented and formalized in registered agreements to facilitate tax negotiations.
4. *Bona fide* cost-sharing agreements, supported by documented cost details, in support of research and development costs, would assist considerably in the eventual determination of P's income tax liability.

Subsidiary in Italy

1. The Italian authorities would make an independent assessment of any royalties or other charges in respect of the remuneration of intangibles. As a general guideline, the following recommendation has been made by the Finance Ministry:

a. Fees up to 2 per cent of sales could be accepted by the Authorities when:
   i. the transaction derives from a written contract prior to the payment of the fee;
   ii. the use and, consequently, the substance of the cost incurred is sufficiently documented.
b. Fees varying between 2 per cent and 5 per cent could be considered adequate when, in addition to the conditions mentioned in the previous paragraph:
   i. the 'technical' data justify the rate reported (execution of research and experiments, obsolescence more or less than one year, technical life, originality, results obtained, etc.);
   ii. the 'juridical' data of the contract justify the rate reported (exclusive right, right to grant sub-licences, right to exploit discoveries or developments of the intangibles, etc.);
   iii. the real usefulness obtained by the licensee be proved.
c. Fees higher than 5 per cent of sales could be accepted only in exceptional cases justified by the high technological level of the economic sector in question or by other circumstances.
d. Fees of any amount paid to companies resident in low taxation countries could be deducted and considered reasonable only under the more onerous conditions stated under paragraph (c).

2. There is no procedure whereby an Italian taxpayer may obtain a tax deduction of a foreign allocation.
3. It is unlikely, for the reasons explained under B(4), that this circumstance could ever occur.

D. Services

Assumed Facts

P is a large multinational concern which wholly owns foreign subsidiary S. Both P and S are engaged in manufacturing and sales activities. P's headquarters division performs general management services for P's multinational operations including services which directly relate to S. The services performed for S include periodic visits by P's executives to review S's operations, financial analysis of S's future requirements, engineering services in connection with S's manufacturing activities and marketing services in connection with S's sales activities. P does not charge S for such service.

Parent in Italy

1. An adjustment to taxable income in respect of imputed benefits provided by the parent to its subsidiaries could conceivably arise if the parent fails to enter into satisfactory contractual arrangements with such subsidiaries or if the amount of such remuneration is not reasonable in relation to 'normal value'. Given the subjective nature of many of the relevant factors in terms of measuring arm's length considerations, the nature of the services is likely to be determining in terms of an eventual assessment by the tax authorities.
2. It is to be expected that any approach is likely to be based on an allocation of costs – both direct and indirect – and perhaps a minimal profit markup, but after the recovery of localized services chargeable to relevant subsidiaries on a cost-plus basis.

Subsidiary in Italy

1. The authorities would not accept an allocation made retroactively by P's country. Such charge would require formalization in an appropriate registered agreement drawn up and completed prior to the raising of the charge on a current basis. The amount of this charge could be the subject of separate determination by the Italian authorities.
2. To the extent that such a charge is a reimbursement of incurred expenses, there would be no withholding tax requirement.

E. Loan Guarantees and Rentals

Assumed Facts

P is a multinational company whose main business is manufacturing and selling. P plans to establish foreign sales subsidiary S located in country S. P capitalizes S with $500,000 and guarantees a loan to S of $500,000 obtained from an independent bank. Land and a warehouse which P owns in country S will be used as a site for S's operations. P plans to make this land and warehouse available to S at a fee of $1 per year for 99 years.

Parent in Italy

1. No income will be allocated to P for P's guarantee of the loan to S, but if P has to pay a bank commission to provide this guarantee, the cost would not be tax deductible.

As regards the use by S of P's land and warehouse, an income would certainly be allocated to P, as the authorities would require that such a transaction should be treated for tax purposes on an arm's length basis.

In making such imputation, the tax authorities would take into account the actual rent values of equivalent property.

Subsidiary in Italy

1. If the subsidiary is not charged for the guarantee provided by the foreign parent there would be no income adjustment. Where a charge is to be raised, the subsidiary is required to obtain prior approval from the exchange control authorities before entering into the guarantee contract (to get approval of the proposed rate, etc., which will clearly have to be lower than that applied within the Italian system). Furthermore, when paying such commission, S will be required to withhold, and pay over, tax at 15 per cent of the relevant commission (unless special tax treaty provisions apply).

2. With respect to the nominal rental charged by the parent for S's occupation of land and buildings, the charge of $1 would be accepted in relation to the subsidiary. However, since P has property in Italy, P would be considered to be maintaining a permanent establishment in Italy. As a consequence, P would be assessed on the basis of presumed rental income which would be fixed in relation to local official rating scales ('catastale') and would be expected to file an annual tax return, paying corporate and local income taxed at a combined rate of 46.368 per cent.

PART III. TAX TREATIES

A. Tax treaties which Italy has entered into with other countries all contain a provision for a mutual agreement procedure for settling questions regarding the allocation of income and expense between related parties located in the treaty countries.

B. It would appear that this procedure is not yet fully functioning (ie applications filed have not yet been brought to a conclusion), and we are not aware of any guidelines which might be applied by the Italian competent authority for the allocation of income and expenses. Generally, Italian tax authorities apply the domestic law or the treaty provisions where these expressly have overriding effect.

C. Treaty provisions must be invoked by the taxpayer seeking protection under the treaty. In some instances, it would also be advisable for the related party of the other country to file an appeal with his own competent authority so as to notify this authority of such imputations of income as have been made.

D. The taxpayer should file a claim with the Italian Ministry of Finance. There are no established guidelines which define when the application has to be made in order to be accepted.

E. If the competent authorities of the two treaty countries fail to reach a settlement, the taxpayer will suffer double taxation.

F. There are no existing provisions under which a taxpayer might appeal against a settlement made between two competent authorities.

G. If agreement is reached, adjustments and payments will be allowed without further tax consequences.

H. As previously stated, little is known as to the procedures adopted in competent authority negotiations, nor are details known of any settlements reached. Claims have been filed but would appear to date to have remained unanswered.

PART IV. SPECIAL SITUATIONS

A. 1./2. The Italian tax authorities would not accept allocation of expenses if the Italian entity has no gross income or has incurred a loss, unless it can be proved that such expenses were unequivocally and necessarily incurred in the interest of the Italian entity and would contribute toward the generation of income even if only in the long term.

3./4. The normal allocation rules should not be modified whether tax rates of the countries involved are substantially equal or whether they differ significantly (eg in the case of income allocations in a low tax rate country).

B. The Italian tax authorities will closely examine all related party transactions and, in particular:

1. Intercompany purchases

2. Intercompany sales
3. Royalties
4. Management fees and administrative services
5. Interest payable or receivable

Any amounts deemed to be in excess of the so-called 'normal value' (ie unrelated transfer prices) will be added back to profit and the Italian subsidiary or branch could be charged with having illegally evaded taxation and created capital abroad. This would give rise to charges under criminal law if the amount involved is material.

Japan

Makoto Ishihara

PART I. GENERAL RULES

A. 1. Adjustments to reallocate income and expenses between related companies are made mainly for the purpose of preventing tax avoidance.

2. Arm's length prices are the basis for the determination of adjustments; however, there are in practice only a few cases of such adjustments, as it is very difficult for Japanese tax authorities to prove the reason for disapproval of such adjustments when transactions involve related companies in different countries.

3. There are regulations and circulars regarding transactions which cover rentals on real property and interest on loans. There is a formula to calculate the reasonable rental price of land.

As for interest on loans, 10 per cent per annum is allowed under the Commercial Code as an acceptable rate. A lower rate can be used if the loan is funded with lower interest borrowings from the bank. No other safe havens are provided for.

4. The same rules apply for transactions between domestic taxpayers and for transactions between residents and non-residents.

B. Under Japanese tax laws, a person is related to a company if the person is a shareholder of a family corporation whose shares are held, directly or indirectly, in the amount of 50 per cent or more by three or fewer shareholders, or if the person is defined in the tax law as a person who has a special relationship with shareholders of that corporation. All affiliated companies and persons are considered as one shareholder.

C. Specific transactions between the Company and related persons of a family corporation are subject to adjustments, and attributable income is subject to adjustments.

D. There is no statute of limitations applied to the making of allocations.

E. There are no regulations which govern a correlative adjustment when changes are made to the income or tax of a related person in another country.

F. 1. Foreign subsidiaries located in countries designated as tax haven countries are, under certain circumstances, taxed on a consolidated basis.

The Finance Ministry has designated certain countries or areas as tax havens, which are then classified into three categories:

a. Where no income tax is assessed or income tax rate is exceptionally low, such as Bahamas, Hong Kong, etc.
b. Where (a) above applies on foreign source income, such as Venezuela, Panama, etc.
c. Where (a) applies on specified source of income, such as holding company operations in Switzerland.

2. If dividends are paid by that foreign company, that portion would not require consolidation, and a foreign tax credit on dividends or on taxation on the consolidation basis is available. Japan grants FTC for foreign withholding tax and underlying profits tax.
3. Payment of the allocated amounts is not required.

G. When a foreign tax credit is available, adjustments are affected for five consecutive tax years following the year in which the foreign tax was paid. Japan would always make income or expense adjustments in the underlying transaction year.

H. There is no system in Japan whereby a taxpayer can initiate an adjustment under the allocation rules by specific request to the tax authorities.

PART II. SPECIFIC EXAMPLES

A. Sale of Goods

Assumed Facts

Assume P is a manufacturer which sells finished products to S which is located in a different country. P sells these products to S at cost. P also sells these products to unrelated parties at cost plus 10 per cent mark-on. Both S and the unrelated parties incur the same selling and promotional expense and both resell P's products at the same price per unit.

Parent in Japan

1. The difference in selling price which is considered unreasonable in comparison with P's selling price to unrelated parties will be added to P's taxable income.

2. The tax authorities will request P to revise its selling price to S. If P does not agree, the assumed income of P will be treated as a contribution from P to S out of after-tax income and income taxes will be assessed.
3. It is unlikely that the allocation would be made by the tax authorities if there were no sales to unrelated parties, as the burden of proof is on the Japanese tax authorities. Also, if special circumstances which force P to sell at a lower price could be presented, the authorities would take this into consideration; for example, where S is obliged to pay sales promotion expenses or where S is trying to increase its market share in a foreign country.

Subsidiary in Japan

1. If the determination of P's country is reflected in contracts between P and S, and if S's formula was considered reasonable, it may be approved by tax authorities.
2. S will be allowed to deduct the allocation, if it is considered reasonable as compared to similar transactions with unrelated parties.
3. If deductions are disallowed by tax authorities, S's payment to P would be treated as a contribution to P. However, the payments would only be regarded as a dividend subject to withholding tax in certain cases, such as payments in the course of S's reorganization.

B. Loans and Advances

Assumed Facts

P and S are manufacturers located in different countries. P loans S money on open account without interest so that S can expand its operations. P is not engaged in the business of lending money.

Parent in Japan

1. P will be required to record interest income on loans. The applicable rate will be the normal borrowing rate from financial institutions (usually prime rate) if P has long-term borrowings from them. The imputed interest income would not be more than the legally acceptable rate under the Commercial Code, currently 10 per cent.
2. The answer would be the same even if the loan was evidenced by a non-interest-bearing note, as interest must be imputed on all loans even those without interest.
3. Since the loans and equity investments fall under different legal procedures, the loan cannot be considered an equity investment.

Subsidiary in Japan

1. Transactions will be reviewed independently based on contracts between P and S.
2. Loan transactions will be treated only as loans.
3. S will be required to record interest expense on loans. The applicable rate will be the same as stated for parent above. Deductions will be allowed for interest expense only where interest is legally required under a loan agreement.
4. In the case that S borrows from P at a rate which prevails in P's country but is higher than S's country as a means of avoiding tax, the difference between that rate and the bank rate in S's country might be disallowed as a deduction, but no withholding tax would apply to the disallowed interest payments.
5. The loan would always remain treated as a loan.

C. INTANGIBLES

Assumed Facts

P and S are manufacturers located in different countries. P performs research and development which has led to P's ownership of certain intangibles consisting of patents, trademarks and know-how. P makes available to S exclusive right to use in S's country all of P's intangibles. P does not charge S for the use of P's intangibles.

Parent in Japan

1./2./3. Income will not be allocated to P, the reason being that S's benefits will eventually return to P. Capitalization is recognized only when the required legal procedures are carried out.
3./4. Allocation of research and development costs would not be allocated to S for the above reason. However, if the technology being developed is for use solely in S's country, research and development costs could be reallocated to S (denied to P).

Subsidiary in Japan

1./2. Since transactions are based on contracts between P and S, acceptance of any allocation would be based on whether the allocation was reasonable or inequitable.
3. A lump sum payment or a running royalty will be subject to a withholding tax. As for a sharing of costs, the regulations are different depending on whether the payment is consideration for the transfer of intangibles or is a payment for the performance of personal service, and withholding tax would

be collected according to the source of income or based on the articles of the tax treaty. Withholding tax also applies to outright purchases of patents, trademarks, etc, unless that is overridden by treaty.

D. Services

Assumed Facts

P is a large multinational concern which wholly owns foreign subsidiary S. Both P and S are engaged in manufacturing and sales activities. P's headquarters division performs general management services for P's multinational operations including services which directly relate to S. The services performed for S include periodic visits by P's executives to review S's operations, financial analysis of S's future requirements, engineering services in connection with S's manufacturing activities and marketing services in connection with S's sales activities. P does not charge S for such service.

Parent in Japan

1. An allocation of income would be required for direct expenses. There is generally no difference in the computation of the charge based on the nature of the services.
2. P's direct costs would be considered. An allocation of profit would not be required.

Subsidiary in Japan

1. A separate determination would be made by Japan based on whether, 1) services are provided based on contracts, 2) the basis of computation is provided in the contract, and 3) P or S could verify that such services were actually provided. S would be allowed a deduction for the amount which S could verify, based on the above three requirements.
2. Payments by S to P would not be subject to a withholding tax in Japan if such services were provided in P's country. This is true even with a profit element in the charge.

E. Loan Guarantees and Rentals

Assumed Facts

P is a multinational company whose main business is manufacturing and selling. P plans to establish foreign sales subsidiary S located in country S. P capitalizes S with $500,000 and guarantees a loan to S of $500,000 obtained from an independent bank. Land and a warehouse which P owns in country S will be used as a site for S's operations. P plans to make this land and warehouse available to S at a fee of $1 per year for 99 years.

Parent in Japan

1. An allocation of income would not be required for P's guarantee of the loan to S. For S's use of P's land and warehouse, the amount of rental computed at 8 per cent per annum of the market value of land and fair market rental value of warehouse must be allocated to P.
2. Rental income would be allocated to P. P would never be regarded as having made an equity investment in S.

Subsidiary in Japan

1. Japan would make a separate determination.
2. The amount of the allocation for the use of land would be determined in the same way as mentioned above for a Japanese parent.
3. Payments in the form of rental would be subject to a 20 per cent withholding tax. No withholding tax applies to guarantee fees.

PART III. TAX TREATIES

A. The tax treaties Japan has entered into contain a provision concerning the allocation of income and expenses between related parties; no specific mention is made of a mutual agreement procedure, however. For example, the US–Japan Tax Treaty provides in Article 11(1) that 'where a resident of a Contracting State and any other person are related and where such related persons make arrangements or impose conditions between themselves which are different from those which would be made between independent persons then any income, deductions, credits, or allowances which would, but for those arrangements or conditions, have been taken into account in computing the income (or loss) of, or the tax payable by, one of such persons, may be allocated and utilized in computing the amount of the income subject to tax and the taxes payable by such resident of the Contracting State.'

B. There are no specific guidelines which Japanese tax authorities use, nor details worked out by them with respect to other countries.

C. Taxpayers can file applications with the Japanese government to apply for exemption from or a deduction in withholding tax on certain categories of income under the tax treaty.

D. The procedures for applying to tax authorities for application of treaty provisions are set forth in the Law for Procedures for Implementing the Tax Treaties.

E. If the competent authorities of the two treaty countries did not reach settlement, double taxation will result. However, negotiation of a revision to the tax treaty will be sought by a country which has suffered disadvantages under the treaty.

F. A taxpayer can appeal the facts to the tax tribunal in the other treaty country as well as appeal to the tax authorities in his own country, but no appeal exists from the decision of the competent authorities.

G. Adjustments and payments would be allowed without further tax consequences where Japanese authorities have agreed to adjustments.

H. In our experience, the Japanese tax authorities rarely concede in negotiations. Negotiations would be carried on intermittently for one or two years.

PART IV. SPECIAL SITUATIONS

A. 1./2./3. The conclusions are not affected by these circumstances.
4. Those countries in which tax is exempt or tax rates are substantially lower than those in Japan are designated as tax haven countries, and retained profits of subsidiaries located in these tax haven countries are included in taxable income of the parent companies on a consolidated basis. Japanese shareholders in such companies are given a foreign tax credit for any tax paid in such countries.

B. The allocation of interest costs of financial institutions has been examined. In June, 1983, new ruling on corporation tax of foreign corporations were issued; however, rulings on financial institutions are not included. The present guidelines are as follows:
1. Interest on loans between home office and Japan branch of foreign bank is deductible to the limit of the discount rate of the central bank in the country of the home office.
2. Interest on Euro-dollar funds drawn from home office or branch abroad is limited to Reuter closing rate of the day when funds were drawn.

PART V. OTHER CONSIDERATIONS

Exchange rates to be used in the conversion of foreign currency transactions should be the rate when the transaction is made (or the average rate for the month). Inter-company rates which are often used between a parent and subsidiaries would be subject to correction when they are fixed and considered unreasonable by the tax authorities.

Mexico

Humberto Ortiz

PART I. GENERAL RULES

A. The general rule in Mexico for making allocations of income and expenses between related companies is the fair market value of the service or products sold between such companies.

1. The main reason for such adjustments is to prevent tax avoidance.
2. The standard used will be arm's length rates.
3. The transactions specifically covered by the income tax law are the following:
   (1) Selling goods or services at less than fair market value.
   (2) Buying goods or services at higher than fair market value.
   (3) Selling goods or services at original cost or below cost. There are exceptions when the seller can demonstrate that the selling price is similar to fair market value, or when the goods are damaged, obsolete, etc.
   (4) In connection with any import or export transaction, the tax authorities always have the right to estimate prices involved. Experience up to now is that such estimation is done basically considering fair market value and arm's length rules. The Mexican tax authorities have discretion to establish what they believe are fair market value prices, and then Mexican taxpayers have the opportunity to submit arguments, proof and any kind of support. Also, taxpayers can challenge tax resolutions in the Courts.
   (5) Any payment abroad for technical services, royalties, interest, etc.
   (6) Under certain conditions or circumstances, interest payments may be considered as dividends by tax authorities (see Part V-3).
4. The same rules are applicable for domestic and cross-border transactions; the only exception is the one mentioned in 3.6 above.

B. For the purpose of making allocations, the Mexican Income Tax Law has the following concept of related persons:

1. When company 'X' is the owner of enough shares of company 'Y' to control or vice versa.
2. When a third person or company is the owner of enough shares of both companies 'X' and 'Y' to control both.

C. The principal approach in making adjustments is a transactions basis.

D. The general statute of limitation is five years after filing of tax returns.

E. If Mexico increased the income of a Mexican parent company, Mexico would allow the foreign subsidiary to pay the adjustment to the Mexican parent company at a later date without imposing any Mexican tax, except an export tax if it is applicable.

F. An adjustment made to a related company located outside Mexico does not have any affect on the taxable income of the Mexican company, but the foreign tax credit involved might be changed if the Mexican company owns more than 10 per cent of the shares of the other company.

G. The adjustments are made to the tax years in which the underlying transaction took place.

H. A taxpayer cannot initiate an adjustment.

PART II. SPECIFIC EXAMPLES

A. Sale of Goods

Assumed Facts

Assume P is a manufacturer which sells finished products to S which is located in a different country. P sells these products to S at cost. P also sells these products to unrelated parties at cost plus 10 per cent mark-on. Both S and the unrelated parties incur the same selling and promotional expense and both resell P's products at the same price per unit.

Parent in Mexico

1. Mexican tax authorities have the right to allocate additional income to P.
2. The allocation will be made considering:
a. the market value of the goods which, in this case, will be represented by the selling prices to unrelated parties;
b. the normal gross income rate of P.
3. As already mentioned, the Mexican tax authorities have the right to make the allocation but, where S undertakes greater selling or promotional expenses, etc., there will be arguments to avoid such allocation.

Subsidiary in Mexico

1. The allocation of income made in P's country by itself does not determine that it will be accepted by Mexican tax authorities. As in this particular case, if the effect would be a higher cost for company S and, consequently, lower taxable income for income tax purposes, then the Mexican tax authorities will not accept the adjustment. Nevertheless, Mexican import duties might be collected on a higher basis, notwithstanding the incongruity.
2. As above, S will not be allowed any deduction.
3. The charge to S's income will likely not be initiated until a different year from that in which the transaction was made. S is not entitled to make the additional payment and deduct it for income tax purposes in another fiscal year. If S makes such payment, the tax authorities have the right to consider it as a dividend subject to withholding. Note that, after January 1, 1983, dividends are deductible and subject to a 55 per cent withholding tax.

B. Loans and Advances

Assumed Facts

P and S are manufacturers located in different countries. P loans S money on open account without interest so that S can expand its operations. P is not engaged in the business of lending money.

Parent in Mexico

1. Interest income will not be allocated to P but, if P is paying interest on loans received from third parties, the proportional interest expense will not be deductible.
2. The existence of a non-interest-bearing note will not change the result.
3. The loan could not be considered as an additional equity investment by P in S because the legal formalities have not been complied with. There are no tax consequences when the loan is repaid.

Subsidiary in Mexico

1. The characterization of the transaction by P's country will not be accepted by Mexican authorities.

For Mexican tax purposes, S will have a liability which reduces the opportunity of S to take a special deduction granted by income tax law relating to certain monetary assets and liabilities.
2./5. The transaction will always be considered as a loan.
3. Interest will not be allocated to S.

4. The transaction will only be characterized as a loan free of interest and, if S pays the interest allocated to P by P's tax authorities, such amount will be considered as a dividend and subject to withholding tax. Starting January 1, 1983, such dividends are subject to a 55 per cent withholding tax and the payor can deduct the dividend for tax purposes.

C. Intangibles

Assumed Facts

P and S are manufacturers located in different countries. P performs research and development which has led to P's ownership of certain intangibles consisting of patents, trademarks and know-how. P makes available to S exclusive right to use in S's country all of P's intangibles. P does not charge S for the use of P's intangibles.

Parent in Mexico

1./2. If P makes available to S the exclusive right to use in S's country all of P's intangibles without charging any amount for this, the Mexican tax authorities will not have a basis to allocate income to P nor to treat this as an equity contribution to S. (See Answer 1 in connection with P's services.)
3. Mexican income tax law does not provide for allocation in connection with intangibles; the worst thing that could happen is that some of the research costs incurred by P would not be accepted as a fiscal deduction but, actually, this is considered a very remote possibility with a weak legal basis.
4. If P and S entered into a *bona fide* cost sharing arrangement with respect to the research and development costs incurred by P, the Mexican tax authorities might then not accept the deduction of P's costs, when the proportion absorbed by P seems too high and unfair.

Subsidiary in Mexico

1. Mexican tax authorities do not accept P's country's allocation as an adjustment to S's taxable income.

When P's country makes an allocation to P, the only way to resolve future problems will be for P and S to enter into a royalty and knowhow agreement and from that date forward Mexican company S may deduct the payments to P. If this happens, a withholding tax is applicable on such payments.
2. The allocation of P's country to P by itself does not have any effect on Mexican company S. The agreement mentioned in 1. above is the way to resolve this situation, and the corresponding payment must be approved by

Mexican authorities who control the transfer of technology. If this authorization is not granted, S cannot deduct those payments.
3. Yes, when S makes this type of payment to P, there is a withholding tax of 42 per cent and, under certain circumstances, the tax will be 21 per cent.

D. Services

Assumed Facts

P is a large multinational concern which wholly owns foreign subsidiary S. Both P and S are engaged in manufacturing and sales activities. P's headquarters division performs general management services for P's multi-national operations including services which directly relate to S. The services performed for S include periodic visits by P's executives to review S's operations, financial analysis of S's future requirements, engineering services in connection with S's manufacturing activities and marketing services in connection with S's sales activities. P does not charge S for such service.

Parent in Mexico

1. Yes, income will be allocated to P for the performance of such services. The computation of such allocation will depend on the circumstances and evidence of the extension of the services performed.
2. Direct and indirect costs will be considered together with a profit element. Lump sums might also be considered if that type of payment was ever received by P from other parties.

Subsidiary in Mexico

No allocation of income to P will be accepted as a deduction to S. If S makes payments to P for services, the withholding tax will be 21 per cent.

E. Loan Guarantees and Rentals

Assumed Facts

P is a multinational company whose main business is manufacturing and selling. P plans to establish foreign sales subsidiary S, located in country S. P capitalizes S with $500,000 and guarantees a loan to S of $500,000 obtained from an independent bank. Land and a warehouse which P owns in country S will be used as a site for S's operations. P plans to make this land and warehouse available to S at a fee of $1 per year for 99 years.

Parent in Mexico

1. Income will not be allocated to P for P's guarantee of the loan to S. Mexican tax authorities will, however, allocate income to P for the land and warehouse used by S and will consider the market value of such properties and the rents normally paid in S's country.
2. This situation will not be considered as an additional equity investment by P because of the lack of legal formalities.

Subsidiary in Mexico

1. The characterization of the transaction by P's country will not be accepted by Mexico.
If Mexican tax authorities make a separate determination (which is not probable), they may impute some rental income to P but, even in this case, there will not be a legal basis for such determination because the income tax law does not have a provision for allocation of income to non-residents.
2. The allocation to P will be determined considering the actual value of the properties and the normal rents paid in Mexico but, as previously mentioned, this is not probable.
3. The payment will be subject to a 21 per cent withholding tax and, in order for S to obtain the benefit of deducting the rental expense, an agreement should be entered into between P and S. Guarantee fees are subject to the same withholding tax as interest payments.

PART III. TAX TREATIES

Mexico has no tax treaties.

PART IV. SPECIAL SITUATIONS

Mexico would not apply its tax rules differently to cross-border transactions just because one of the related companies had no gross or net income or because the tax rates in the two countries were substantially the same or substantially different.

PART V. OTHER CONSIDERATIONS

1. As Mexico is an underdeveloped country, there are not a large number of investments by Mexican corporations in other countries. Consequently, the income tax rules are basically directed to protect Mexican tax where foreign corporations have Mexican subsidiaries.

2. Interest paid by a Mexican company to a related foreign company might be considered as non-deductible dividends subject to withholding tax when:
   a. the foreign company is entitled to collect the loan whenever it wants to,
   b. the loan can be converted into shares of the Mexican company,
   c. in the case of default by the Mexican company, the foreign company is entitled to take over the management of the Mexican company, or
   d. interest payments are conditional on the existence of profits in the Mexican company.

The Netherlands

Jan M. van der Beek

PART I. GENERAL RULES

A. In Dutch tax law, there are no specific provisions dealing with the transactions between related companies. It is, however, a generally accepted principle that prices for transactions between related companies shall be the same as those between independent parties (arm's length price) in order to be acceptable for tax purposes. This principle arises from the notion of profit itself, as contained in Article 7 of the Income Tax Act: 'profit is the amount of aggregate benefits accruing to an enterprise by whatever description and in whatever form they may arise'. If a company has a benefit because of a price that is not 'arm's length' this benefit is, in principle, included in the profit.

1. In a 'non-arm's length' situation an adjustment will be made therefore, not only to take into account expenses properly, but also to reflect income clearly. They are not used only to counter tax avoidance.
2. It is very difficult most of the time to establish an arm's length price or rate. Although the phrase 'prices which would have been agreed upon between unrelated parties engaged in the same or similar transactions under the same or similar conditions in the open market (OECD "Transfer Pricing And Multinational Enterprises" report)' seems simple, there are a number of complications involved. Even when there are unrelated parties engaged in the same or similar transactions, factors like market position, price and production cartel, assortment problems, dumping, etc., have to be taken into account; seldom an easy task. The determination of an arm's length price is, for that reason, in practice often a matter of bargaining with the tax inspector. If the bargaining does not result in agreement, the inspector will issue an assessment on the basis as he sees it. A taxpayer can then go through the objection and appeal procedures available to him in the tax law. These procedures are outside the scope of this paper.
3. In some cases, eg finance transactions and royalties, it is possible to obtain an advance ruling from the tax inspector whereby the basis of a minimum income is agreed upon and no adjustments will be made if the income is not less than such imputed amount.
4. In theory, it makes no difference whether the transactions take place between domestic taxpayers or between residents and non-residents. All

transactions are judged within the framework of the profit notion mentioned above. In practice, however, the tax inspector will more closely examine transactions between residents and non-residents, especially if the tax rate is lower in the foreign country, to which a 'non-arm's length' benefit appears to have been channelled, than in Holland.

B. For the determination of whether parties are related, Dutch tax law does not contain firm guidelines. In practice, however, the same definition as in Article 9 of the OECD Model Treaty is being used: a related party situation arises whenever 'an enterprise participates directly or indirectly in the management, control or capital of another enterprise or the same persons participate directly or indirectly in the management, control or capital of two or more enterprises'.

C. The principle approach in making adjustments is a transaction basis. In the case of rendering services or of sales operations in which profit may ordinarily be expected, however, net income adjustments are made or agreed upon by the tax authorities usually by imputing a percentage of operating expenses as income, on the basis that no unrelated party is considered to be prepared to accept terms which would not lead to profits in the long run.

D. The law contains two forms of time limitations on adjustments. The inspector must issue an assessment within three years from the period in which the tax became due, but this term is extended to five years if a hitherto unknown fact becomes apparent affecting the assessment. If, therefore, within the five-year period an incorrect allocation, caused by a fact the inspector could not have known, is discovered he has the right to issue additional assessments and make an adjustment in the years for which an assessment has not yet been issued. The right to adjust arises from Article 7 Income Tax Act mentioned above: during the existence of the company *all* profits must be taxed. The time limits are imposed by law in order to protect the taxpayer. His tax position as the tax administration sees it is determined within a reasonable period. Irrespective of the limitation for issuing assessments the principle of the so-called 'Balance Sheet Continuity' forms part of Dutch tax law. The inspector establishing that a correction needs to be made to the fiscal financial position of a taxpayer may make this correction in any one year for which he has not yet issued an assessment, even if such corrections refer to earlier years.

E. If an adjustment is made to the income of a foreign related company, this does not mean that automatically a correlative adjustment is made to the Dutch company's profit. The tax inspector will independently judge the relevant facts and, if necessary, make his own adjustment. In the case of income adjustments in a treaty country, the mutual agreement procedure (Article 25 OECD Model Treaty) could be set into motion if no satisfaction is obtained from the independent judgement by the inspector. Also, the normal objection and appeal routes are open to the taxpayer under these circumstances.

F. If an adjustment is made by the Dutch tax authorities to prices charged for goods or services by or to a related company located outside the Netherlands the only company affected as far as the Dutch tax administration is concerned, is the Dutch taxpayer company. The authority of the Dutch tax inspectorate does not extend beyond Dutch borders. The related foreign company does not become a resident taxpayer in The Netherlands because it has charged, or has been charged, prices for goods or services not acceptable to the tax authorities in Holland. On the other hand, if a foreign tax administration makes an adjustment to a foreign company in respect of prices charged for goods or services by a domestic company, the domestic company's tax position is not affected automatically either. If reversing entries result from such adjustment they may or may not be accepted. Again, under both circumstances, the competent authorities procedures can be set into motion if, because of the adjustments, double taxation occurs.

1. A related foreign company cannot form part of a fiscal unity. This Dutch form of consolidated tax returns is only available to Dutch wholly-owned groups of companies. Adjustments to pricing for goods or services from or to foreign subsidiary companies are, therefore, not set-off as a result of fiscal consolidation.
2. Benefits from investments in participations (ie principal holdings of at least 5 per cent) remain untaxed in The Netherlands. If a subsidiary supplied goods free of charge or below market to the parent company, this latter company enjoys a benefit from its participation, which is not taxable. If a parent provides goods free of charge or below market to a foreign subsidiary it will be taxed on the non-arm's length portion of the transaction. Foreign tax credits are not affected by cross-border transactions between legal entities. Such credits are only applicable in relation to permanent establishments (ie branch operations).
3. An adjustment made by the Dutch inspectorate to inter-company transfer pricing does not require the other related party affected to make payment of the amount adjusted.

G. In principle adjustments are made to the tax years in which the underlying transactions took place. Only if that is not possible because of the statute of limitations, adjustments are made to the earliest tax year for which no assessments have yet been issued.

H. If a taxpayer wants to make an adjustment to inter-company prices he does not have to file a specific request. He can incorporate this adjustment in his tax return. He can also have returns already submitted amended provided that the inspector has not yet issued an assessment thereon.

PART II. SPECIFIC EXAMPLES

A. Sale of Goods

Assumed Facts

Assume P is a manufacturer which sells finished products to S which is located in a different country. P sells these products to S at cost. P also sells these products to unrelated parties at cost plus 10 per cent mark-on. Both S and the unrelated parties incur the same selling and promotional expense and both resell P's products at the same price per unit.

Parent in Netherlands

1. In principle, income will be allocated to P with respect to its sales to S for a price less than the arm's length price. If it can be shown that P granted the benefit of the lower price to S purely for reasons flowing from P being a shareholder (eg wishes S to be more securely established in the foreign country), the difference between the actual price and the arm's length price could then be considered an informal capital payment by P to S. It increases therefore both the cost of the investment in S and the income of P. The benefit enjoyed by S, once remitted back to P through dividends, is not taxed because of the participation exemption (see I F.2).

2. The Netherlands has accepted the OECD 'Transfer Pricing and Multinational Enterprises' Report of the Committee on Fiscal Affairs of March 12, 1979. It is therefore reasonable to assume that the Dutch tax authorities, in their judgement of arm's length prices, will be guided by this Report and in particular by the methods of ascertaining an arm's length price more fully dealt with in the OECD Report. These methods are:

- comparable uncontrolled price method
- resale price method
- cost plus method
- any other method found acceptable.

In most cases, in actual practice, the problem will be solved by bargaining discussions with the tax inspector.

3. If there are no sales of the particular goods in S's country to independent parties, the same methods as mentioned above can be followed. Even if the identical goods are not on the market, a comparison with similar or substitute articles with appropriate price adjustments can be made. If S incurs greater selling or promotional expenses than an independent trader, a lower price charged by P to S could be considered an adjustment to bring that price to a comparable market level. A lower price by P to S because S operates at below market prices in order to establish a market could also be interpreted as 'payment' by P for marketing its products and need not necessarily result in an adjustment to its profits.

Subsidiary in Netherlands

1. The Dutch tax authorities will make an independent determination of the arm's length price when a Dutch subsidiary purchases goods from a foreign parent company.
2. S will be allowed to deduct from its taxable income a later allocation of costs by P if and insofar as it is in line with the arm's length price.
3. Only payments in excess of the arm's length price, from the Dutch point of view, are treated as dividend payments subject to withholding tax if applicable.

B. Loans and Advances

Assumed Facts

P and S are manufacturers located in different countries. P loans S money on open account without interest so that S can expand its operations. P is not engaged in the business of lending money.

Parent in Netherlands

1. Depending on the terms and conditions of the non-interest-bearing loan, it can be considered an informal capital contribution by P to S and no interest will be allocated. If, at a later stage, 'interest' is paid on such informal capital contribution, such interest will be treated as a dividend distribution. If it is considered to be a loan, however, interest income will be allocated to P at the market rate for a similar loan.
2. If the loan is evidenced by a non-interest-bearing note with a fixed maturity date, the loan itself cannot be considered an informal capital payment and interest income will be allocated to P.
3. If the loan will be considered an informal capital contribution and, therefore, an additional equity investment by P in S, a subsequent repayment would reduce the tax value of the investment but would not attract tax.

Subsidiary in Netherlands

1. S's country will make an independent determination of the character of the transaction.
2. It will depend on the terms and conditions of the loan whether it will be treated as informal capital or as a loan. If the loan is evidenced by a non-interest-bearing note with a fixed maturity date it will be considered a loan and not an informal capital payment. If there is no such note, it still depends on the other conditions of the loan whether it is deemed an informal capital payment or not.

3. Once the transaction has been characterized as a loan, interest expense can be deducted from income by S at the normal market rate even though no legal obligations existed to pay such interest. The imputed interest itself becomes an informal capital contribution by P and attracts 1 per cent capital duty. If the imputed interest related to years which were statute-barred, the interest deduction could not be granted.
4. If S actually pays more interest to P than the amount allocated in S's country on the basis of the market rate, the excess will be considered a profit-distribution subject to dividend withholding tax. The excess is not deductible.
5. a. If the transaction is characterized in country S as an additional equity investment, repayment of the loan will not have any corporate tax consequences. However, a repayment of capital is treated as a dividend if and to the extent that there are accumulated profits, unless the amount of authorized and paid up capital is statutorily reduced accordingly.
b. If P's country characterizes the transaction as a loan, and S pays the amount of interest allocated as income in P's country while the loan is considered informal capital in S, these payments will be considered a profit distribution subject to dividend withholding tax.

C. Intangibles

Assumed Facts

P and S are manufacturers located in different countries. P performs research and development which has led to P's ownership of certain intangibles consisting of patents, trademarks and know-how. P makes available to S exclusive right to use in S's country all of P's intangibles. P does not charge S for the use of P's intangible.

Parent in Netherlands

1. If P makes available to S the exclusive right to use in S's country P's intangibles without charging S for it, it can be assumed that P does this only because of its being a shareholder of S. Income will be allocated to P on the basis of an arm's length price of such intangibles. If P transfers the intangibles to S once and for all and without a charge, a capital contribution increasing the investment in S and creating income in the form of the disposal of the intangibles is raised. If the intangibles are retained by P, but the use thereof is granted to S free of charge, annual licence fee income would be allocable to P with a corresponding increase in the investment in S.
2. As explained above it depends on the terms of the intangible transfer whether income will be allocated in the form of annual royalties or a lump-sum. The computation in either case follows the OECD guidelines. If the same

services are obtainable from third parties, a comparable uncontrolled price can be established and this price can be used to allocate income to P.

If a comparable uncontrolled price is not available, the charge must at least cover the costs insofar as S has benefited from it. It is very likely that a profit margin has to be included. This will depend on the facts and the outcome of the discussion with the inspector. If the country of S does not allow payment for the use of intangibles, a transfer free of charge would be advisable. P should, under these circumstances, sell the intangibles or charge a royalty at an arm's length price and write-off the S receivable as uncollectible. If payments are allowed, P's tax position would not be affected by the non-deductibility by S and the payments would have to be treated as income.

3. A portion of the research and development costs incurred by P should be allocated to S.

4. The recovery by P of its cost for intangibles will be more acceptable if P and S entered into a *bona fide* cost-sharing arrangement with respect to P's research and development costs. However, if such a contract were entered into retroactively, that would not likely deter the tax authorities from insisting on a profit element in the charge from P to S.

Subsidiary in Netherlands

1. S's country will judge the allocation and its basis of the expense allocated to S.

2. Irrespective of the nature of the payment, which depends on the terms of the transfer of the intangibles, the tax authorities in their judgement are guided by the arm's length price principles on the basis of the OECD report. Again, if there is a comparable uncontrolled price, this price will be used for the allocation and be deductible. If there is no such price, the determination of the amount to be allocated can be difficult. Negotiations with the tax inspector will in any case often be the only solution. Excessive payments would be considered partly distributions and be subject, to that extent, to dividend withholding tax.

3. There is no withholding tax on royalty payments, lump-sum payments or sharing of costs.

D. Services

Assumed Facts

P is a large multinational concern which wholly owns foreign subsidiary S. Both P and S are engaged in manufacturing and sales activities. P's headquarters division performs general management services for P's multi-national operations including services which directly relate to S. The services performed for S include periodic visits by P's executives to review S's operations, financial analysis of S's future requirements, engineering services in connection with S's manufacturing activities, and marketing services in connection with S's sales activities. P does not charge S for such service.

Parent in Netherlands

A distinction must be made as to the nature of the services:
a. General Services
1. Costs made in connection with a substantial participation in a foreign subsidiary (see IF[2]) as such are deductible. Such costs would include:

- costs connected with controlling the participation,
- interest on debts incurred in acquiring the participation,
- costs connected with the dividends.

Income will not be allocated to compensate for these costs. For other general services, income will be allocated by P if and insofar as these services are in the interest of and for the benefit of the subsidiary. For general services which are in the interest of the whole group, income could also be allocated by P, eg on the basis of turnover.

2. The amount of the allocation will depend on whether the services are made available by third parties. If that is the case, the comparable uncontrolled price will be used. If not, which will be usual, the allocated income will equal the actual costs of the services with or without an imputed profit margin, depending on the facts and subject to the discussions with the tax inspector. It will in practice also depend on the outcome of the discussion with the inspector whether certain expenses will be classified as actual costs of the services, be they direct or indirect.
b. Specific Services
1. With specific services such as periodic visits by P's executives to review the operation of S, financial analysis of S's future requirements, etc., it must be decided whether the services were rendered for the benefit of the subsidiary. If that is the case, income will be allocated by P.
2. If there is a comparable uncontrolled price, this price will be used for the allocation. If not, the allocation will at least amount to the actual cost of the services and the observations in the foregoing subsection a(2) will apply here as well.

Subsidiary in Netherlands

1. S's country will not automatically accept the allocation by P, but it will judge the reasonableness and acceptability of the allocation on the basis of the arm's

length principle. If the services are obtainable from third parties, the amount of the allocation will be the comparable uncontrolled price. If there is no market price, the costs of the services may be deducted insofar as it can be shown that they were incurred for the benefit of the subsidiary. The deduction allowed would be limited to what is agreed with the tax administration on the basis of the arm's length principle; any excess would be considered a distribution and, as such, subject to dividend withholding tax.
2. The payments by S to P are, therefore, only subject to a withholding tax insofar as they exceed the arm's length price; only this part of the payment is considered a hidden profit distribution and subject to withholding.

E. Loan Guarantees and Rentals

Assumed Facts

P is a multinational company whose main business is manufacturing and selling. P plans to establish foreign sales subsidiary S located in country S. P capitalizes S with $500,000 and guarantees a loan to S of $500,000 obtained from an independent bank. Land and a warehouse which P owns in country S will be used as a site for S's operations. P plans to make this land and warehouse available to S at a fee of $1 per year for 99 years.

Parent in Netherlands

1. Income will be allocated to P for P's guarantee of the loan to S and for S's use of P's land and warehouse. The allocation will be based on the price that is normally charged between independent parties.
2. Since the amount of the allocation is neither charged to nor paid for by S, it is considered an additional equity investment in or informal capital contribution to S. The allocated amount is included in taxable income of P on the one hand and increases on the other side the tax value of the investment in S. The land and warehouse itself will not be treated as an additional equity investment but remain operating assets of P. The imputed income from these assets is allocated under most treaties and under the unilateral measure for the avoidance of double taxation to the non-domestic income of P and, therefore, not taxed in country P but in country S.

Subsidiary in Netherlands

1. The Netherlands will judge separately the determination of the character and the amount of the transaction.

2. The Netherlands determination of the character will not likely differ from P's country. The amount for the transaction must follow the normal arm's length price rules. If the amount is not charged to S, this benefit will be treated as an informal capital payment and, as such, deducted from income and added to additional capital paid-in. The land and warehouse itself will not be treated as an investment of S.
3. Payments from S to P are subject to (dividend) withholding tax only insofar as they exceed the arm's length price determined by The Netherlands. There is no withholding tax on reasonable payments for anything other than dividends.

PART III. TAX TREATIES

A. With an occasional exception the tax treaties Holland has entered into contain a provision for a mutual agreement procedure on the basis of Article 25 of the OECD Model Treaty. Disputes in the allocation of income and expense between related parties located in treaty countries can be dealt with under this provision.

B. Answers to previous questions are not modified by treaty provisions. The competent authorities use the same rules for allocation of income and expenses as described above. The competent authorities are bound by local tax law; their interpretation may not be contrary thereto. Treaties do reduce the withholding tax rate on dividends from 25 per cent to a range of zero to 15 per cent.

C. Treaty protection is not invoked automatically. The taxpayer will have to send a request to the competent authority explaining the situation.

D. There are no guidelines as to when application to the competent authority will be accepted. Whenever double taxation is threatening or has already taken place, the procedure can be started in line with the OECD model, simultaneously with the legal objection and appeal procedures. The competent authority will first try to find a solution within the scope of the Dutch law and, only if that solution cannot be found, contact the competent authority of the other state involved.

E. If no settlement is reached the effect will be double taxation.

F. No appeal is possible against a settlement made between the competent authorities.

G. In case of agreement as to the correct allocation, confirming adjustment and payments can be made without further tax consequences. In most cases settlement has been reached on a mutually acceptable allocation. Competent authority negotiations can carry on for periods varying from two to seven years.

PART IV. SPECIAL SITUATIONS

A. 1. The rules as described above are in theory applied in all cases, irrespective of the situation of the company involved. The tax inspector will, however, be more critical in all situations where tax evasion can be expected; for example, when the tax rate in the foreign country is substantially lower than in Holland.

As to the specific situations, the following comments are added:

(1) In cases of no gross income of the related party providing the service free of charge an imputed income is allocated by the tax inspector usually by mutual agreement and in the form of a ruling. The income is imputed on the basis of a percentage of the corporation's expenses varying from 10 to 35 per cent, with a minimum amount of Dfl.10,000.

(2) An operating loss in any one year does not affect the principle of related companies transfer pricing since it remains based on the arm's length principle also under these circumstances.

(3) Where the tax rate in both countries are substantially equal, the inspector will be less suspicious about tax evasion, but again the basis of his actions remains the same: is the relation between the two parties arm's length?

(4) If the tax rate in the country to which the income is allocated is substantially lower than in Holland, the inspector will be suspicious of tax evasion and demand more extensive proof of the arm's length principle being applied than if the situation were the other way.

B. 1. In respect of the following intermediate companies, it is normal to obtain tax rulings in advance in order to avoid questions on the allocation or imputation of income later on:
- holding companies
- finance companies
- royalty companies

2. The tax inspector normally watches closely inter-company prices for goods and services. Advance rulings for the basis in respect of services can sometimes be obtained.

PART V. OTHER CONSIDERATIONS

In the area of related companies and, in particular, where use is made of Dutch intermediate holding, finance, or royalty companies, tax inspectors ask for the identity of the ultimate owners of the parent company of the intermediate company before granting an advance ruling. Although no actions are known to have resulted from the 'Article 16 U.S. Model Treaty' mentality, it is a sign of the way things are also moving in Holland.

New Zealand

P. Ross Cook/D. B. MacMorran

INTRODUCTION

1.0. Income tax is imposed under domestic law by the Income Tax Act 1976 (the Act) and, pursuant to this Act, New Zealand maintains double taxation agreements with its major trading partners. The Act is administered by the Inland Revenue Department (the Department). The head of the Department is the Commissioner of Inland Revenue (the Commissioner) and he determines the administrative policies of the Department.

Objections to income tax assessments made by the Commissioner may be made in the first instance to the High Court or the Taxation Review Authority, with provisions for subsequent appeals to be made to the Court of Appeal and, finally, to the Privy Council in London.

2.0. New Zealand has historically been an importer of investment capital and, as a result, New Zealand's experience on the allocation of income and expenses between related companies in different countries has primarily focused on New Zealand subsidiaries with foreign parents.

PART I. GENERAL RULES

3.0. The general rule concerning allocation of income and expenses between related companies is that the assessable income produced by the New Zealand business must be *commercially realistic*. This presupposes that the intercountry transactions between related companies are recorded at a rate consistent with arm's length transactions.

The practical application of this rule by the Commissioner involves the determination that the Department receives its equitable share of income tax arising from business entities involved in such transactions. The Commissioner generally has the option to approach this determination on a:

- net income basis, or a
- specific transaction basis.

4.0 Net Income Approach

4.1. Section 22 of the Act provides the Commissioner with the power to issue an arbitrary income tax assessment where a business carried on in New Zealand but controlled by non-residents appears to produce an insufficient taxable income or excessive loss. The arbitrary assessment, can however, be challenged in the courts based on the facts of the case. This section has been used to combat inventory transfer pricing whereby a New Zealand subsidiary or associate company of a multinational company appears to be paying an excessive price for its inventory purchases.

4.2. Before the Commissioner is able to invoke this section, however, he must determine that the business being carried on in New Zealand is:

- controlled exclusively or principally by non-residents,
- carried on by a non-resident company (eg a branch operation) or a company under the control of non-resident, or
- carried on by persons having control of a non-resident company,

and that, in his opinion, it has produced an insufficient taxable income or an excessive loss. He may recalculate the taxable income on the basis of:

- total receipts of the business (cash or credit), or
- such proportion as the Commissioner determines of the total purchases of the business (cash or by the granting of credit).

4.3. In relation to the recalculation of an excess loss, the Commissioner is empowered to determine a loss he considers 'fair and reasonable'.

4.4. There is also a safeguard within the section to ensure that it is not applied to deem income onto a New Zealand taxpayer where another taxpayer within this jurisdiction is assessable and liable to pay income tax on the deemed insufficient income.

4.5. The provisions of Section 22 can only apply where the required degree of control is present between the New Zealand business and the non-resident. Thus, a company will be treated as under the control of non-residents if those non-residents:

- hold more than 50 per cent of shares, nominal capital, paid-up capital or voting power of the company,
- have control of the company by any other means, or
- are entitled by reason of shareholding at the end of the income year to more than 50 per cent of the profits for the year if they were distributed by way of dividend at the end of the year.

For the purposes of calculating control, shares held by a nominee on behalf of another person are deemed to be held by that other person.

5.0 Minimizing the Effect of Section 22

5.1. The crucial component of this section is the requirement that the New Zealand business be controlled by a non-resident. This encompasses the situations of a non-resident branch operation in New Zealand or a subsidiary company operation. A New Zealand branch will always be controlled by a non-resident by its very nature and will, therefore, be susceptible to this section. It is suggested that a resident company controlled by non-residents would be able to circumvent the requirements of this section by the insertion of a non-operating New Zealand incorporated holding company between:

- the non-resident shareholders, and
- the resident trading company.

The reasoning behind this concept is:

- the trading company is owned by a resident company, and
- the application of the definition of 'controlled' is believed not to extend beyond the shareholders of the trading company, ie the non-operating holding company. This principle has yet to be tested in a court of law.

5.2. Notwithstanding this arrangement, the Commissioner may nevertheless see fit to argue that it would come within the ambit of Section 22 because the meaning of control includes 'control . . . by any other means' and he may consider that the non-residents, via the resident holding company, have control of the New Zealand resident trading company. This concept was considered in an Australian case, *F.C. of T.* v. *Commonwealth Aluminium Corporation Limited* 80 ATC 4371, where the High Court was required to determine the meaning of 'controlled'. Their Honours found in this case that the taxpayers' business was actually controlled by its directors and, since the majority of them were Australian, it could not be said the business was controlled by non-residents. If the precedent established in this case is followed in New Zealand, it would mean the Commissioner will be required to look at the actual and *de facto* day to day control of the company such as the control which may, in fact, be exercised by the directors. It would be incorrect for the Commissioner to merely have regard to the capacity to control the company such as the power to control the company in a general shareholders' meeting.

5.3. We believe it would be prudent for a person contemplating a corporate structure of the type described, to ensure the New Zealand resident holding company is controlled by a majority of New Zealand resident directors. This would considerably weaken any argument advanced by the Commissioner that the New Zealand trading company is controlled by non-residents.

5.4. Provision is also made in this Section 22 to deal with the situation where New Zealand taxpayers carry on business in this country and control a non-resident company. This provision may be avoided by ensuring that the non-resident takes a form other than a company: a trust, for example.

6.0 Other Considerations

6.1. Reference was made in paragraph 4.1 to the observation that the Commissioner, in the main, applies Section 22 to situations involving inventories being purchased by New Zealand businesses at excessive prices.

6.2. This section could have equal application, however, to a New Zealand business controlled by non-residents which:
- sells inventory to the non-residents at a price which is below a fair market value, and
- is charged excess management fees or research and development costs by the non-residents.

7.0 Specific Transaction Approach

Section 22 requires the Commissioner to make an arbitrary assessment of income based on the total receipts or payments of the business. This can present difficulties to the Commissioner as it requires the use of a predetermined industry standard to arrive at the arbitrarily assessed income. For example, the Commissioner may determine that companies in Industry A produce a profit which equates to 5 per cent of the sales, and he may then use that percentage in making an arbitrary assessment for a similar company under Section 22. The difficulty for the Commissioner, however, is a determination of the appropriate percentage to use as this will vary between companies as a result of product mix, pricing policies, marketing policies, management policies and advertising strategies. It is for this reason that the Commissioner may choose to adopt a specific transaction approach to transactions between related companies in different countries. In this context, 'related' companies would have the same meaning as 'controlled' companies, referred to in paragraph 4.5.

8.0 Difficult to Disallow Excess Inventory Costs

We have commented that Section 22 is mainly used to combat transfer pricing involving the purchase of inventories into New Zealand. The alternative ground upon which the Commissioner could attempt to upset this type of arrangement would be the disallowance as a deduction for the portion of the purchase price of the inventory considered to be excessive.
8.1. The criteria which permits New Zealand taxpayers to deduct expenditure from assessable income is contained in Section 104 of the Act. This section states that in calculating the assessable income of any taxpayer, any expenditure or loss *to the extent* to which it is necessarily incurred in carrying on a business for the purpose of gaining or producing the assessable income for any income year may, except as otherwise provided in this Act, be deducted from the total income derived by the taxpayer in the income year in which the expenditure or loss is incurred.
8.2. Neither the Courts nor the Commissioner are able to disallow a deduction for the purchase of trading stock on the grounds that the amount paid for it was

excessive. However, the dictum of the Privy Council in Europa (No. 1) indicated that expenditure is deductible only to the extent that it is a genuine business expenditure. In other words, to the extent it was a sham, it would be disallowed as a deduction. In the case referred to, the Commissioner was able to disallow the portion of the deduction for trading stock which was held to be inflated by reference to costs imposed by the Bermuda company, of which the taxpayer was a 50 per cent shareholder.

8.3. Whether this line of attack is still open to the Commissioner is subject to debate because a subsequent Privy Council Case, Europa (No. 2), has held that the deductibility of expenditure is dependent on the legal enforceability of the rights acquired by the taxpayer in return for making the expenditure. Thus, where the only right of the purchasing taxpayer is to acquire the goods, it appears that the expenditure is deductible in full. In these circumstances, it would seem that the Commissioner could not rely on Section 104 to rectify the excessive purchase price paid for trading stock by a New Zealand business, and would have to adopt the net income approach under Section 22 if he wished to alter the assessable income of the New Zealand business.

9.0 Inadequate Consideration for Inventory

Transfer pricing may also involve sale from New Zealand of inventory for an inadequate consideration. While Section 22 permits the Commissioner to make an arbitrary assessment of income where transactions involve related companies, Section 91 of the Act allows the Commissioner to approach the situation by deeming the sale price of the inventory to be market price or, where there is no market price, such prices as he determines. The difficulty (consistent with a problem with Section 22) in this approach is arriving at the market price of the inventory because the actual sale price may reflect the taxpayer's marketing strategy, or the inventory sold to the non-resident related company may represent goods which could otherwise not be sold on the New Zealand market. Section 91 is not restricted in its application to transactions involving related companies but the Commissioner would be unlikely to invoke it in circumstances involving arm's length transactions between third parties.

10.0 Management Fees

10.1. Management fees for services *not* rendered in New Zealand in the nature of financial advice, engineering services, design advice, technical advice and production assistance are frequently charged by non-resident companies to New Zealand resident subsidiary companies. In general, these payments by New Zealand companies are deductible. To the extent that these payments are blatantly excessive and unjustifiable, a deduction for a portion of these payments may be prohibited. However, these fees may, if care is not taken, give rise to assessable income to the recipient.

10.2. The Act defines various categories of income which are deemed to be derived from New Zealand and, therefore, subject to New Zealand tax. These include:

i. income derived from contracts made or wholly or partly performed in New Zealand,
ii. royalties paid from New Zealand, and
iii. income derived directly or indirectly from any other source in New Zealand.

If management services relate to a contract made outside New Zealand and performance of the services is rendered out of the country, the Commissioner would not be able to deem management fees to be income in terms of categories (i) or (iii) above. However, he may be able to deem the payments to be royalties.

10.3. Included within the general definition of a royalty is a payment of any kind to the extent to which it is derived as consideration for:

- the supply of scientific, technical, industrial or commercial knowledge or information,
- the supply of any assistance which is furnished as a means of enabling the application or enjoyment of anything referred to . . . in this definition.

This definition of royalty is so extensive, there is a consensus of opinion that it could be deemed to cover and include any sort of supply of information or management services. Notwithstanding this opinion, the Commissioner has attempted to differentiate between the rendering of services (not considered a royalty) and the supply of know-how (considered a royalty). This distinction is, in many cases, extremely hazy but the Commissioner views the difference as:

> 'The main distinction between know-how and services is that the former is an asset and, as such, is something which is already *in existence* and is not brought into being pursuant to a particular contract. Thus if a contract is one for supply, for the use of the buyer, of what might be broadly termed here a "product" which is already in existence, or substantially so, it is a contract for supply of know-how, and payments will be taxed as royalties.
>
> 'On the other hand, if a contractor is required to supply his special skills and knowledge in order to bring "the product" into existence for the buyer, payments under the contract would be considered to be for services and would not constitute a royalty.'

10.4. This concept may be expressed another way. Payments for access to pure information which can be retained and used by the recipient in a number of cases, would be considered a supply of 'know-how'. This may be contrasted with a pure provision of services on a once-of basis, such as design fees for a particular project or management services or any other form of once-of professional services performed outside New Zealand.

10.5. Clearly, royalties would include any fees paid for technical assistance, design fees, managerial services which are charged to a New Zealand company in relation to the amount of product produced or sold in New Zealand, or which are based on turnover in New Zealand. The continuing nature of the base on which payments are calculated would be indicative that the payment is made in respect of an 'access' type payment and be deemed a royalty. In practice, the terms 'administrative charges', 'head office expenses', 'management fees' and 'technical fees' are used by companies to describe amounts which may be for services, knowhow or a combination of knowhow and services. It is not sufficient to merely look to what account a payment has been charged, but also to consider whether a payment is for services or know-how in light of the above.

10.6. Typically, payments for the supply of know-how and connected services will be for the supply of technical data such as models, plans, designs, processes, formulas, publicity, construction material and marketing material, together with such services from time to time as are necessary to enable the New Zealand payer to use the knowhow. These services can take various forms, eg the training either in New Zealand or overseas of the payer's staff, the sending to New Zealand of specialized personnel to advise on the use of the technical data, the sending of written answers to queries on the technical data issues by the New Zealand taxpayer, and so on. Under domestic law, these payments will be treated as falling within the definition of royalty.

10.7. Payments for the supply of services unconnected with the supply of know-how or other royalties will be treated as not falling within the definition of royalties, and will not be subject to non-resident withholding tax. To the extent that the services are not performed in New Zealand, the payments will not be subject to New Zealand income tax. If, however, a portion of these services are performed in New Zealand, the payment may be assessable to New Zealand tax, subject to apportionment between the New Zealand content and the overseas content.

10.8. It may be claimed that a composite payment is made (either on a royalty basis or as a lump sum) for the use of patents, trademarks, know-how, services connected with know-how, and services unconnected with the transfer of that know-how. As a general rule, unless the taxpayer can truly demonstrate that a significant part of the payment relates to services unconnected with the patents, trademarks or know-how supplies, then the entire payment should be treated as relating to those items, and therefore falling within the definition of a royalty.

10.9. Where a payment of management fees is considered to be a royalty, the payment is subject to 15 per cent withholding tax. This withholding tax is a minimum final tax with the recipient of the 'royalty' being subject to annual assessment on this royalty income, with tax being imposed on the net income at the rate of 50 per cent.

10.10. The important issues which arise are:

i. If the payment for management fees relates to services provided in connection with knowhow and to services provided unconnected with know-how, it is essential that separate agreements be effected to record the situation. This will ensure that the payments unconnected with the supply of know-how are not subject to New Zealand withholding tax as a result of the payment being deemed a royalty.

ii. The double tax treaty between the recipient country and New Zealand will require careful evaluation. The more recent double taxation treaties signed by New Zealand contain a more restrictive definition of royalties. For example, in many cases, the phrase:

> 'Supply of any assistance which is furnished as a means of enabling the application or enjoyment of anything referred to . . . in this definition', is not present.

Furthermore, the protocol to several treaties specifically excludes from the definition of royalties any payments made for services. For example, the French/New Zealand treaty states at paragraph 6 of the protocol:

> 'In respect of (royalties) payments received as a consideration for technical services, including studies or surveys of a scientific, geological or technical nature, or for engineering contracts including blueprints related thereto, or for consultant or supervisory services shall be deemed not to be payments received as a consideration for information concerning commercial or scientific experience.'

The double tax treaties can, therefore, considerably restrict attempts to deem payments to overseas companies for management fees to be royalties.

10.11. To summarize:

i. The management fee will generally be deductible to the New Zealand company.

ii. If the management fees are not deemed to be royalties, and relate to services performed outside New Zealand, the recipient will not be subject to either New Zealand profits tax or withholding tax.

iii. If a portion of the fees relates to services performed in New Zealand, this portion may be taxed unless a double tax treaty exempts the income.

iv. The Commissioner is currently attempting to treat most management fees as royalties. It is, therefore, necessary to examine closely the content of the management fees, and the applicable double taxation treaty.

11.0 Research and Development Costs

11.1. In the same way that management fees are charged to New Zealand companies by non-resident affiliates, research and development costs incurred by non-residents are also frequently charged to New Zealand businesses.

11.2. Consistent with the approach adopted with management fees, payment by the New Zealand business presents no tax problems in regard to its deductibility provided exchange control approval is received. The contentious issue is again whether payments of these costs result in:

i. the payment being deemed income to the recipient, and
ii. consequently, subject to withholding tax and annual assessment.

11.3. In paragraph 2 of Management Fees, we set out the relevant categories of income which are deemed to be derived from New Zealand and, consequently, subject to tax. Provided payment for the research and development costs is made pursuant to a contract made outside New Zealand or in relation to costs incurred outside New Zealand, payment may only be deemed to be income if it can be classified as a royalty. Royalties are also deemed to include a payment of any kind to the extent to which it is derived as consideration for:

- the use of, or the right to use, any copyright, patent, trademark, design or model, plan, secret formula or process or other like property.

11.4. To the extent that any research and development cost payments will result in the ownership or right to use any patents, trademarks or designs for the New Zealand payer which may result from the research, these payments would be considered to be royalties and be subject to withholding tax and annual assessment. If payment from New Zealand is entirely reimbursing, it is probable that the deduction of withholding tax will not give rise to a corresponding tax credit in the country where these costs were incurred because the payee will have no assessable income against which to offset this tax deduction.

11.5. If the payment of any research and development costs did not give rise to ownership or the right to use patents, trademarks or designs resulting from the research, the Commissioner could argue that these costs were not incurred in deriving income and disallow a deduction to the New Zealand company.

12.0 Intercompany Loans

12.1. Loans made by non-resident companies to related companies in New Zealand will attract the following tax consequences:

Non-Resident Lender

If the loan is made interest-free, no tax consequences would arise to the lender or the borrower. If the loan is made with an interest charge, payment of interest to the lender would be subject to non-resident withholding tax of 15 per cent and the total interest income earned from the loan would be subject to an annual income tax assessment. This assessment would make allowance for costs incurred by the non-resident company in loaning the money to New Zealand, and the net income would be taxed at 50 cents on the dollar. The non-resident pays the greater of the 15 per cent on gross or 50 per cent on net income.

Interest-bearing loans by non-resident companies to affiliate New Zealand companies should be channelled through a country with whom we have a double tax treaty which restricts the amount of income tax that may be imposed on such interest income. In these circumstances the withholding tax charged on the interest income will be a final tax.

Resident Borrower

The cost of the borrowing will be deductible.

12.2. Loans made by resident companies to related companies in different countries have to satisfy exchange control requirements imposed by the Reserve Bank of New Zealand. These requirements, in practice, mean that the loan must result in some future benefit to New Zealand and usually this results in the loan being made at commercial interest rates. Interest income flowing back to New Zealand would be assessable income with due allowance for any foreign tax incurred.

13.0 Intercompany Leasing Charges

The Commissioner has the power to deem an adequate rent where he considers the rental charge between parties inadequate. It is likely that this power would only be used in circumstances where a New Zealand business is not charging a market rental in relation to property leased to a non-resident affiliated company.

On this point, paragraph 3(b) of Part V (Other Considerations) should be referred to. The rental, in respect of a contract activity, of equipment to a New Zealand entity by a non-resident person will be subject to withholding tax at the rate applicable to non-resident contractors.

14.0 Effect of Income or Expense Allocation by Foreign Income Tax Authorities

14.1. An allocation of income or expenditure in a foreign tax jurisdiction would have no direct income tax consequences for a New Zealand taxpayer, for the Act has no provision to permit the Commissioner to recognize these adjustments. It is probable that the Commissioner would take cognisance of any such adjustments, however, and permit a corresponding amendment to the New Zealand returned income:

i. On receipt of persuasive evidence substantiating it, eg correspondence with the foreign tax authorities, invoice from non-resident supplier;
ii. On a determination that the allocated deduction was a permissible deduction in terms of the Act, or the allocated income was properly assessable in New Zealand; and
iii. The adjustments were reflected in the financial records of the New Zealand company. This would involve either a payment or crediting of an allocated

deduction to the intercompany current account or a receipt or debiting of allocated income to the intercompany current account.

These adjustments would be permitted more readily where they originated from countries with whom New Zealand maintains double tax treaties and these treaties contain a mutual agreement procedure.

14.2. New Zealand resident companies are not grouped with non-resident companies for tax purposes although a foreign branch of a New Zealand company would be taxed in this country with an appropriate credit for foreign tax paid. Dividends received by a New Zealand parent company from non-residents are free of New Zealand tax.

15.0 Year of Adjustment

15.1. Where, as a result of an allocation of income or expenditure by a foreign tax authority or by the Commissioner, an adjustment is made to a New Zealand taxpayer, this adjustment will be reflected in the income year to which it relates. The Commissioner is restricted to amending assessments prior to four years after the end of the year of assessment, unless there is evidence to suggest that the return was fraudulent or wilfully misleading. In these circumstances, he may amend any assessment made after April 1, 1958.

15.2. The period of four years after which the Commissioner may not generally alter assessments may, however, be amended by double tax treaties where the amendment period may be modified.

15.3. A New Zealand taxpayer can initiate an adjustment to cross-border transactions by making application to New Zealand tax authorities.

16.0 Summary

The New Zealand approach to transfer pricing has been to ensure that multinational corporations operating in the country contribute an equitable share of tax revenue to the government. The main weapon of the Commissioner to administer this task is his right to issue arbitrary assessments to New Zealand businesses controlled by non-residents where he believes such businesses are generating insufficient income. However, the Commissioner also has the ability to attack various transactions on a specific transaction approach. For example, the purchase of goods for an inflated purchase price may result in a disallowance of a deduction for the New Zealand business. Payments for management services, research and development costs, once they pass exchange control scrutiny, do not cause problems for the New Zealand businesses but the payments may give rise to income being deemed onto the non-resident recipients by the Commissioner and care must, therefore, be taken with payments of this nature. Finally, any companies involved in transactions with related companies in New Zealand must be aware of the implications of the relevant double tax treaty before any such transactions are affected.

PART II. SPECIFIC EXAMPLES

A. Sale of Goods

Assumed Facts

Assume P is a manufacturer which sells finished products to S which is located in a different country. P sells these products to S at cost. P also sells these products to unrelated parties at cost plus 10 per cent mark-on. Both S and the unrelated parties incur the same selling and promotional expense and both resell P's products at the same price per unit.

Parent in New Zealand

1./2. Prima facie, the Commissioner would be able to allocate income to P in respect of its sales to S. This could be achieved by either:
- a determination by the Commissioner that P has returned insufficient income and, as a consequence, an arbitrary assessment could be issued to P under Section 22 (paragraph 4);
- a determination that the finished products sold to S were sold for inadequate consideration. In this case, a deemed market price would be allocated to these finished products, and the difference between this price and cost would be allocated to P (paragraph 9).

3. If S were to incur greater selling or promotional expenses or resold P's products at a lower price per unit so as to establish a market, it would be more difficult for the Commissioner to allocate income to P because the transactions could be justified on a commercial arm's length basis (paragraphs 7 and 9). This is, of course, a recurring problem for the Commissioner and one reason why inventory transfer pricing is difficult for him to combat.

If P made no other sales to unrelated parties and all sales to S were made at cost, P would not in general terms be considered to be in business. However, this would not preclude the operation of Section 22.

Subsidiary in New Zealand

1./2. If P's country allocates income to P as a result of the sale of finished

products, the Commissioner would accept this determination provided the criteria enunciated in paragraph 14.0 were met. As noted in that paragraph, S would be allowed to deduct the allocation from its taxable income if the allocation is recorded by way of payment to P or by crediting P's intercompany account with S.
3. Payment of the allocated amount to P would not be treated as a dividend subject to withholding tax.

B. Loans and Advances

Assumed Facts

P and S are manufacturers located in different countries. P loans S money on open account without interest so that S can expand its operations. P is not engaged in the business of lending money.

Parent in New Zealand

1. P would not be allocated interest income on its advance to S provided there was evidence to confirm that the loan would ultimately result in increased or maintained benefits deriving from S to P. This may be an increased dividend flow, increased market share in S's country resulting from the expansion of S's business, or simply maintaining the status quo. There may be a greater danger, however, of denying a deduction for P's interest costs related to making the low-interest loan.
2. This position would not alter if the loan was evidenced by a non-interest-bearing note with a fixed maturity date.
3. If no interest income was allocated to P, the Commissioner would not determine that the interest-free advance was an additional equity investment unless the transaction was obviously a 'sham'. This is extremely improbable.

Subsidiary in New Zealand

1. The Commissioner would, in this case, make a determination that the loan without interest is a loan regardless of any separate determination made by the relevant tax authorities in P's country of the transaction.
2. Interest-free loans are not regarded as additional equity investment in New Zealand.
3. Interest would not be automatically allocated to an interest-free advance to S.

4. The Commissioner would not allocate the interest to an interest-free advance. If P's country were to allocate interest income to the advance, this would be accepted by the Commissioner as a deduction in New Zealand, provided the criteria discussed in paragraph 14 were met. The acceptance by the Commissioner of a deduction for S, for the interest income imputed to P would, as a corollary, result in the net income P derives from the advance being assessed for tax in New Zealand.
5. The transaction would not be regarded as equity in New Zealand and there would be no New Zealand tax consequences on repayment of the loan.

C. Intangibles

Assumed Facts

P and S are manufacturers located in different countries. P performs research and development which has led to P's ownership of certain intangibles consisting of patents, trademarks and know-how. P makes available to S exclusive right to use in S's country all of P's intangibles. P does not charge S for the use of P's intangible.

Parent in New Zealand

1. The Commissioner would be unlikely to allocate income from this transaction to P although he may be able to invoke Section 22. He would not be able to treat the free use of patents, trademarks or know-how by S as a contribution towards the capital of S unless shares were issued in exchange.
2. Income would not be allocated to P. The tax treatment in country S would not affect New Zealand's position.
3./4. If P were to allocate a portion of its research and development costs to S or to enter into a *bona fide* cost sharing arrangement with S in respect of these costs, the effect of these arrangements would be to increase the taxable income of P in New Zealand by decreasing the expenses of P. There would be no other tax consequences for P.

Subsidiary in New Zealand

1. The Commissioner would not make a determination on the characterization of this transaction unless P's country determined that income or expense should be allocated. In this case, the Commissioner would determine independently whether the characterization by P's country was acceptable.

2. A deduction would be permitted for the amount of the allocation on the basis discussed earlier in paragraph 14. Other considerations are:
Lump Sum Payment – A contract specifying the amount of the payment would be required. The payment of it would be deductible to S but would also be assessable income to P in New Zealand.
Annual Royalty – A contract specifying the amount of the annual royalty would be required – generally annual royalties in excess of 5 per cent of S's annual sales would not be permitted by the Reserve Bank. The annual royalty would be deductible to S, but would also be assessable to P.
Reduction of Expenses – An invoice detailing the basis of calculating S's share of the expenses would be required to substantiate a deduction on this basis for the Reserve Bank.
3. The payment by S to P of a lump sum or annual royalty would attract withholding tax at the rate of 15 per cent. This rate of withholding tax may be reduced by a double tax treaty to 10 per cent.
The treatment of the expense reimbursements is more complex. The definition of 'royalty' as discussed in paragraph 11.3 includes a payment of any kind, whether periodical or not and, however described or computed, to the extent to which it is derived as consideration for the use of, or the right to use, any copyright, patent, trademark, design or model, plan, secret formula or process, or any other like property or right.

To the extent that the cost sharing arrangements result in S having the right to use any patents, trademarks or know-how, any payment would be considered a royalty and would, therefore, be subject to withholding tax at the rate of 15 per cent (subject to a rate adjustment under the treaties).

If the cost sharing arrangement did not result in S having the right to use future patents, trademarks, or know-how, the payment would not be a royalty, and would not be subject to withholding tax. In this case, however, the deduction would not be incurred in deriving assessable income, and would be disallowed as a deduction to S.

D. Services

Assumed Facts

P is a large multinational concern which wholly owns foreign subsidiary S. Both P and S are engaged in manufacturing and sales activities. P's headquarters division performs general management services for P's multinational operations including services which directly relate to S. The services performed for S include periodic visits by P's executives to review S's operations, financial analysis of S's future requirements, engineering services in connection with S's manufacturing activities and marketing services in connection with S's sales activities. P does not charge S for such service.

Parent in New Zealand

1./2. Income in the form of a charge for services rendered would not be allocated to P. It may be possible for the Commissioner to disallow a deduction for the cost of the services rendered to S on the grounds that the costs were not incurred in deriving assessable income for P but such a possibility is unlikely.

Subsidiary in New Zealand

1. The Commissioner would accept the determination made in P's country provided the conditions discussed in paragraph 14.0 were met. In these circumstances, S would be permitted a deduction.
2. The payments by S of management services would not attract tax to the extent that they were performed outside New Zealand in relation to a contract made outside New Zealand and provided the payments were not considered to be royalties (paragraph 10).

The portion of the service charge which related to services performed in New Zealand (the periodic visits by P's executives to review S's operations) may nevertheless be subject to income tax as ordinary income, unless it can be shown that it is a wholly reimbursing payment, or a relevant double tax agreement determines that profits of this nature are exempt from New Zealand tax because of the absence of a permanent establishment by the payee in New Zealand.

E. Loan Guarantees and Rentals

Assumed Facts

P is a multinational company whose main business is manufacturing and selling. P plans to establish foreign sales subsidiary S located in country S. P capitalizes S with $500,000 and guarantees a loan to S of $500,000 obtained from an independent bank. Land and a warehouse which P owns in country S will be used as a site for S's operations. P plans to make this land and warehouse available to S at a fee of $1 per year for 99 years.

Parent in New Zealand

1./2. Income would not be allocated to P for P's guarantee of the loan. The Commissioner would, however, be able to deem an adequate rental payable by

S to P and to assess P on that deemed rental payment. The Commissioner would determine what was an adequate rental in terms of prevailing market rates.
2. The non-allocation of income for the loan guarantee would not result in the guarantee being regarded as an additional equity investment in S.

Subsidiary in New Zealand

1. The characterization of the transactions by P's country would only be of concern to the Commissioner if they involved the allocation of income to P. This characterization would be accepted by the Commissioner provided the conditions discussed in paragraph 14.0 were met.
2. The payment of these allocated costs from S to P would not be subject to withholding tax in New Zealand. P would, however, face profits tax on its rental receipts from New Zealand. No New Zealand tax would apply to the guarantee fees.

PART III. TAX TREATIES

A. New Zealand has entered into double tax agreements with the following countries:

- Australia
- Belgium
- Canada
- Denmark
- Fiji
- Finland (not yet ratified)
- France
- West Germany
- Italy
- Japan
- Korea
- Malaysia
- The Netherlands
- Philippines
- Singapore
- Sweden
- Switzerland
- United Kingdom
- USA

These tax treaties entered into by New Zealand contain a mutual agreement procedure concerning the allocation of income and expenditure between related parties in treaty countries. However, this procedure does not provide the Commissioner with any further assistance in his determination of the procedure to follow in allocating income and expenses because the treaty provisions may not extend the domestic law contained in the act. The treaties may restrict the application of domestic law but they cannot serve to broaden the taxing provisions already imposed by the domestic law.

The tax treaties also contain an Article which concerns transactions between associated enterprises. This Article is based on Article 9 in the OECD Model Double Taxation Convention on Income and Capital. As noted above, a double tax agreement may not impose more stringent taxing measures than domestic law and, as a result, this Article does not give the Commissioner any additional grounds upon which to rectify transfer pricing between associated enterprises. The Commissioner must rely on Section 22 and other measures discussed in this paper.

B. The tax treaties are of particular importance to non-resident companies entering into transactions with New Zealand companies. In particular, the treaties

a. define what income items are to be included within the meaning of industrial or commercial profits;
b. define in what circumstances these profits are taxable in New Zealand. For example, unless the non-resident has a permanent establishment in New Zealand, industrial or commercial profits would not be taxable in New Zealand. If the management services rendered to a New Zealand company were not deemed to be a royalty and there was a profit component to the non-resident company, it would seem that in most situations the existence of a double tax agreement would preclude the Commissioner taxing this commercial profit.
c. define, in generally a more restrictive manner, the meaning of royalties. The trend in the more recent treaties signed by New Zealand has been to specifically exclude in the Protocol to the treaty the concept of 'services' from the definition of royalties. This step has removed any doubt as to whether such services as technical, consultant or supervisory services may be deemed to be royalties by the Commissioner. An example of this is the West German agreement, where paragraph 5 of the Protocol states:

  > 'In respect of paragraph 3 of Article 12 (which defines royalties), payments received as consideration for technical services, including studies or surveys of a scientific, geological or technical nature, or for engineering contracts including blueprints related thereto, or for consultant or supervisory services, shall be deemed not to be payments received for information concerning industrial, commercial or scientific experience.'

  Similar Protocols are found in tax treaties with France and The Netherlands.
d. contains a clause which may restrict the amount of withholding tax deductible from royalty payments.

A company rendering management services or charging a subsidiary company for research and development costs would be well advised to study the applicable tax treaty before proceeding with the transaction to determine the appropriate tax treatment it will be afforded.

C./D. Taxpayers who desire to seek protection under a tax treaty are advised to approach the Department on this basis. This approach is normally made when the income tax returns are filed. It would be unusual for the Department to invoke a tax treaty unless specifically requested to do so. Applications made on this basis will be accepted by the Department where it is apparent that the circumstances are complementary with the tax treaty requirements.

E./H. If the Department was not able to reach an accord with the competent authorities of a different country, it would have to make a determination of the New Zealand tax due as it sees fit. The taxpayer would have the right to object to the income tax assessment issued in the normal manner. In our experience, disputes with the Commissioner involving different income tax jurisdictions rarely reach the stage where negotiations are required between the Department and competent authority from another country. It is usual for the dispute to be settled in New Zealand to the satisfaction of the Commissioner.

F. New Zealand taxpayers cannot appeal decisions of the competent authorities.

G. Conforming adjustments would be permitted without further tax consequences provided the criteria discussed in paragraph 14.0 are complied with.

PART IV. SPECIAL SITUATIONS

A. The general rules for allocation of income and expenses would not be subject to variation in circumstances where the New Zealand related company did not have gross income or has an operating loss. The Commissioner may invoke Section 22 regardless of whether the business coming within its ambit is carried on for a profit or otherwise. However, the Commissioner may be reluctant to accept allocations of expenses to a New Zealand company from a non-resident affiliate where the New Zealand company is already incurring a loss or producing no gross income.

The rules of income and expense allocations are not affected by the comparable tax rates charged by competent authorities in different countries.

Nevertheless, the Department would scrutinize transactions between a New Zealand company and a related company in a tax haven country, or in a country with a lower rate of corporate tax, in more depth to confirm the reasonableness of the transactions than it would scrutinize similar transactions between countries of similar corporate tax rates. As discussed, the types of transactions which will be subject to special scrutiny are inventory transfer prices, management fees, royalties, and research and development cost allocations.

PART V. OTHER CONSIDERATIONS

Withholding Taxes on Non-Resident Contractors

The government has recently introduced a withholding tax on payments to overseas contractors undertaking contract activities in New Zealand. The main features of this withholding tax are:

1. Rate of Tax and Application Date

The rate is 15 per cent of gross payments made to non-residents whether they are companies or individuals (other than employees), in respect of specified contract activities or services. It applies to payments made on or after January 1st, 1982.

2. Interim Tax

The withholding tax is not an additional tax but a payment on account of the non-resident's annual income tax liability. This tax is neither a minimum nor a final liability. The non-resident's final tax liability will be determined by annual assessment in the normal way. Any refund or further tax to pay will be determined when the tax return for the year is filed.

3. Liable Payments

The withholding tax will be required to be deducted from payments to non-residents in respect of any 'contract activity'. A 'contract activity' is:

a. work carried on in New Zealand in relation to:
   - construction, installation, assembly and similar projects, or
   - consultancy, advisory and other professional or technical services in respect of such projects;

b. the hire of personnel or equipment to be used in New Zealand.

4. Exempt Payments

   a. Payments which are a direct reimbursement of the non-resident's costs will be exempt from the withholding tax except where the non-resident and the payer are associated persons.

b. Payments which are 'royalties' within the meaning of the Tax Act. (Note: Royalty payments to non-residents are subject to Non-Resident Withholding Tax)

5. Exemption Certificates

Exemption certificates may be granted, on written application by the non-resident contractor, where:

a. the Commissioner is satisfied that, by reason of a double tax treaty or for any other reason, the income is exempt from New Zealand tax.
b. the non-resident contractor provides a bond or other form of security satisfactory to the Commissioner, securing payment of any tax which is, or may become, payable in respect of the contract activity. The Department's current attitude is that the bond must equate with 15 per cent of payments being exempted.
c. the Commissioner is satisfied that the non-resident contractor has complied with his tax obligations in the twenty-four months immediately preceding the application and will continue to comply in the future.

6. Special Rate Certificates

The Inland Revenue Department can issue, on application by a non-resident contractor, special tax rate certificates authorizing lower or higher rates of withholding tax. An amended rate would normally be based on a certified budget of expected revenues and expenditures or on the basis of previous years' tax returns. Any special rate would be for a limited period and be reviewed in the light of actual results.

Conclusions

The general rule for the allocation of income and expenses applied by the Commissioner concerning transactions involving trans-national corporations is that the transactions must be performed at arm's length rates. The general rule is complementary with the treatment accorded to the payment of management fees and research and development costs where, in certain circumstances, income will be allocated to the non-resident recipient by deeming the payments to be royalties.

Companies involved with transactions with related companies in different countries must also be aware of the implications of double tax treaties which affect the tax treatment of these transactions to ensure maximum benefit is obtained from any relief from tax resulting from the treaty.

Norway

Helge Ostvold

FOREWORD

It should be appreciated that the laws and practice concerning cross-border transactions is a grey area. Internal Norwegian law gives the tax authorities the right to make adjustments if a taxpayer seeks to avoid taxation through transactions carried out at other than arm's length prices. At the same time, it is left to the taxpayer to provide proper documentation for deductible costs/ expenses. However, the tax treaties normally provide for reduction in income if a related party in another country has had its income increased.

In many cases, it is difficult to determine proper allocations as an open market does not exist for the particular commodity traded.

PART I. GENERAL RULES

A. 1. In principle, adjustments are made to properly reflect income and to stop tax avoidance. However, in practice, allocations are only likely to be made in order to prevent tax avoidance.

2. Arm's length rules are the basis for making adjustments.
3. Sale of oil production companies is the only area where special rules exist. The price of oil is fixed by the authorities. No other safe havens are provided for.
4. For domestic companies within the same group, it is possible to make contributions (subvention payments) with tax effect for both companies.

B. Any persons with a 'participating interest' in another corporation would be regarded as related persons and thus subject to adjustment if they do not deal at arm's length prices.

A person/corporation is considered to have a 'participating interest' when he is in a position to influence directly the income or costs of the other company in order to manipulate the taxation of that company. Limits are vague but, in practice, ownership or influence down to 30 per cent has been regarded as enough to show a 'participating interest'.

C. Any adjustments that would be made would be on a transactions basis.

D. There is no statute of limitations for this purpose. However, there is a practical limit in that companies need not retain their books and supporting records beyond 10 years.

E. When Norway initiates adjustments to, say, a Norwegian parent company, no adjustments are made automatically which would affect subsequent dividends or foreign tax credits flowing back from the foreign subsidiary.

F. When a foreign tax authority makes an adjustment to a foreign subsidiary's tax owing:
1. Norway does not allow consolidated reporting or subvention payments between Norwegian and foreign companies;
2. no special adjustments are made to the dividends or foreign tax credits flowing back to the Norwegian parent;
3. Norway does not require payment to or from Norway to reflect the adjustments.

G. Adjustments are made to the year in which the transactions took place.

H. A Norwegian taxpayer can only ask his tax authorities to adjust cross-border transactions if an allocation has already been made to a related foreign company.

PART II. SPECIFIC EXAMPLES

A. Sale of Goods

Assumed Facts

Assume P is a manufacturer which sells finished products to S which is located in a different country. P sells these products to S at cost. P also sells these products to unrelated parties at cost plus 10 per cent mark-on. Both S and the unrelated parties incur the same selling and promotional expenses and both resell P's products at the same price per unit.

Parent in Norway

1. The tax authorities may increase P's income in this case.
2. The allocation will be based on the arm's length principle.
3. In principle at least, there should still be an increase to P's income even where S incurred greater selling or promotional expenses or was trying to establish a market in country S.

Subsidiary in Norway

1. Norway would make an independent determination of S's income.
2. S can only deduct the extra cost if they are invoiced by P, and Norwegian authorities agree the charge was fair.
3. If S pays the extra charge to P, Norway would levy a withholding tax on the payment.

B. Loans and Advances

Assumed Facts

P and S are manufacturers in different countries. P loans S money on open account without interest so that S can expand its operations. P is not engaged in the business of lending money.

Parent in Norway

1. Income will be allocated to P using market rates of interest.
2. The existence of a non-interest-bearing note would not affect the result.
3. The loan might be regarded as an additional equity investment in S. Pay-back of the loan might be regarded as dividend and taxed at 50.8 per cent.

Subsidiary in Norway

1. A separate determination will be made of S's income.
2. The transaction would most likely be regarded as a loan from P to S.
3. Norway would normally accept a retroactive interest charge if P actually charged S at open market rates.
4. If S pays P more interest than Norway felt was a fair charge to S, the excess amount would probably be regarded as dividend and subjected to withholding tax.
5. Norway would not regard the loan as an equity investment in S.

C. Intangibles

Assumed Facts

P and S are manufacturers located in different countries. P performs research and development which has led to P's ownership of certain intangibles consisting of patents, trademarks and know-how. P makes available to S

exclusive right to use in S's country all of P's intangibles. P does not charge S for the use of P's intangibles.

Parent in Norway

1. In principle at least, income should be allocated to P.
2. Very difficult to say if Norway would impute a lump sum or annual royalties, etc., to P. Either could happen, depending on the circumstances. The treatment in S would not affect the treatment in P.
3. Yes, as an alternative a portion of P's costs could be allocated to S.
4. If the contract adhered to arm's length rules, the contract would govern and no allocation would take place.

Subsidiary in Norway

1. A separate determination of S's income would be made.
2. S would be granted deductions but these must be based on properly documented *bona fide* charges from P.
3. Yes, Norway will levy a whithholding tax on payments to P for intangibles, unless Norway accepted those payments as reasonable charges to S.

D. SERVICES

Assumed Facts

P is a large multinational concern which wholly owns foreign subsidiary S. Both P and S are engaged in manufacturing and sale activities. P's headquarters division performs general management services for P's multinational operations, including services which directly relate to S. The services performed for S include periodic visits by P's executives to review S's operations, financial analysis of S's future requirements, engineering services in connection with S's manufacturing activities and marketing services in connection with S's sales activities. P does not charge S for such services.

Parent in Norway

1. In principle, P's income could be increased in this case. Practical problems would probably prohibit such allocations.
2. In principle, the allocation should be the same if the services had been sold to a third party.

Subsidiary in Norway

1. A separate determination of S's income will be made, and probably no allocation will be made.
2. Norway would levy a withholding tax on any service payments from S to P which were in excess of deductible amounts under 1.

E. Loan Guarantees and Rentals

Assumed Facts

P is a multinational company whose main business is manufacturing and selling. P plans to establish foreign sales subsidiary S located in country S. P capitalizes S with $500,000 and guarantees a loan to S of $500,000 obtained from an independent bank. Land and a warehouse which P owns in country S will be used as a site for S's operations. P plans to make this land and warehouse available to S at a fee of $1 per year for 99 years.

Parent in Norway

1. In principle at least, income should be allocated to P for both the guarantee and the rentals of its property in country S.
2. It is most unlikely that Norway would regard P as having made an equity investment in S.

Subsidiary in Norway

1. A separate determination would be made of S's income.
2. No allocation to S is likely to be accepted.
3. Norway would levy a withholding tax on payments from S to P for loan guarantees or rentals.

PART III. TREATIES

A. Most treaties contain a provision that the state in which the taxable income is too high shall make an appropriate adjustment. However, such adjustment is not to be made automatically and the authorities may determine the adjustment independently.

B. Yes, the treaties will alter domestic tax laws in some cases. However the treaties can never expand domestic taxation. Basically, where internal tax law does not prescribe a reduction of income, such reductions can be made according to the treaties.

C. In most treaties no automatic adjustments are made by tax authorities. The Norwegian taxpayer must apply, normally in response to an adjustment already made in a foreign country.

D. No general guidelines exist for initiating the competent authority procedures.

E./F. If competent authorities fail to agree, double taxation can result. However, the case can always be taken to court in the respective countries.

G. Yes, when two competent authorities reach agreement, conforming adjustments will be allowed without any abnormal tax consequences.

PART IV. SPECIAL SITUATIONS

A. The response of Norwegian tax authorities to cross-border transactions would not differ just because one of the companies had no gross or net income, or because the two companies were facing substantially similar or substantially different tax rates.

B. Oil producing companies. Income is fixed through standard prices on oil assessed by the authorities.

Saudi Arabia

Munir Ahmad

PART I. GENERAL RULES

Saudi Arabia Tax Regulations have not made very significant or sophisticated 'strides' in the concept and treatment of related party transactions, and thus there are no general rules for making allocation of income and expenses between related companies as there are in the US and some other countries.

As a matter of fact, the very concept of 'allocation' of costs or income is one which is generally not acceptable to the Saudi tax authorities.

In no case is the taxpayer allowed to deduct costs which are other than the following:

1. Those directly related to his business activities in the kingdom.
2. Those which represent *actual*, *true*, *definite*, and proveable expenses.

Circular 3 of 1389, issued by the tax authorities, specifically prohibits deduction of any amount in respect of indirect expense which represents the proportion of, say, a foreign parent company's costs that are attributable to the activity in the kingdom, and the circular further reiterates that the profits from the local sources in the kingdom should be affected only by expenses directly related to those profits.

The concept of 'allocation or imputation' of income between related parties (which arises when *no* actual financial transaction takes place between them, ie when the parent or subsidiary do not charge each other for the goods or services) is presently virtually non-existent in Saudi tax regulations (although the gradual awakening of the tax authorities and eventual introduction of this concept should not be ruled out).

The assessment of tax only arises when the charge for the goods and services has been recognized/accrued and accordingly reflected in the audited financial statements.

Since Saudi Arabia's economy is predominantly an importer of goods and services (excluding oil) this paper will mainly concern itself with the situation where subsidiary S is set up in Saudi either as a branch or a limited liability company/partnership reporting to the Saudi tax authorities and receives goods and services from parent/affiliates P situated outside Saudi Arabia.

In accordance with international accounting standards, the related party transactions have to be disclosed in the audited financial statements. These are then required to be analyzed in the taxpayer's returns in order to provide details of the transactions, eg names and addresses of payee P, amounts paid by S, nature of the transaction and, in the case of services, place of performance of work. Copies of agreements between the parties are also required to be provided with the tax returns.

The Saudi tax authorities function more or less in a 'vacuum', completely unconcerned and unconnected with any tax implications or tax assessments that may result from parent (payee) country's tax regulations. Saudi tax authorities strictly look into the determination, assessment and collection of tax on the taxable entity based in Saudi in accordance with the Saudi Arabian tax regulations.

Most of the situations envisaged in the questionnaire provided to assist in preparing this paper do not currently apply in Saudi but, having identified related party transactions, the resulting Saudi Arabian tax implications may be summarized as follows:

Technical Services Rendered Outside the Kingdom

Charges billed by parent or affiliated P to S for service performed wholly outside Saudi Arabia and for the exclusive benefit of the Saudi Arabian project are deductible costs against Saudi source revenues, and payments made by S will not be taxable in the hand of the recipient parent P.

However, there is the need to support the charge (recorded in accounts) by a certification from P's auditors confirming that the charges billed by P to S are in accordance with the books and records of the billing company P, and that the staff billed for have worked in the parent company's offices wholly ouside the kingdom of Saudi Arabia.

The hourly rates billed must contain no element of administrative charge or profit and must be only the direct costs of the individual plus a proportion thereof in respect of direct overheads (utilities etc.).

PART II. SERVICES RENDERED INSIDE THE KINGDOM

Payments made by S to P in connection with services performed by P inside the kingdom will be held taxable in the hands of the recipient P. Unless P is registered with the Saudi Arabian tax authorities and settles its tax directly with them on an accounts basis, S will be held liable for P's tax liability. P is taxed on the imputed profit element in the payment received, and the percentage of the payment which is deemed to be profit may vary from 15 per cent to 100 per cent.

Payments for other services, eg hire of equipment, etc., would attract deemed profit tax at 15 per cent but there is always the probability that related parties may attract tax at an imputed profit rate which is greater than 15 per cent.

Net profits accruing to a non-Saudi taxpayer are taxed at following rates:

First SR	100,000	– at 25%
next	400,000	– at 35%
next	500,000	– at 40%
above	1,000,000	– at 45%

Management fees paid by a subsidiary in Saudi to a parent are deemed to be 100 per cent profit in the hands of the recipient and taxed at the above rates.

However, if fees are paid, under the terms of an arm's length service agreement, as compensation for services rendered and the compensation paid stands the 'reasonableness test', then the fees are allowed as a deductible charge in the payor's accounts, with the tax liability determined by the place where the services are rendered. If rendered wholly outside the Kingdom, then they should not attract tax.

If services are rendered inside the Kingdom, or partly inside and partly outside, then the gross payments made are held taxable on a deemed profit rate which can vary between 15 per cent and 100 per cent. The deemed profit is then taxed at the above rates in order to arrive at the tax liability.

Foreign Source Income of Saudis

Income from carrying out operations both inside and outside the Kingdom at the same time will be subject to Saudi profits tax. Thus, foreign source dividend income will be subject to Saudi tax.

PART III. GOODS

'Supply only' operation, where goods are consigned to the port of entry, is classified as trading with Saudi Arabia and does not attract tax, provided that the supplies are charged to the Saudi branch/company S at international or P's home country market value at the date of dispatch and this fact is confirmed by the parent (supplying company's) auditors.

Supply, erection and installation contracts are subject to tax even if the foreign supplies are quantified and shown clearly in the contract. Therefore, the taxpayer is required to account for the whole value of the contract.

PART IV. LOANS/GUARANTEES

Advances/loans made by P to S are treated in the same manner as advances from banks, ie interest paid/payable attracts a tax on a deemed profit where the minimum acceptable rate of imputed profit is 15 per cent, and to this figure the normal tax rates apply.

In accordance with the current practice, interest free loans are not assessed an imputed profits tax. It is far from certain, however, how long the tax authorities will permit such a situation to prevail. There have recently been reservations expressed by the tax authorities whether interest on loans paid by S to P should even qualify as a tax deductible expense in S's tax return.

PART V. INTANGIBLES

Research and Development

A one-time payment from Saudi, made in the first year of an arrangement with a Saudi taxpayer and which is capitalized and written off over the years, will not attract tax.

Royalties paid and charged as such will attract tax in the hands of the recipient on a 100 per cent imputed profits basis.

Singapore

Graham R. Clark

PART I. GENERAL RULES

A. The fundamental principle for making allocations of income and expenses between related companies is that there must be a matching of income and expenditure and, because income tax is an annual tax, that income and expenditure must be matched in the same period. The general rule on deductibility of expenses is that all expenses wholly and exclusively incurred in the production of (assessable) income, except those expenses specifically prohibited by the Income Tax Act, may be charged off as a deduction. The Singapore Tax Code has no provision for filing consolidated tax returns for associated or related companies and, consequently, allocations of income and expenses are made not only between resident and non-resident companies, but also between companies which are both resident in Singapore. Because allocations can be used as a means of shifting profits, Revenue gives much attention to internal as well as cross-border transfers.

1. Whilst prevention of tax avoidance is the main thrust of the interest by Revenue (they are frequently ambivalent in that they seek to have resident companies include a profit element when charging foreign companies, whilst accepting charges from foreign companies only on a cost-recovery basis), the principal purpose is to arrive at an equitable result, even where no tax avoidance is present.
2. In the absence of any specific legislation, the well-worn phrase 'arm's-length' is the generally accepted basis for making adjustments. The nature of the Singapore economy is such that many of the manufacturing and trading companies are related to or are subsidiaries of foreign corporations and, consequently, inter-company transactions are frequent. Provided it can be demonstrated that the basis of allocation is universally followed by all companies within the same group and such basis is consistently observed, then there is little likelihood of Revenue seeking to impose any variation. The weight of emphasis is plainly directed towards payments made by resident companies to non-resident companies with comparatively little attention being devoted to recoveries being made from non-resident entities.
3. Special rules and safe havens – to enable withholding tax to be imposed on

certain payments made to non-residents, such payments are deemed to have a source in Singapore; for example, payments for assistance in the management of any trade or business and rent or other payments for the use of any movable property. By concession, however, there is no withholding tax applied to management fees where the services are provided entirely from outside Singapore and the charge is essentially a cost-recovery. The general withholding rate is at 40 per cent, although it is open to negotiate a lesser rate on a case-by-case basis. The Act specifically provides for a tax adjustment to be made where, owing to the close connection between a resident and a non-resident person and to the substantial control exercised by either party (or some other party over them both), the profits derived by the resident are less than the ordinary profits which might be expected to arise. The Act provides that the non-resident person shall be assessable and chargeable to tax in the name of the resident person as if the resident person were an agent. In practice, however, the negotiated adjustment is made to the profits of the resident company.

4. Although greater emphasis is given to cross-border transactions, the absence of group relief in Singapore gives rise to close scrutiny of domestic transactions where one of the parties concerned is in a loss position. There is an inherent inconsistency in the tax authorities' practice in that domestic companies are expected to recover expenses in such an amount as to yield a profit margin of not less than 5 per cent, whereas payments made to non-residents should not include any profit element. If there is a profit element in the latter instance, there will invariably be an attempt to tax the non-resident recipient on the profit margin.

B. There is no statutory definition of related persons for purposes of making allocations. In practice, parties will be treated as related if either controls the other; both are subject to third-party control, such control either being effected by 50 per cent of more voting control or *de facto* management control where the shareholding is less than 50 per cent. Payments made between unrelated parties are *prima facie* regarded as being at arm's-length and seldom subject to queries.

C. When adjustments are made, these are normally on a transactions basis. Where imbalances arise between different categories of transactions, it may be sufficient to show that there was a 'trade-off' thus not requiring any tax adjustments to be made, but it would be unwise to rely on this being acceptable in every case. For instance, Revenue might not accept that the granting of a soft loan is balanced by trade goods being supplied back by the other party on unusually favourable terms.

D. There is no specific statute of limitations, other than the 12-year period open to Revenue to renew assessments, but the accrual basis of accounting requires recognition of all relative income and expenditure of the basis period.

The inclusion of expenditure relating to a previous basis period may be denied, as may also be a claim to re-open earlier financial statements.

E. Where an adjustment is made by Singapore authorities, there is no requirement that any correlative adjustment be made to the income of the non-resident person.

F. When a foreign country initiates an adjustment, Singapore law permits the assessment of the non-resident on his extra income by assessing the resident person as agent. However, the practice is to adjust the profits of the resident person. Only where Revenue is unable to negotiate agreement with the taxpayer will the assessment be raised in the statutory manner.

There is no consolidated basis of reporting permitted. Dividends and foreign tax credits are not affected by adjustments to a related company (eg subsidiary in a foreign country). The tax adjustments which are made in all cases do not require an actual payment between those companies of the amounts allocated.

G. Adjustments are made to the underlying transaction years and not to the year when the adjustment is initiated.

H. Generally, the taxpayer has no right to seek allocation where this has not been incorporated in the statutory audited financial statements. The only exception to this is between branch and company under the terms of a tax treaty.

PART II. SPECIFIC EXAMPLES

A. Sale of Goods

Assumed Facts

Assume P is a manufacturer which sells finished products to S which is located in a different country. P sells these products to S at cost. P also sells these products to unrelated parties at cost plus 10 per cent mark-on. Both S and the unrelated parties incur the same selling and promotional expense and both resell P's products at the same price per unit.

Parent in Singapore

1. The sale to the subsidiary at cost is not acceptable. A profit margin would be allocated to the parent.
2. Initially, Revenue may be expected to attribute to P the same profit margin as is achieved in sales to unrelated parties. Other factors to be taken into account, however, are the credit risk attaching to sales to the unrelated parties,

whether such orders are regular and in sizeable numbers, and the relative terms of payment. These may warrant a lesser profit margin being accepted.
3. Revenue would not normally accept a zero profit margin on P's sales to S. If it can be shown that S derives a lesser profit than that achieved by unrelated parties, then a lower selling price to S would be acceptable.

Subsidiary in Singapore

1. Allocations made by foreign authorities are not given recognition in Singapore. The only exception would be where, unusually, it was possible to invoke the non-discrimination article in a tax treaty.
2. Whilst retroactive allocations would not be deductible in S, subsequent adjustments reflected in the financial statements of S would be allowed if Singapore authorities agreed that the adjustment was justified.
3. If S makes a payment of the allocated amount to P, whilst the payment would not be deductible as a business expense, the payment would not be treated as a dividend.

Although Singapore has no withholding tax *per se* on dividends, there is a danger in having a payment classed as a dividend payment. Singapore's imputation system works similar in concept to ACT in the UK, and the Singapore payor must in effect remit to the government an amount equal to 40 per cent of its dividend payments, as a non-refundable instalment against its profits tax.

B. Loans and Advances

Assumed Facts

P and S are manufacturers located in different countries. P loans S money on open account without interest so that S can expand its operations. P is not engaged in the business of lending money.

Parent in Singapore

1. There are no provisions in the Singapore Tax Act to allocate interest income. What is done, however, is to deny a deduction to P of any interest expense incurred by P in financing the loan to S. Such interest expense would be disallowed on the grounds that it is not an expense incurred in the production of income since the funds have been loaned on terms which do not yield income.
2. The answer would not differ if the loan was evidenced by a non-interest-bearing note with a fixed maturity date.

3. The loan would not be regarded as an equity investment by P and there are no tax consequences on the repayment of the loan.

Subsidiary in Singapore

1./2. There are no tax implications on the acceptance of an interest-free loan by a subsidiary company in Singapore.
3. There will be no notional interest expense attributed to S on the loan.
4./5. Any amount paid by S would not be allowed as a deduction unless it arose out of the loan agreement itself. If S pays the amount allocated by P's country, this will be a non-deductible expense and not treated as interest or a distribution of profit.

C. INTANGIBLES

Assumed Facts

P and S are manufacturers located in different countries. P performs research and development which has led to P's ownership of certain intangibles consisting of patents, trademarks and know-how. P makes available to S exclusive right to use in S's country all of P's intangibles. P does not charge S for the use of P's intangibles.

Parent in Singapore

1./2. No income would be allocated to P, although it would suffer a restriction of any related expenses incurred in the current accounting period.
3. Whilst no prior year costs would be allocated to S such current costs would be allocated effectively by way of disallowance of the expense to P.
4. A cost sharing arrangement would be in accordance with the principles of the Singapore Tax Code and would be adhered to if reasonable. No retroactive adjustments could be made.

Subsidiary in Singapore

1. Singapore would not accept an allocation made by P's country. No retrospective deduction would be allowed.
2. A payment made in respect of prior years would be denied as a deduction. An annual royalty would be permitted as a deduction although this royalty would be subject to withholding tax, either at the standard rate of 40 per cent or at a lower rate if provided by a tax treaty. If P's allocation was on a cost recovery basis, then the payment would be tax deductible to S (but subject to

withholding) provided that it was shown that the allocation to S was on a reasonable and consistent basis.
3. Singapore imposes withholding tax on royalties, technical assistance and service fees at the rate of 40 per cent or such lesser rate as provided for in any tax treaty.

Even if S was buying capital assets such as patents, trademarks, etc., such payments must be approved. Depreciation allowance at 20 per cent per annum straight-line is granted on capital expenditures in acquiring approved know-how or approved patent rights. Approval status is given by the Minister of Finance. If the know-how or patents were so approved, this would also result in exemption being given from withholding tax. Even if no approval was given to the patents or know-how, it would still be open to apply for exemption from the withholding tax although it is unlikely one exemption would be granted without the other. It is to be noted that the withholding tax can only be applied to royalty payments if the payment is income in the hands of the recipient. The fact that the expenditure is capital is not indicative that the receipt is also capital. The Revenue would observe the principles laid down in *Jeffrey* v *Rolls Royce Ltd* (UK Tax Cases Vol.40) and *Evans Medical Supplies* v *Moriarty* (UK Tax Cases Vol.37) in determining this point.

D. Services

Assumed Facts

P is a large multinational concern which wholly owns foreign subsidiary S. Both P and S are engaged in manufacturing and sales activities. P's headquarters division performs general management services for P's multi-national operations including services which directly relate to S. The services performed for S include periodic visits by P's executives to review S's operations, financial analysis of S's future requirements, engineering services in connection with S's manufacturing activities and marketing services in connection with S's sales activities. P does not charge S for such service.

Parent in Singapore

1. No charge will be allocated to P for the performance of services but there will be a disallowance of the costs incurred in rendering the services.
2. There is no statutory basis for calculating the disallowance. In practice this might be calculated by prorating the costs of the headquarters by reference to S's turnover as a fraction of group sales.

Subsidiary in Singapore

1. No deduction would be allowed to S unless this charge has been levied on a current basis and recognized in the audited financial statement.
2. Any payments made by S to P (on a current year basis) would not be subject to withholding tax if it were demonstrated that P was effecting a cost recovery with no profit margin. Where made to a treaty country, the payment would normally be tax protected by the Business Profits Article. Where withholding tax is applied, this would normally be to the profit margin only.

E. Loan Guarantees and Rentals

Assumed Facts

P is a multinational company whose main business is manufacturing and selling. P plans to establish foreign sales subsidiary S located in country S. P capitalizes S with $500,000 and guarantees a loan to S of $500,000 obtained from an independent bank. Land and a warehouse which P owns in country S will be used as a site for S's operations. P plans to make this land and warehouse available to S at a fee of $1 per year for 99 years.

Parent in Singapore

1. No income would be allocated to P either for the guarantee or rent of the land and warehouse. If, however, P had incurred any interest expense in borrowing money to capitalize S then that interest expense would be disallowed, unless the investment in the subsidiary company yielded income by way of dividend. Likewise, if any interest expense had been incurred in borrowing money with which to buy the land and warehouse, a similar interest expense restriction would be imposed.
2. This transaction would not be treated as an additional equity investment by P in S.

Subsidiary in Singapore

1. The actions by P's country would not be recognized by Singapore.
2. No income would be allocated to P in respect of the facilities afforded to S. Any amounts allocated to P and paid by S would not be recognized as tax deductible expenses.
3. If income is allocated to P and S makes payment of the allocated amounts to P, no withholding tax would apply.

PART III. TAX TREATIES

A. Singapore has entered into tax treaties with twenty-two other States. Each of these agreements has an article on transactions between 'associated enterprises'.

B. Under the mutual agreement procedure in the treaty, it would be open to the aggrieved party in Singapore to make representations to the Singapore fiscal authority to negotiate with the other fiscal authority where taxation has been imposed and is not in accord with the convention. Singapore gives general observance to the official commentary on the OECD Model Agreement. The domestic law of Singapore gives precedence to the provisions of the double tax agreement where the subject matter is cognizant to both.

C. The provisions of the treaty will only be invoked at the instigation of the taxpayer. There is normally a three-year time limit in which to lodge the complaint.

D. There are no published guidelines on the procedure to be adopted for applying to competent authority. In practice, having received the complaint and determined the facts, the authority will enter into written correspondence with the other authority with a view to reaching mutual agreement.

E. Should the authorities fail to reach agreement, Singapore would normally grant unilateral relief where it is satisfied that hardship has been suffered.

F. The domestic law has no provisions to appeal against a settlement made between the two authorities, except where its subject matter is capable of appeal under the domestic law. In such events, it is improbable that it would have been possible to invoke the mutual agreement article in the first instance.

G. Where agreement is reached as to the correct allocation, conforming adjustments and payments can be made with no adverse tax consequence.

H. Competent authority negotiations are something of a rare event. Negotiations have most frequently been carried on between Singapore and Malaysian authorities, this no doubt resulting from the substantial inter-company trade and business carried on. Negotiations have extended for as long as four years. In our experience, agreements have eventually been reached to the satisfaction of the taxpayers.

PART IV. SPECIAL SITUATIONS

A. The normal allocation rules are not modified or applied differently:
1. if either of the related companies does not have any gross income;

2. if either of the related companies has an operating loss for the year;
3. where the tax rates of the countries involved are substantially equal;
4. where the tax rate of the country to which the income is to be allocated is substantially lower than the rate of tax in the country where the income was originally reported.

B. Transactions between financial institutions are, on occasion, closely examined because of the ease of profit shifting by way of interest rates on charges and payments. Manufacturing concerns are also subject to scrutiny on transfer-pricing, there being a large number of companies in Singapore which manufacture or assemble on behalf of foreign corporations.

PART V. OTHER CONSIDERATIONS

The probable response by the Singapore Revenue to situations of the kind dealt with in this paper is fairly predictable. Accordingly, it should normally be possible to arrange matters in advance so as to avoid intervention by the Authority. Revenue is not unduly aggressive and would normally only exercise its powers in cases where there is a flagrant attempt to drive out profits.

Singapore is a regional service centre and many service-type companies have been established. It is expected by Revenue that such companies should earn a marginal profit of approximately 5 per cent. If this is done, it is unlikely that any further questions would be directed as to the specific nature of the services.

This soft approach by the Authority is probably attributable to the economic desire to enhance the development of the State as a business and financial centre in South East Asia.

South Africa

Chris K. Hassall/Patrick K. Quarmby

PART I. GENERAL RULES

A. 1. An arm's length standard is adopted for adjusting transactions between related parties. The Act does contain an anti-avoidance provision where tax is avoided through abnormal transactions.
2. Adjustments may be made only to prevent tax avoidance.
3. All types of transactions are covered and no safe havens are proclaimed.
4. From a tax viewpoint, domestic transactions are treated the same as international transactions. However, certain cross-border transactions are limited due to exchange control restrictions.

B. There is no statutory definition of arm's length or related persons in South Africa. Each transaction would be judged on its own facts, ascertaining whether the parties are acting as persons dealing at arm's length. This is not based on any particular relationship between the parties, although a close corporate relationship may be a presumption for a non-arm's length relationship.

C. Transactions basis is the principal approach in making adjustments.

D. Assessments cannot be reopened more than three years after the date of an original assessment, unless there has been non-disclosure of material facts.

E. When South Africa or another country adjusts one side of an international transaction, South Africa will not normally make any correlative adjustment to the other side of the transaction. However, Revenue has the discretion in a tax avoidance situation of taxing as it deems fit within the boundaries of the law.

F. If an adjustment was made to a company located outside South Africa:
1. no consolidation basis or other group relief is available;
2. dividends are not affected and foreign tax credits would not be affected by foreign profits tax, only by withholding tax on dividends;
3. payment of allocated amounts is not required.

G. The adjustments would be made to the years in which the transactions took place.

H. A South African taxpayer cannot initiate an adjustment under these allocation rules.

PART II. SPECIFIC EXAMPLES

A. SALE OF GOODS

Assumed Facts

Assume P is a manufacturer which sells finished products to S which is located in a different country. P sells these products to S at cost. P also sells these products to unrelated parties at cost plus 10 per cent mark-on. Both S and the unrelated parties incur the same selling and promotional expense and both resell P's products at the same price per unit.

Parent in South Africa

1. Only if Revenue applies anti-tax avoidance legislation could this income be reallocated (section 103). However, in practice, this would rarely happen.
2. If it was an avoidance scheme an arm's length price would be used, using other unrelated sales as a measure.
3. If P made no sales to independent parties, or S incurred greater selling/promotional expenses, then Revenue authorities would be hard pressed to show that this was actually a tax avoidance measure. As there is no comparable price, the imputation of an arm's length price would be difficult.

Subsidiary in South Africa

1. The allocation of income as determined by P's country would not be accepted by South Africa.
2. Only if the price is charged through to S can it be acceptable as a deduction in South Africa.
3. If S actually pays the amount charged by P, then if the amount is seen to be a distribution of profits it will be a dividend and subject to withholding tax. If it can be allocated to the cost of the stock, a deduction from income will be granted and no withholding applies.

B. Loans and Advances

Assumed Facts

P and S are manufacturers located in different countries. P loans to S money on open account without interest so that S can expand its operations. P is not engaged in the business of lending money.

Parent Company in South Africa

1. No interest income will be allocated or imputed to P. However, certain problems could be encountered because of South Africa's exchange controls.
2. The existence of a formal note would not affect P's treatment. Also, prior exchange control approval would have to be sought.
3. No, the loan cannot be considered an additional equity investment by P.

Subsidiary in South Africa

1. South Africa would make its own determination of whether S is entitled to any tax deductions.
2. The transaction would be characterized as a loan.
3. Interest would not be allocated to S, except if the interest is actually charged by P to S. The charge would have to be legally binding. Problems might be encountered with the deductibility of the interest if the rate is not market-related.
4. Problems with the deductibility by S might be encountered where South Africa disagrees with P's allocation. However, the amount disallowed would still be subject to withholding tax.
5. This transaction would always be viewed as a loan, not equity.

C. Intangibles

Assumed Facts

P and S are manufacturers located in different countries. P performs research and development which has led to P's ownership of certain intangibles consisting of patents, trademarks and know-how. P makes available to S exclusive right to use in S's country all of P's intangibles. P does not charge S for the use of P's intangibles.

Parent in South Africa

1. At present, income would probably not be allocated for the free use of intangibles.
2. If made, the allocation would probably be a royalty calculated on an arm's length basis. The tax position of S would not effect any change.
3. If properly incurred by P, the R and D costs will not be allocated to S. Problems might be encountered with the deductibility of the costs as they would not be incurred in the production of income. Dividends are not considered 'income' as defined for tax purposes when received by a company.
4. If P and S entered a cost-sharing agreement, no royalties would be payable, but costs would be allocated to S.

Subsidiary in South Africa

1. South Africa would make its own determination, and would only react to an actual fee being charged.
2. Only if the amount was actually charged through to S would it rank as a deduction. The royalty would be deductible. If it was a lump sum payment, the South African authorities would have to be satisfied that the payment did not ensure an 'enduring benefit', thereby forcing it to be of a capital nature and thus not deductible.
3. The amount paid in respect of the use of trademarks, patents or know-how will be subject to withholding tax depending, however, on the relevant Double Tax Treaty. Note that payments of this nature are deemed to be from a South African source and are subject to South African normal tax. The withholding tax is merely an advance payment against this tax.

D. SERVICES

Assumed Facts

P is a large multinational concern which wholly owns foreign subsidiary S. Both P and S are engaged in manufacturing and sales activities. P's headquarters division performs general management services for P's multinational operations including services which directly relate to S. The services performed for S include periodic visits by P's executives to review S's operations, financial analysis of S's future requirements, engineering services in connection with S's manufacturing activities and marketing services in connection with S's sales activities. P does not charge S for such service.

Parent in South Africa

1. No charge will be allocated to P for such services.
2. Not applicable. However, if Revenue became aware that certain activities were not designed to produce income, the deduction in respect thereof could fall under question.

Subsidiary in South Africa

1. A separate determination will occur, unless there is a corresponding charge from the holding company. These charges always fall under the scrutiny of the Exchange Control authorities who would require justification of the amount. S will only be allowed a deduction of an actual charge.
2. No withholding tax applicable. The only problem being that of exchange control.

E. Loan Guarantees and Rentals

Assumed Facts

P is a multinational company whose main business is manufacturing and selling. P plans to establish foreign sales subsidiary S located in country S. P capitalizes S with $500,000 and guarantees a loan to S of $500,000 obtained from an independent bank. Land and a warehouse which P owns in country S will be used as a site for S's operations. P plans to make this land and warehouse available to S at a fee of $1 per year for 99 years.

Parent in South Africa

1. No income will be allocated to P.
2. Only if the company could arrive at a value of the service could there be an additional equity investment. If a value is accepted, the amount would be taxable in P's hands.

Subsidiary in South Africa

1. South Africa would make a separate determination of whether S could deduct any allocations initiated in country P.
2. Only an actual charge could be accepted, providing it was reasonable.
3. No withholding tax would be applicable to S's payments of rentals or guarantee fees to P.

PART III. TAX TREATIES

A. Yes, the tax treaties which South Africa has entered into do contain a provision for mutual agreement procedure, but only in the areas where there has been double tax.

B. The tax treaties would not affect a change to the answers previously given. Domestic law would have to be applied in a negotiation.

C. The taxpayer will have to seek protection under the treaty. There are no regulations setting out procedures.

D. No procedural guidelines have been issued for initiating mutual agreement provisions of treaties.

E. If there is a failure to reach an agreement between the competent authorities regard would have to be had to domestic law. It would appear that, in extreme circumstances, double taxation could prevail.

F. A taxpayer cannot appeal against a settlement made between two competent authorities.

G. Where agreement has been reached, conforming adjustments and payments will be allowed.

H. Our experience in this area is quite limited. In our few experiences, delay has always been encountered, especially when the negotiations involve the repayment of money. However, the matters are usually favourably resolved.

PART IV. SPECIAL SITUATIONS

A. 1. There will be no change in the normal allocation rules just because one company has no gross income.
   2. If income is injected into a company solely for the utilization of an assessed loss, no set-off is allowed. Other than that, no change to previous answers.
   3. The fact that the tax rates in the two countries involved were substantially equal would not alter South African treatment of the transaction.
   4. The fact that the tax rates in the two countries involved were substantially different would not alter South Africa's treatment of the transaction. Unless it was part of a tax avoidance scheme, in which case section 103 could be applied to tax the income in the hands of whichever company Revenue deem fit.

B. 1. Where one of the companies is in an assessed loss position, the authorities will analyze more carefully the generation of income in that company.

2. Due to exchange controls, all payments made from South Africa in respect of royalties, interest, management fees, and technical assistance fees are carefully scrutinized.

3. Also where it is possible to ascertain an overpricing policy designed to transfer funds overseas, the exchange control authorities investigate carefully and base their attacks on other arm's length prices if available.

Spain

Jaime Lopez-Chicheri

PART I. GENERAL RULES

A. The basic rule is that established in Article 16 of the 1978 Corporation Tax Law. The wording of this article is as follows:

> 'Art.16. Valuation of Income and Expenses.
> ONE. Income and expenses will be valued at the amount recorded in the books of account, providing that these reflect at all times the true value to the company.
> TWO. (Not applicable)
> THREE. Despite the foregoing, in the case of transactions between related companies, their valuation for the purpose of this tax will be in accordance with those prices that would be agreed in normal market conditions between unrelated companies.
> FOUR. The preceding provision shall always be applied to:
> a. *companies associated directly or indirectly with others not resident in Spain*;
> b. transactions between a company and its shareholders, board members, or persons who form part of their respective family units, defined in accordance with the fifth article of the law governing the personal income tax;
> c. transactions between two companies in which the same members or persons making up their respective family units own at least twenty-five percent of their capital, or when the said persons carry out functions in both companies which imply the exercise of the power of decision.
> FIVE. For the purposes of the provisions of the two preceding sections it will be understood that there is affiliate relationship between two companies *when one holds directly or indirectly at least twenty-five percent of the share capital* of the other, or when, without this circumstance existing, one company *carried out functions in another which imply the exercise of the power of decision*.'

This provision applies to transactions made after January 1st, 1979 (date on which the Corporation Tax Law came into force) and has been implemented by Royal Decree 2361/1982 of October 15, 1984, section 39. Although five years have elapsed, we still have had little experience since the tax authorities do not apply these provisions unless the values of transactions are very highly affected by the relationship of the partners. This makes the problem of allocation of income and expense between related companies very unclear, not only for the taxpayer but also for the tax authorities themselves.

Some examples of the main points in doubt are the following:

a. May the taxpayer make the adjustments in his tax return or do they have to be made by the tax authorities?
b. Is this provision only applicable to income and expenses or is it also applicable to capital for capital gains and losses? This appears to have been resolved by sec.39 of regulations, which is headed 'Operations between related companies'. The corresponding section of the law was headed 'valuation of income and expenses'.
c. Must adjustments made by other government bodies (ie customs authorities) be recognized by the tax authorities?

   This is very important because the majority of Spanish subsidiaries import goods from their foreign parent company. In most cases, import prices are adjusted by the customs authorities for import duty purposes. May this adjustment be used also for fiscal purposes to reduce the taxable income of the Spanish subsidiary?
d. What happens in the case of a tax inspection? Do the inspectors have to examine two or more related companies at the same time?

   If not, what effect do the hypothetical adjustments proposed by the inspectors to one company have on an affiliated Spanish company?
e. Do the adjustments, if made by the company, have to be recorded on the books of account or just shown in the tax computations when the tax return is filed?

All these important problems, and others not mentioned above, have not yet been resolved; therefore, many decisions taken by the taxpayer might be opposed by a tax inspector.

Bearing in mind all these limitations, we comment below on the above-quoted provision:

1. In principle, the adjustments are aimed at preventing tax evasion or the transfer of profits between related companies. Normally an adjustment made by the taxpayer will be accepted by the tax inspectors if the result is an increase in the taxable amount. On the other hand, if the result is a higher expense it could be opposed upon inspection.
2. The basis for the adjustments is the normal market prices that would be agreed upon between independent companies dealing at arm's length.
3. In principle, the regulations of transactions between related companies covers income and expenses of any nature as well as capital gains and losses. However, the following transactions are normally examined in more detail by the inspectors:
   - intercompany financing

– intercompany sales
– intercompany services

4. The present legislation does not differentiate between resident and non-resident companies. Nevertheless, in some cases the fact that the transaction takes place between a resident and a non-resident company has different effects.

   For example, in the case of a loan between domestic companies bearing no interest or with a low interest, this could be adjusted up to the market rate. On the other hand, if one of the contractors is non-resident there is a widespread opinion that the interest could not be adjusted since the loan conditions require previous approval from the Spanish foreign exchange authorities.

B. This point has been contemplated in A. above. In general terms, when a company owns directly or indirectly at least 25 per cent of the share capital of another company, or both are owned (again, at least 25 per cent) by a third company, it is understood that they are related for fiscal purposes. The power to make decisions is also determinant even if the minimum percentages of ownership are not met. For certain branches of foreign entities a net income of 15 per cent of expenses incurred is established.

C. The adjustments are normally made on a transaction-by-transaction basis. However, in certain types of Spanish companies whose only activity is rendering services to the parent company, the tax authorities generally accept that they invoice at, say, total cost plus 10 per cent, which means adjusting on a net income basis.

D. The statute of limitations is the same as for tax inspections – five years.

E. It seems to be the criteria of the tax authorities to make the adjustments on a company-by-company basis and only when they involve a higher income. Therefore, a corresponding adjustment to the income of the related company will not normally be accepted when it gives rise to higher expense. Although in our opinion this criterion is not in accordance with the law, it is the one that most probably will be applied by the tax inspectors.

Take, for example, a Spanish company whose activity is import–cxport with foreign affiliates at prices below market. In the case of imports, although the prices will probably have been adjusted upwards for import duty purposes, the inspectors will probably not accept an adjustment to the cost of sales. However, in the case of an export, a higher income will be imputed.

This highlights the importance of using proper prices in transactions between related companies (be they domestic or between resident and non-resident companies) because, in addition to the risk explained above, a penalty of at least 33 per cent (25 per cent plus 8 per cent interest) will be imposed on inspection on underpayments of tax.

F. In principle, the adjustment made to a subsidiary located outside of Spain would not have any effect in the domestic company tax computation, except if the foreign entity is a branch of the domestic one, in which case they will be taxed in Spain on a consolidated basis. A Spanish company is taxable on foreign source dividends but a foreign tax credit is granted equal to lessor of foreign tax paid and the normal Spanish tax on the dividend (33 per cent).

G. Adjustment should affect the year in which the transaction took place.

H. We have no experience as yet with this subject but, in principle, the taxpayer should be able to request Spanish tax authorities to make adjustments.

An example is the situation explained in C. above (Spanish subsidiaries rendering services at cost to their foreign parents), in which case the company could propose to the tax authorities a fee (cost plus) to be charged to the parent. The total fee should be collected.

PART II. SPECIFIC EXAMPLES

A. Sale of Goods

Assumed Facts

Assume P is a manufacturer which sells finished products to S which is located in a different country. P sells these products to S at cost. P also sells these products to unrelated parties at cost plus 10 per cent mark on. Both S and the unrelated parties incur the same selling and promotional expense and both resell P's products at the same price per unit.

Parent in Spain

1. In principle, a tax inspector could adjust the income in P, since all the circumstances of Article 16 (see above) are met.
2. The basis for the adjustment, as stipulated in the provision, is 'the price that would be agreed in normal market conditions between unrelated parties'. That is to say if the market price is the selling price to the unrelated parties, in principle this would be the standard taken by the inspector. Of course, special circumstances would be taken into account: for example, where P sells to S 80 per cent of its production, the selling market prices for the last unit sold would arguably be lower than that for the earlier units sold, but this should be treated as a discount for sales volume.
3. The same result should occur even where there are no comparable sales to unrelated parties but the tax inspector would have to prove the basis for the adjustment.

The allocation to P would probably be the same even if S had agreed to absorb some of the marketing and promotional expenses.

Subsidiary in Spain

1. The allocation of income from S to P would not be accepted by Spain. If the higher price is used by customs authorities in Spain, there is an argument that the higher price can also be expensed by S for income tax purposes. Although we feel this argument should succeed, the tax authorities oppose it.
2. The higher allocation to P would not be tax deductible in Spain.
3. No payments that were not included in the import licence could be made. Otherwise, a monetary offence would be committed. Of course, S could distribute dividends out of its profits which would attract the normal withholding tax on dividends.

B. Loans and Advances

Assumed Facts

P and S are manufacturers located in different countries. P loans to S money on open account without interest so that S can expand its operations. P is not engaged in the business of lending money.
Note: In principle, the treatment would be different in the case of a formal loan to that of a loan on current account. In both cases, exchange control regulations must be taken into consideration.

Parent in Spain

1. Interest income could be allocated to P at a rate approximating the market rate in the case of a current account. However, due to strict exchange control in Spain, current account financing of a non-resident entity without government authorization would be an administrative infringement.
2. A loan between resident and non-resident companies has to be authorized by the government. In this case, the authorization covers the conditions of the loan, amongst which is included interest. In fact, it is normal that, when the borrower is a Spanish resident, the loan is approved without interest, but not so in the opposite case. We are of the opinion that if the goverment has approved a non-interest bearing loan, no allocation should be made to the Spanish parent.

Subsidiary in Spain

1. The treatment of the transaction in P's country would not affect the treatment in S's country.
2. In principle, Spain would not treat the transaction as an equity investment. If the financing is not approved, there is a risk that the government will not authorize the repayment. In this case, and providing that the company can prove that the money was received from abroad, it could apply for the capitalization of the debt.

If the loan is duly formalized and approved with no interest, the transaction would be characterized as a loan.
3. No interest deduction would be allowed to S.
4. Exchange controls would prevent interest payments by S.
5. If the transaction is characterized as an additional equity investment in the sense of 2. above, the loan could not be repaid as such but only indirectly through dividend distributions or when the company is liquidated, always subject to the fiscal treatment of such type of transaction.

In the case where the debt is transferred to capital stock a 3 per cent transfer tax would be levied.

C. Intangibles

Assumed Facts

P and S are manufacturers located in different countries. P performs research and development which has led to P's ownership of certain intangibles consisting of patents, trademarks and know-how. P makes available to S exclusive right to use in S's country all of P's intangibles. P does not charge S for the use of P's intangibles.

Parent in Spain

1. In principle, royalty income could be allocated to P, although this possibility is more theoretical than real because of the lack of control by the Spanish government. However, following an application to the government it could also be treated as a capital contribution.
2. In our opinion, this particular case should be treated, in the absence of a specific contract, as a lump sum income for P, regardless of the treatment in S's country.
3. We do not believe a portion of P's R&D costs would be allocated to S.
4. If a *bona fide* cost sharing agreement had existed, this would modify the preceding answers. In that case, the costs would be allocated proportionally. However, if P becomes the sole owner of the patents, etc., we would arrive at the same conclusion as in 1. above.

Subsidiary in Spain

1. No allocation or payment would be accepted by Spain, not even in the case where a contract exists under which S has to pay P a royalty (except if such contract is approved by Spain's exchange authorities).
2. The only possibility of S deducting and paying a part of the expense would be to apply to the Spanish government for authorization to share expenses. This sharing would be computed taking into consideration factors such as worldwide and domestic capital and turnover, as well as the criteria of allocation, all of which would have to be certified by independent auditors. Spanish tax authorities would not likely accept such a cost sharing for R and D costs, whereas they may do so for overhead and administrative costs.
3. Withholding tax in Spain will only be applicable in the case of a royalty payable under a duly approved contract as explained in 1. above. Since 1983, withholding also applies to reimbursement of parent company expenses allocated to the Spanish subsidiary, unless a tax treaty prevents this treatment.

D. Services

Assumed Facts

P is a large multinational concern which wholly owns foreign subsidiary S. Both P and S are engaged in manufacturing and sales activities. P's headquarters division performs general management services for P's multi-national operations including services which directly relate to S. The services performed for S include periodic visits by P's executives to review S's operations, financial analysis of S's future requirements, engineering services in connection with S's manufacturing activities and marketing services in connection with S's sales activities. P does not charge S for such service.
Note: In principle, the position is similar to that relating to intangibles.

Parent in Spain

1. Two different consequences could arise:
   a. Allocation of income to P;
   b. Non-acceptance of the expenses incurred in connection with services rendered to S as tax deductible because they are not directly related to P's income.

2. It would not be easy for a tax inspector to determine the amount to be allocated. In theory, it should be calculated on the direct costs plus a mark-up calculated to absorb the indirect costs.

Subsidiary in Spain

1. There are two possibilities for S deducting and paying a charge beyond which any deduction or payment would represent a monetary offence –
a. to obtain Spanish government approval of the contract, or
b. to obtain authorization for paying to P a part of the expenses, the amount being calculated in the way explained in the case of intangibles.

Only in these two cases would a deduction be allowed on the amount shown in the contract or in the application.

2. Withholding tax will apply as in the case of intangibles.

E. Loan Guarantees and Rentals

Assumed Facts

P is a multinational company whose main business is manufacturing and selling. P plans to establish foreign sales subsidiary S located in country S. P capitalizes S with $500,000 and guarantees a loan to S of $500,000 obtained from an independent bank. Land and a warehouse which P owns in country S will be used as a site for S's operations. P plans to make this land and warehouse available to S at a fee of $1 per year for 99 years.

Parent in Spain

1. Income could be allocated to P with respect to the land and warehouse.

Theoretically, the amount of the allocation would be determined taking into account a price that could be agreed in normal market conditions between independent parties.

We think that no income would be allocated on guarantees.

2. These transactions would not be regarded as an equity investment by P in S.

Subsidiary in Spain

The transaction will be treated in S's country without considering the characterization made by P's country. If no contract between the parties has been signed or no amount has been agreed to be paid, no deduction will be allowed to S, although P's country has allocated income to P.

If S is allowed to make payments to P, these will be subject to withholding tax in Spain.

PART III. TAX TREATIES

Most of the tax treaties into which Spain has entered follow the OECD model. That model contains several provisions concerning transactions between related companies: specifically, Article 7.2 (with respect to permanent establishments), Articles 11.6 and 12.4 (by which interest and royalties, paid in excess of those that would have been agreed between independent parties dealing at arm's length, are not covered by the reduced rates applicable under the tax treaties), and Article 9 (for related companies in general). The latter includes a provision similar to that established in Spanish Corporation Tax law but it seems to be applicable only in the case of non-reported revenues which would have been obtained dealing at arm's length, but does not apply to non-reported expenses.

There is no specific provision for a mutual agreement procedure concerning the allocation of income and expense between related parties, but this seems to fall under the sole competence of the country of residence. However, there are provisions similar to Article 25 of the OECD model tax treaty.

PART IV. SPECIAL SITUATIONS

A. Spanish tax rules would not be applied any differently to cross-border transactions just because one of the companies had no gross or net income, or because the tax rates in the two countries was substantially the same, or substantially different.

B. As has been said, due to the newness of the law in this area, the treatment of several aspects of cross-border transactions is unclear. However, we feel the following situations are usually more closely watched by the tax authorities:

a. A Spanish company whose income arises from billing to a non-resident parent company and is only based on actual costs or expenses. Although we are mainly thinking of services, export of tangible products cannot be excluded. This should be more evident in the case where the parent's country is a low rate or tax haven.

b. Transfer of shares of a Spanish company between non-resident companies. Although this type of transaction cannot be directly controlled by the tax authorities, the fact that the new investor has to officially appear before authorities facilitates control of related party transactions.

PART V. OTHER CONSIDERATIONS

We conclude this report with three following considerations:

A. There is little experience in our country as to the behaviour of the tax authorities with cross-border transactions because of:

- the newness of the Corporation Tax Law;
- the lack of implementing rules on transactions between related parties together with the obscurity of the existing provisions;
- the unsystematic approach of the tax inspectors themselves who are still unsure of the way in which these rules are to be applied.

B. The interpretation of the tax authorities regarding the application of the implementing rules is that they apply only when they could have as a consequence an increase in the Spanish tax base of the taxpayers involved. Together with most of our colleagues, we consider this to be illegal because it would be against the spirit of the Law.

C. When the transactions take place between companies residing in different countries, it is most important to take into account the very strict exchange control regulations in force in Spain, under which few payments can be made without prior authorization, nor even accounted for. This means that an allocation of income made in another country has no effect in Spain except where specifically authorized.

Sweden

Nils von Koch

PART I. GENERAL RULES

A. 'Arm's-length' rules are the basis for adjusting cross-border transactions.

1. The Swedish tax law contains a provision to counteract the shifting of profits to a person who is not subject to tax in Sweden with respect to such shifted profits.

   The provision provides that if the income of a person (including a company) who carries on a business is reduced as a result of an agreement to conditions which deviate from what would have been agreed between independent businessmen, the income shall be computed as the amount it would have been if those deviating conditions had not existed, provided:

   a. the person to whom the income is transferred is not subject to tax in Sweden in respect thereof;
   b. there are reasonable grounds to assume that an economic relationship exists (ie active participation in the other's management) between the businessman and the person with whom the agreement was made; and
   c. for existing circumstances do not suggest that the deviating conditions have been agreed to for reasons other than the economic relationship.

   Arm's length rates are the basis for adjusting cross-border transactions.
2. Adjustments can be made either to prevent tax avoidance or to clearly reflect income.
3. All transactions between a Swedish company and a foreign related company (not liable to tax in Sweden) are specifically provided for. No safe havens are provided.
4. *Swedish* companies in the same group may transfer income by subvention payments, which are tax allowable for the donor and taxable income for the receiving company.

B. For the purpose of applying the provisions mentioned in A.1, an economic relationship is deemed to exist if the taxpayer, directly or indirectly, participates in an active way in the management or supervision of the enterprise of another person or owns part of the capital of such an enterprise; also if the same persons, directly or indirectly, participate in the management or supervision of both enterprises or own part of the capital of both enterprises.

C. The principal approach in making adjustments is a transactions basis.

D. Adjustments may be made for six years prior to the year under investigation.

E. No, a correlative adjustment is not made to the accounts of a foreign taxpayer when Sweden initiates an adjustment to a Swedish company's tax payable.

F. If a foreign country initiates an adjustment to, say, a foreign subsidiary's tax payable:
1. No, that company is not taxed on a consolidated basis with any Swedish company.
2. The dividends flowing back to Sweden from that subsidiary, or the related foreign tax credits, are not affected in any way.
3. Sweden does not require the reallocated amounts to be paid to or from Sweden.

G. Adjustments are made to the tax years in which the underlying transaction took place.

H. A taxpayer can normally only initiate an adjustment by notifying the tax authority before the return is checked. However, a taxpayer may, under certain specific circumstances, initiate an adjustment after the authorities have checked the return. In both cases the taxpayer must give the reasons for the desired adjustment.

PART II. SPECIFIC EXAMPLES

NB Swedish tax law prescribes that an arm's-length basis shall be used, but permits divergence from this general rule if required between interested parties for sound marketing reasons. Also, in practice, *since onus of proof lies with the tax authorities, reallocation of income is extremely rare in practice*. The answers given below are therefore very theoretical.

A. Sale of Goods

Assumed Facts

Assume P is a manufacturer which sells finished products to S which is located in a different country. P sells these products to S at cost. P also sells these products to unrelated parties at cost plus 10 per cent mark-on. Both S and the unrelated parties incur the same selling and promotional expense and both resell P's products at the same price per unit.

Parent in Sweden

1. Income should be allocated to P.
2. The price used in sales to unrelated parties will be the guiding principle for the judgement.

The tax authorities will claim that P's revenues from the subsidiary should be raised by 10 per cent.
3. The answer should not differ even if there were no sales to independent parties. In order to determine what is a reasonable price, the tax authority always can order the Parent to hand over whatever information and other material they need.

However, if the lower price is necessary for S to cover its current expenditures (eg when a new market is being established) there will be no adjustment of P's income. Comparison can be made with the situation where P itself was developing the new market.

Subsidiary in Sweden

1. Sweden will make an independent determination of S's income.
2. Under no circumstances will S be allowed to deduct the allocation from its taxable income.
3. If S makes payment to P for the extra income allocated to P, Sweden will treat the 'excess' payment as a dividend subject to withholding tax.

B. Loans and Advances

Assumed Facts

P and S are manufacturers located in different countries. P loans S money on open account without interest so that S can expand its operations. P is not engaged in the business of lending money.

Parent in Sweden

1. Interest income should be allocated to P. The rate will lie between the normal business rate in Sweden and that in S's country.
2. The answer would not differ even if the loan was evidenced by a non-interest-bearing note with a fixed maturity date.
3. The loan cannot be considered as an additional equity investment.

Subsidiary in Sweden

1. Sweden will make an independent determination of S's income.

2./5. The transaction will be characterized as a loan. It does not make any difference if the loan is evidenced by a non-interest-bearing note. No tax consequences when loan repaid.
3. Interest will not normally be allowed as a deduction to S. However, reasonable amounts may be accepted.
4. If S pays the amount that P's country allocates and this exceeds an acceptable rate of interest, the excess will be considered to be a dividend subject to withholding tax.

C. Intangibles

Assumed Facts

P and S are manufacturers located in different countries. P performs research and development which has led to P's ownership of certain intangibles consisting of patents, trademarks and know-how. P makes available to S exclusive right to use in S's country all of P's intangibles. P does not charge S for the use of P's intangibles.

Parent in Sweden

1. There is an article in Swedish tax law making it possible for the tax authorities to allocate income to P. P cannot be treated as having made a contribution to the capital of S.
2. Allocation will most likely be made annually. In principle the annual allocation will be computed with respect to P's direct and indirect costs plus a mark-up for the profit element. Comparison will, if possible, be made with a market royalty. (This question has not been dealt with in practice).

It does not make any difference if S's country does not allow payments for the use of intangibles or if S's country allows payments but does not allow a deduction for tax purposes.
3. P is allowed to allocate a portion of the research and development costs to S.
4. If P and S entered into a *bona fide* cost sharing arrangement, there should be no additional allocation of income to P.

Subsidiary in Sweden

1. Sweden will make a separate determination of S's income.
2. S is not automatically permitted a deduction for the income allocated to P. However, Swedish authorities may accept reasonable amounts.
3. If S makes a payment to P of the amount allocated, any amount in excess of a reasonable market rate might be considered as a dividend. Sweden will subject that payment to withholding tax.

D. Services

Assumed Fact

P is a large multinational concern which wholly owns foreign subsidiary S. Both P and S are engaged in manufacturing and sales activities. P's headquarters division performs general management services for P's multi-national operations including services which directly relate to S. The services performed for S include periodic visits by P's executives to review S's operations, financial analysis of S's future requirements, engineering services in connection with S's manufacturing activities and marketing services in connection with S's sales activities. P does not charge S for such service.

Parent in Sweden

1. Income should be allocated to P for the performance of services. There will be no differences in how the charge is calculated for the different services.
2. The amount of allocation will be computed with respect to P's direct and indirect costs plus a mark-up for a reasonable profit element, and the extent of the services performed for the subsidiary.

Subsidiary in Sweden

1. Sweden will make a separate determination of S's income. S is allowed a deduction for expenses. Note, however, if no deduction is claimed at first and S then tries to make a claim as a result of a tax assessment in P's country, this claim will not be allowed (see General Rules, H above).
2. Payments of this type from S to P will not normally be subject to withholding tax. However, if non-deductible payments are made, these are regarded as dividends and subject to withholding tax.

E. Loan Guarantees and Rentals

Assumed Facts

P is a multinational company whose main business is manufacturing and selling. P plans to establish foreign sales subsidiary S located in country S. P capitalizes S with $500,000 and guarantees a loan to S of $500,000 obtained from an independent bank. Land and a warehouse which P owns in country S will be used as a site for S's operations. P plans to make this land and warehouse available to S at a fee of $1 per year for 99 years.

Parent in Sweden

1. For such a time as is necessary for S to establish a new market there will be no allocation of income to P.

When S is established, income can be allocated to P. The amount of allocation would be calculated with respect to P's direct and indirect costs for the warehouse. No income will be allocated because of P's guarantee of the loan.

2. P cannot be treated as having made an additional equity investment in S.

Subsidiary in Sweden

1. Sweden will make a separate determination of S's income.

2. As long as S only pays $1 per year, the Swedish authorities will make no separate assessment (because this would only decrease S's taxable income). If S later pays more rent, the Swedish authorities will assess the reasonableness.

3. Reasonable rent is deductible for S and not subject to withholding tax. The excess is treated as a dividend and is subject to withholding tax.

PART III. TAX TREATIES

A. All except a few very old tax treaties do contain an article for mutual agreement procedure.

B. Yes. The principal guideline is that the State shall make an appropriate adjustment of tax charged on profits which have been allocated to the other State.

The competent authority is, however, required to apply domestic laws.

C. Treaty protection concerning income tax will always be considered when a Swedish taxpayer so requests. Normally, the Swedish taxpayer applies but the Swedish competent authority could also initiate a review.

D. The latest tax treaties state that the case must be presented within three years from the first notification of the action. There are no established guidelines which define when application will be accepted. The taxpayer must make a written application to have the terms of a tax treaty applied.

E. If the authorities of the two countries fail to reach a settlement, the result is international double taxation.

F. A taxpayer cannot appeal against a settlement made between two competent authorities.

G. If an agreement is reached as to the correct allocation this agreement only concerns a specific case. In that case, conforming adjustments and payments are allowed without any abnormal tax consequences.

H. Settlements are usually reached when Swedish and other tax authorities negotiate. The time taken is from one to three years.

PART IV. SPECIAL SITUATIONS

A. The Swedish tax rules would not be applied differently to cross-border transactions just because one of the companies had no gross or net income, or because the tax rates in the two companies were substantially the same, or substantially different.

Note, however, that if a company has no gross income or makes losses because it is in the 'establishment phase', special considerations apply.

B. A holding company located outside Sweden but owned by Swedish residents is, for tax purposes, considered a Swedish co-operative society. Such a company is liable to tax in Sweden.

A foreign company which does not have any operations is suspected to be a company only used for tax evasion. Transactions with such a company will be closely examined.

PART V. OTHER CONSIDERATIONS

No allocation of income to a Swedish Parent (P) will be made if P is supporting its wholly-owned Subsidiary (S) located in a different country. The form in which this support is arranged (eg non-interest loan, low prices etc.) does not matter for tax purposes. This support is allowed only to give S the ability to cover its current expenditures. When S shows a profit from its business, this principle is not valid any more.

The National Tax Board has established a special group for assessing cross-border transactions of multinationals. This new group has aggressively attacked transfer pricing and thin capitalization, and it will take some Supreme Court decisions to establish new guidelines.

Switzerland

Rudolf Sigg/Francis A. Zoller

PART I. GENERAL RULES

A. Switzerland does not have explicit legislation in respect of the allocation of income and expenses between domestic and foreign companies except for the provisions in the various double taxation treaties which, however, are of a general nature and which are predominantly based on the OECD Model Double Taxation Convention.

As the primary goal of a company is to achieve an adequate profitability, especially multinational companies which aim to minimize the overall tax burden of the company as a whole through tax planning instruments, the Swiss tax authorities have established certain administrative practices in this area. The practices, however, are not uniform throughout the country. This is due to the fact that there are 26 cantons and half-cantons with individual tax laws and, in addition, the federation also has a tax law of its own. Thus, the rules applied are derived from interpretations of the various laws, through special regulations issued by the tax authorities and through negotiations with the tax authorities.

The general rule is that transactions which are economically justified are tax accepted, whereas transactions which do not reflect economic facts are adjusted.

The Swiss authorities do not make adjustments to prevent tax avoidance but to reflect the true income which would be achieved if the company would deal with third parties.

The principle used for allocation of income and expenses is the principle of 'dealing at arm's length'.

There are neither specific transactions covered by any specific tax law nor are specific safe havens provided for.

The rules applicable to transactions between domestic taxpayers and transactions between residents and non-residents are principally the same.

B. A related person is defined as being a so-called '*nahestehend Person*', which means a party which has a close relationship to another and can influence its financial position. In most cases, that means at least a 51 per cent ownership by a parent, and sister companies would then also be regarded as related companies.

C. Generally, the original approach in making adjustments is on a net income basis. The federal tax authorities have, in this context, established a regulation (*Kreisschreiben* No. 14) which deals with the taxation of domestic companies which belong to an international group or whose main activity is outside Switzerland. This regulation sets forth rules which the Federal tax authorities can apply in cases where the income obviously does not reflect an arm's length basis. In such cases, the tax authorities can levy taxes on a certain mark-up (which can be negotiated) on expenses. This mark-up is usually between 10–20 per cent of expenses or, in specific cases, a percentage of salaries or 1–5 per cent of turnover (which latter case is rarely applied).

There are some cases where adjustments are made on a specific transaction basis. This applies mainly to the interest spread of inter-company loans.

D. Generally, a return may be audited for a five-year period from the date when the tax payment was due. Consequently, adjustments can be made in the same five-year period. A return may be approved by the tax inspector before the five-year period lapses. In this event, no changes can be made by either the tax inspector or the taxpayer after the final assessment unless new (previously unknown) facts arise to re-open the assessment.

In a normal situation, the tax authorities will make an assessment of tax liability and present a tax bill based on the information contained in the return. If no appeal is made, the assessment becomes final.

The initial objection to an assessment is a review by the tax authority of its assessment. A taxpayer must file its objection within 30 days of receipt of the assessment; for cantonal or communal purposes, one must object within 60 days. Full details of the objection to the assessment must be included. This review does not suspend the liability for tax (including any interest and penalties) but does prevent the tax authority from requiring payment. The tax authority may review not only those items objected to but the taxpayer's entire tax liability. Even the withdrawal of the objection and payment of the original assessment cannot prevent a new assessment.

The second stage of appeal is a legal one. The exact procedure may vary with the canton and the tax involved, but the complaint is usually filed with a special tax board (*Rekurskommission/Commission cantonale de recours*). The tax board has the power not only to examine the objections in the first instance and any changes in the review, but the taxpayer's entire liability. This appeal will normally be final for cantonal and communal taxes.

The final appeal of an assessment of the FDT and cantonal tax is to the Federal Court (*Bundesgericht/Tribunal Fédéral*). A taxpayer must file its appeal within 30 days of the receipt of the tax board's assessment. This determination is final.

E. Neither the internal law or the double taxation treaties provide for an effective protection from double taxation. Thus, if an adjustment is made in a company in Switzerland, a correlative adjustment is not automatically made in the related non-resident company. Adjustments in both companies can usually only be achieved by appealing to the competent authorities.

F. An adjustment made to a non-resident company has practically no effect to the related domestic company. In Switzerland, companies do *not* and for tax purposes are not allowed to prepare consolidated financial statements. Each legal entity is taxed individually. The physical payments of allocated amounts are not necessarily required. They can be accumulated in form of inter-company loans which, of course, have to bear interest.

G. In most cases the adjustments are made to the tax year in which the underlying transaction took place. There are possibilities through negotiation to make catch-up adjustments at later stages.

H. A taxpayer can always initiate an adjustment as long as he has valid arguments. Swiss tax authorities are generally open to discussion.

PART II. SPECIFIC EXAMPLES

A. Sale of Goods

Assumed Facts

Assume P is a manufacturer which sells finished products to S which is located in a different country. P sells these products to S at cost. P also sells these products to unrelated parties at cost plus 10 per cent mark-on. Both S and the unrelated parties incur the same selling and promotional expense and both resell P's products at the same price per unit.

Parent in Switzerland

1. Income will be allocated to P with respect to its sales to S at least in the amount of the mark-up realized by sales to unrelated parties.
2. As there exists a third part comparison in this example, the amount to be allocated can be clearly determined. A higher price could probably be claimed if P performs some centralized promotional functions.
3. Generally, there would be no differences if there were no sales to independent parties or if S incurred greater selling or promotional expenses or would resell P's products at a lower price than market. The difficulty arising from this situation is the determination of the market price by which P would have to sell to S.

Subsidiary in Switzerland

1. As the mark-up of 10 per cent is based on third party transactions Switzerland would accept it in the books of S. They would make an independent determination in the case where no third party is involved.
2. S would have to book the allocation in the respective year. Unbooked transactions are generally not tax deductible.
3. If the payment of the allocated amount to P is the agreed third party mark-up, this would not be treated as dividend subject to withholding taxes.

B. Loans and Advances

Assumed Facts

P and S are manufacturers located in different countries. P loans S money on open account without interest so that S can expand its operations. P is not engaged in the business of lending money.

Parent in Switzerland

1. Interest will be allocated to P. For Swiss franc loans, the tax authorities have established interest rates which are adjusted periodically. For loans in foreign currencies, interest is applicable based on market conditions. Presently, the interest rates for Swiss franc loans are between 6½ and 7½ per cent.
2. The tax authorities might consider the non-interest bearing loan as additional equity (*verdeckte Kapitaleinbringung*) subject to 3 per cent stamp tax. A repayment of the loan would be considered as repayment of capital.

Subsidiary in Switzerland

1. If the interest rates applied are in line with the rules set forth by the Swiss tax authorities it would be accepted as a deduction in S.
2. If Switzerland makes a separate determination, the loan might be considered as an additional equity investment. It makes no difference if the loan is evidenced by a non-interest bearing loan.
3. As long as acceptable Swiss standards are applied, the interest allocated would be tax deductible.
4. If the interest amount to be charged to S in Switzerland has been determined to be lower than in P's country, the excessive payment would be considered as hidden distribution of profits subject to 35 per cent withholding taxes. Reasonable payments of interest would not attract a withholding tax except if paid on Bank Accounts or bonds.

5. If Switzerland has determined that the loan is effectively additional equity investment the repayment has no tax consequences. The payment then just reduces the investment.

C. Intangibles

Assumed Facts

P and S are manufacturers located in different countries. P performs research and development which has led to P's ownership of certain intangibles consisting of patents, trademarks and know-how. P makes available to S exclusive right to use in S's country all of P's intangibles. P does not charge S for the use of P's intangibles.

Parent in Switzerland

1. It largely depends how material these intangibles are. If P's net income is largely dependent on the income derived from such intangibles, the tax authorities might ask for an allocation of income from S. As indicated, it is not necessarily done in all cases.
2. Both methods are possible, ie annual royalties or lump sum payments. The *company* should establish an amount based on arm's length principles, or this amount can be negotiated. There are no established regulations or guidelines in this context. What is determined in S's country is irrelevant to Switzerland.
3. Research and development costs could be charged to S. Again, this would represent a part of the negotiations with the tax authorities.
4. The existence of a *bona fide* cost sharing agreement between P and S would normally be followed.

Subsidiary in Switzerland

1. The Swiss tax authorities will make a separate determination. A royalty agreement should be established by the Company and negotiated with the tax authorities.
2. The allocated amount accepted by the tax authorities is deductible.
3. There are no withholding taxes deducted on royalty payments out of Switzerland.

D. Services

Assumed Facts

P is a large multi-national concern which wholly owns foreign subsidiary S. Both P and S are engaged in manufacturing and sales activities. P's headquarters division performs general management services for P's multinational operations including services which directly relate to S. The services performed for S include periodic visits by P's executives to review S's operations, financial analysis of S's future requirements, engineering services in connection with S's manufacturing activities and marketing services in connection with S's sales activities. P does not charge S for such service.

Parent in Switzerland

1. If the costs can clearly be defined, these costs should be charged to S. Again, the principle of materiality is relevant. The tax authorities are open for discussion. They decide from case to case as no fixed rules exist.
2. The Company can come up with its own scheme and present it to the tax authorities for negotiation. The allocation can consist of direct or indirect costs.

As described earlier, the federal and a few cantonal tax authorities provide for special treatment of service type companies which might be taxed at expenses plus a mark-up.

Subsidiary in Switzerland

1. Switzerland would make its own determination based on turnover etc. This determined amount would then be fully deductible.
2. No withholding taxes are deducted from such management fee payments, unless the profit element was blatant.

E. Loan Guarantees and Rentals

Assumed Facts

P is a multinational company whose main business is manufacturing and selling. P plans to establish foreign sales subsidiary S located in country S. P capitalizes S with $500,000 and guarantees a loan to S of $500,000 obtained from an independent bank. Land and a warehouse which P owns in country S will be used as a site for S's operations. P plans to make this land and warehouse available to S at a fee of $1 per year for 99 years.

Parent in Switzerland

1. It is not likely that the Swiss tax authorities would allocate income to P in respect of the guarantee granted. However, the land and warehouse should be rented out at market conditions. The difference between $1 and the rent at market conditions would be allocated to P as income.
2. It could be considered as additional equity investment. See B above.

Subsidiary in Switzerland

1. As long as market conditions are applied Switzerland would accept the amounts determined by P's country. Otherwise a separate determination would be made.
2. An adjustment to actual market conditions would be made.
3. Payments of this nature from S to P are not subject to withholding taxes.

PART III. TAX TREATIES

A. The more recent double taxation treaties Switzerland has entered into contain Art.9 of the general OECD treaty which includes the mutual agreement procedures between the competent authorities.

B. These treaty provisions do not affect the answers previously given. The Swiss competent authority applies domestic law.

C. The taxpayer has to invoke the protection under the treaty.

D. In each double taxation treaty Switzerland has entered into there are clauses providing and describing the procedures for applying to the competent authorities. These provisions require that the application for competent authority consideration be made in writing.

E. If no settlement can be reached between the competent authorities it results in double taxation.

F. No appeal can be made from a decision of two competent authorities.

G. Upon agreement between the competent authorities, adjustments and payments will be allowed for the taxes in question. Income taxes and withholding taxes, however, are administered separately. An adjustment to one does not lead to an automatic adjustment to the other tax system. Both authorities must be negotiated with.

H. The competent authorities procedures are lengthy and can take 1–5 years before a settlement is reached and largely depend on the circumstances and the countries involved. Swiss competent authorities usually obtain satisfactory solutions.

PART IV. SPECIAL SITUATIONS

S. Switzerland has established by practice (as a result of the lack of legal regulations) a general approach which is aimed at the reflection of the true income on the principle of dealing at arm's length. What is determined for companies domiciled outside Switzerland is, in most cases, not relevant to the Swiss tax authorities but could serve as a guideline to determine the Swiss income to be reflected. The questions 1 to 4 would not affect the answers given previously.

B. The Swiss tax authorities are closely monitoring the multinational companies or special types of companies (with special tax agreements) such as domiciliary companies, base companies, auxiliary companies, service companies, etc.

United Kingdom

Philip J. Cooke

PART I. GENERAL RULES

A. 1. The main provisions in the UK tax code governing the allocation of income and expenses between related companies are as follows:

a. S.130(a) Taxes Act 1970 provides 'no sum shall be deducted in respect of any disbursements or expenses not being money wholly and exclusively laid out or expended for the purposes of the trade . . .'. This rule, which applies just as much to transactions between independent parties as it does to transactions between related parties, precludes the deduction of an expense unless it is incurred wholly and exclusively for the purposes of the taxpayer's trade.

b. S.485 Taxes Act 1970 (see appendix 1 for detailed provisions) enables the Inland Revenue, in the case of a transaction between related parties (where one such party is resident in the UK and the other is not so resident), to adjust the taxable income of the UK party if it appears to them that goods or services have been acquired at a higher price, or supplied at a lower price, than would have applied had the transaction been between independent parties dealing at arm's length. It is, therefore, essentially an anti-avoidance provision aimed at preventing shifting profits to countries with relatively lower tax rates. [Note – The provisions of S.485 can apply exceptionally in the case of certain transactions between related domestic taxpayers but this is not the main purpose of the section.]

As stated above, S.485 is an enabling provision and does not operate automatically. S.485(3) actually says that 'the preceding provisions of this section shall not apply in relation to any sale (or purchase) unless the Board (of Inland Revenue) so directs'. Very few directions have been made by the Board since these provisions were first enacted in 1951 but this is simply because most cases are settled by negotiation.

2. The criterion or yardstick which is used by S.485 is the price which might have been expected to apply if the parties had been independent persons dealing at arm's length. The section does not elaborate on the

meaning of an arm's length price and no guidance has yet been given by the Courts. In the 30 or so years that the provisions have been on the statute book, there has been only one decided case and that had to do with the meaning of control. It is accepted in practice, however, that the provision does not mean the same price must necessarily be charged to related persons as would be charged to independents. Whilst the price charged to the independent might be a starting point, allowance must then be made for the fact that the supply to a related party will rarely be on precisely the same terms and conditions as the sale to the independent. All kinds of variations will arise including volume of business, terms of transportation, the responsibility for marketing, burden of servicing, warranties, bad debts and many other factors.

3. The provisions of S.485 cover all types of transactions including
   - sales and purchases of goods, services or other property;
   - grants and transfers of rights, interests or licences; and
   - the giving of business facilities of whatever kind.

   Whilst not specifically referred to in this section, it is generally accepted that the reference to 'the giving of business facilities of whatever kind' includes the granting of loans and the provisions of financial accommodation.

   With one exception (relating to oil companies and dealt with in Part IV B below) no provision is made, either in the legislation or by way of regulations, for any guidelines or safe havens in determining what is an arm's length price and, therefore, one can only have regard to practice and experience. UK Revenue has indicated that it accepts the so-called 'guidelines' contained in the OECD report published in July, 1979 on 'Transfer pricing and multinational enterprises'. However, the report does no more than describe generally agreed practices within the countries of the OECD in determining arm's length transfer prices. It does not lay down any hard and fast rules, neither does it attempt to achieve any degree of harmonization of the varying practices in member countries.

4. As stated above, the basic rule concerning the deductibility of expenses (S.130) applies equally to transactions between domestic taxpayers, and transactions between residents and non residents. S.485 can apply in exceptional circumstances to transactions between domestic taxpayers but it is concerned mainly with cross-frontier transactions.

B. S.485 applies if the buyer is controlled by the seller (or *vice versa*) or both are under common control. Control is as defined in S.534 Taxes Act 1970 and means, in relation to a company, the power of a person to secure either by means of shareholding or voting power or by powers conferred by the regulations governing the company that the affairs of the company are conducted in accordance with a person's wishes. In defining whether a person exercises control, there is attributed to him the rights or powers of a nominee and of certain connected persons (relatives, partners, trustees, etc.) or their nominees.

C. S.485(1) and (2) provide that in computing the taxable profits or losses of the seller or buyer, the *like consequences shall ensue* as would have ensued if the *transaction* had been between independents acting at arm's length. The use of the word 'transaction' (in the singular) implies that Revenue is entitled to make adjustments on a single transaction basis but, in practice, in negotiating with the Revenue one would wish to stress the totality of all the transactions. Similarly, in having regard to the consequences which ensue from a transaction, one would certainly wish to point to any secondary effects such as the flow of any dividend income from the non-resident party.

D. The general rule in the UK is that tax assessments may be made within six years after the end of the chargeable period to which the assessment relates though the limitation period does not apply in the case of fraud, wilful default or neglect. These rules apply equally to assessments or adjustments made under S.485 and Revenue usually issue protective assessments for the chargeable period still in date as soon as they have reason to believe that adjustments may be required. This has the effect of placing the onus on the taxpayer to disprove the additional assessments.

E. If adjustment is made to the income of a company in another country in relation to transactions with a related UK company it is open to the latter to request Inland Revenue to make a corresponding adjustment to its income and such adjustments are sometimes made following due negotiation. Where a corresponding adjustment is refused, it would be necessary to initiate the 'mutual agreement' procedures of the relevant tax treaty with a view to the two competent authorities reaching some agreement as to the effect of the adjustment (see III below).

F. 1. Except in the case of a controlled foreign company situated in a tax haven, the profits of non-resident related companies are not chargeable to UK tax until such profits are distributed to the UK shareholding company by way of dividend. If an adjustment is made to the income of a non-resident related company and no corresponding adjustment is allowed by the UK Inland Revenue, this will result in a measure of economic double taxation.

2. The additional tax paid by the non-resident company would however normally be reflected in the foreign tax credit attaching to any dividend received by the UK shareholding company, but subject to the usual limitation and also subject to there being a liability against which foreign tax credit can be set. [Note – Foreign tax credits cannot be carried forward or back in the UK.]

3. The UK Revenue does not necessarily require payment of expenses allocated to related companies. Such expenses would simply be treated

as non-deductible in computing profits of the UK company. Similarly, if goods or services have been sold or provided to a related company at an under-value by the UK company, income will be imputed to the UK company and it is not necessary for payment to be made by the non-resident company.

G. The general rule is that adjustment will be made to assessments for the years in which the underlying transaction took place. In some cases, however, for the sake of convenience, a composite adjustment might be made in the year in which the adjustment is agreed.

H. As mentioned in E above, if an adjustment is made by the competent authority in the country in which the related party resides, it is open to the UK company to request Inland Revenue to make a corresponding adjustment. There is no statutory basis for such a request and consideration would be entirely at Revenue's discretion. If it was declined, it would be open to the company to initiate the 'mutual agreement' procedure (see III below).

PART II. SPECIFIC EXAMPLES

A. Sale of Goods

Assumed Facts

Assume P is a manufacturer which sells finished products to S which is located in a different country. P sells these products to S at cost. P also sells these products to unrelated parties at cost plus 10 per cent mark-on. Both S and the unrelated parties incur the same selling and promotional expense and both resell P's products at the same price per unit.

Parent in United Kingdom

1. In the absence of any other circumstances distinguishing S's position from that of the unrelated customers, income would almost certainly be imputed to P with respect to its sales to S.
2. The 'comparable uncontrolled price' method is considered by the UK Revenue to be the most appropriate method to use and since, in this case, there is clear evidence of such a price, the adjustment will be by reference to the price charged to the unrelated customers.
3. In the absence of a comparable uncontrolled price and, more particularly, if the position of S is distinguishable from that of unrelated customers, it will be open to P to endeavour to substantiate a different price. Both the 'resale price' (list less discount) and 'cost plus' methods are recognized by UK Revenue, as also is the 'commission on sales' method but in arriving at the ultimate transfer

price due allowance should be made for the costs and responsibilities undertaken by S. Provided the basis of calculation can be justified UK Revenue will recognize most methods of computing transfer prices and will also accept that prices must, in some situations, be reduced even below cost (eg to achieve market penetration).

Subsidiary in the United Kingdom

1. UK Revenue will not accept, as a matter of course, an allocation of income made by another country. If a request is made by S for a corresponding adjustment, Revenue will normally make its own determination though, in practice, the attitude of UK Revenue is often influenced according to the country in which P is resident. Thus, for example, adjustments made by US Internal Revenue in accordance with its transfer pricing regulations would be more readily accepted than those made by certain other countries.
2. Provided agreement can be reached with UK Revenue as to the basis of the allocation and also provided that a corresponding charge is made by P upon S, the adjustment will be reflected in determining the taxable income of S.
3. To the extent that payment of the additional charge referred to in 2 can be justified as a deductible trading expense, it will not be treated in S's country as a dividend or other distribution.

B. Loans and Advances

Assumed Facts

P and S are manufacturers located in different countries. P loans S money on open account without interest so that S can expand its operations. P is not engaged in the business of lending money.

Parent in United Kingdom

1. *Prima facie*, interest income will be imputed to P if a loan is made to S free of interest. The rate will be determined according to open market considerations. In the case of a loan without a fixed repayment date the rate would probably fluctuate in line with market rates over the period (eg linked to the monthly, 3-monthly or 6-monthly rate) and would be determined according to the place and currency in which the loan is made.

It should be noted that it is not uncommon for UK companies to finance overseas investment by way of loans (rather than equity capital) with a view to – (a) facilitating repayment in due course, and (b) reducing impact of capital and withholding taxes. The UK Revenue has been known in practice to recognize an 'equity element' in loan capital in circumstances where loan capital is performing a function normally performed by equity capital. For example, if loan capital is being used to finance fixed capital investment (purchase of buildings, plant and equipment, etc.) it might be possible to persuade Revenue that such loans can be made on an interest-free or lower than market rate basis. Revenue has also been known to accept that a loan from P to S may be treated as effectively constituting equity capital up to the point at which equity (including the parent company loan) is brought into line with external debt. Revenue has also been prepared to concede that, to the extent that the pre-tax income of S does not cover total interest charges (including those on external debt) by at least 3:1, interest will not be imputed to inter-company loans.

2. If the loan by P to S were for a fixed term then the rate of interest which would be imputed would be by reference to the market rate for loans for a comparable period but again determined according to the place and currency in which the loan is made. The same comments apply as in 1 if the loan can be shown to perform an equity function.

3. The fact that P may have been able to resist imputation of interest on the loan made to S because it can be demonstrated that it is performing an equity function, does not thereby cause the loan to be treated as equity capital *per se*. There will be no UK taxation consequences affecting P when the loan is repaid except in circumstances where, because the loan is treated as a 'debt on a security' and it was made in a foreign currency, repayment might give rise to a currency gain (or loss) chargeable (or allowable) for capital gains tax purposes. [Note – For a loan to be treated as a debt on a security it is necessary, *inter alia*, that it be freely transferable.]

Subsidiary in United Kingdom

1. Revenue will not, as a matter of course, accept the characterization of the transaction by P's country and it will make its own determination. Capital contributed as loan capital, however, will normally be treated in the UK as loan capital but, if the interest charged exceeds a commercial rate the excess will be treated as a distribution (dividend) and will be subject to the payment of ACT (advance corporation tax) by S and to the deduction of dividend withholding tax on payment to P. Capital will normally be treated as 'equity' only if subscribed as share capital, but there is a growing practice for overseas parents to contribute capital to UK subsidiaries without taking up additional shares since this avoids liability to capital duty (1 per cent on the value of capital subscribed). Such capital contributions would for all practical purposes be treated as equity capital since they are non-repayable.

2. The loan from P to S will be characterized in the UK as a loan and the position would be no different even if the loan was evidenced by a non-interest bearing note with a fixed maturity date.

3. UK Revenue would not seek to allocate interest if the loan from P to S is non-interest bearing since this would, in most cases, lead to a deduction in computing the profits of S for corporation tax purposes. UK tax authorities will accept a reasonable interest allocation initiated by P's country providing S actually pays the interest. The UK does not insist on legally binding prospective contracts for interest, but they would definitely help.

4. If S is required to pay interest at a rate which exceeds a commercial return for the use of the principal, the excess will be treated as a distribution (see 1 above – S.233(2)(d)(iii) Taxes Act 1970). The UK Revenue is also known to be increasingly concerned about thin capitalization of UK companies and it is possible that they would challenge any payment which, having regard to the gearing, exceeded a reasonable commercial return. There are no guidelines as to an acceptable ratio but it is known that a ratio of 1:1 would be accepted without question. A gearing of up to 3:1 might be tolerated, although (at November, 1984) the UK Revenue is known to be taking a much firmer attitude and much will depend upon the particular circumstances. In this connection the Revenue could, in addition to the provisions of S.485 and S.233, possibly invoke S.38 Finance Act 1976, a provision aimed at restricting relief for interest payments where the sole or main purpose is a reduction of tax. In the case of interest paid to the US, it is also possible that Revenue would invoke Article 11(5) of the UK/US tax treaty.

5. If capital is contributed as loan capital to a UK company, it will continue as loan capital regardless of how it is characterized in relation to interest by either P's country or S's country. Repayment of the loan will not give rise to any charge to tax in the UK.

C. Intangibles

Assumed Facts

P and S are manufacturers located in different countries. P performs research and development which has led to P's ownership of certain intangibles consisting of patents, trademarks and know-how. P makes available to S exclusive right to use in S's country all of P's intangibles. P does not charge S for the use of P's intangibles.

Parent and Licensor in United Kingdom

1. Income would almost certainly be imputed to P if it allows S free use of its intangibles, particularly in the case of patents and technological know-how. The broad view of UK Revenue is that research and development costs and benefits should be matched and this might be achieved in various ways including

- building into product prices an appropriate measure of R&D costs;
- the granting of a licence in return for an appropriate fee or royalty or, in some cases, a lump sum payment;

– the allocation of a portion of R&D costs; or
– the entering into a cost-sharing arrangement.

If S also engages in research and development and the results thereof are made freely available to P, there would be a strong argument for resisting or modifying the imputation of income to P.

The treatment of trademarks will depend upon individual circumstances. If unrelated parties are licensed to use the trademark it would be reasonable to expect related parties also to make payment, unless rights to use the mark or name are long established by the related party. It is not unusual for trademark rights to form part of a wider marketing package under which fees are payable not only for such rights but also for group marketing and advertising services.

P could contribute intangibles to S by way of capital but this would be treated in the UK as a disposal for capital gains tax purposes by P of the relevant assets at a price equal to their market value. If P granted S an exclusive licence to use the know-how only in S's market, the UK would regard this as a taxable disposition by P.

2. The form and basis of allocation of income will depend on the circumstances. If there are comparable unrelated party transactions it is likely that Revenue would require related party transactions to be dealt with in a similar manner. In practice, however, the position is usually open to negotiation and any methods in 1 above might be appropriate. If one is concerned only with current R&D expenditure, UK Revenue is often prepared to accept any reasonable allocation of such expenditure.

The UK Revenue is usually understanding of situations where local exchange control regulations preclude payment or where a deduction for tax purposes is refused in circumstances where there would be no possibility of seeking redress through 'mutual agreement' provisions of the tax treaty.

3. As indicated in 1 above, one of the methods of dealing with the R&D costs incurred by P would be to allocate them to S (and any other subsidiaries) on some equitable basis (eg in relation to turnover).

4. A *bona fide* cost sharing arrangement would be recognized by Revenue provided the basis of operation can be justified. The question of whether there should be a profit mark-up would depend largely upon whether it is the company's primary business to provide R&D services to the group or if such activities are incidental to its own trade. The UK may recognize a retroactive cost sharing agreement where a foreign tax jurisdiction is challenging prior allocations of cost and payments are actually made by the UK company.

Subsidiary and Licensee in United Kingdom

1. UK Revenue will not, as a matter of course, accept an allocation made by P's country. However, if the basis of allocation can be shown to be fair and reasonable and, more especially, if the allocation is supported by an agreement between the two companies, it is likely that it will be accepted by UK Revenue.

2. S will not be permitted a deduction in respect of any allocation made to P unless a payment is actually made. The tax treatment in the UK in respect of payments for intangibles is briefly as follows:

a. Lump sum payment for the acquisition of patent rights – spread equally over the balance of the life (maximum 17 years) of the patent.
b. Lump sum payment for the acquisition of technical know-how – spread equally over a period of six years though, in certain circumstances, the payment might be deductible in the year of payment.
c. Annual royalties payable in respect of the user of UK patents – deductible as an annual charge against profits.
d. Other annual payments (licence fees, trademark fees, etc.) – deductible from trading income.
e. Payment of a proportion of R&D costs – deductible from trading income.

Broadly, the amount of any royalty or fee (or lump sum payment) will be determined on arm's length principles. In the absence of comparable unrelated transactions, some guidance might be obtained from trade practice but regard must be had to particular circumstances.

3. There is a requirement in the UK (S.53 Taxes Act 1970) for withholding tax to be deducted (at the basic rate of 30 per cent) from UK patent royalties though exemption (or a lower rate of tax) may be provided by the relevant double taxation treaty. Withholding tax is also deductible from a lump sum payment made to a non-resident vendor of UK patent rights but, again, subject to any modification provided by the relevant tax treaty and also subject to a claim by the non-resident for relief in respect of the cost to him of acquiring the patent. Withholding tax is not normally deductible from other types of payment (eg licence fees, turnover fees, lump sum payments for know-how and non-UK patent rights).

D. Services

Assumed Facts

P is a large multi-national concern which wholly owns foreign subsidiary S. Both P and S are engaged in manufacturing and sales activities. P's headquarters division performs general management services for P's multi-national operations including services which directly relate to S. The services performed for S include periodic visits by P's executives to review S's operations, financial analysis of S's future requirements, engineering services in connection with S's manufacturing activities and marketing services in connection with S's sales activities. P does not charge S for such service.

Parent in United Kingdom

1. Expenses incurred by P in providing services to S are potentially disallowable to P if such services are provided without charge. The UK Revenue are usually concerned to see that expenses specifically connected with the activities of unrelated companies are recharged but they will normally adopt a more sympathetic attitude in relation to expenses of a general nature, particularly if it is shown that the supply of such service is in the overall interests of the UK company. Indeed, in a recent case (*Robinson* v. *Scott Bader*) the Court held that the costs incurred by a UK parent in seconding an executive to act as managing director of a French subsidiary in order to rescue that company and assure the UK parent of continuing trading connections, was an expenditure incurred wholly and exclusively for the purpose of furthering its own business in France and Europe.
2. Except in a case where a company's business is primarily provision of services to members of the group, Revenue will usually be content to see that direct expenses incurred on behalf of related parties have been recovered. If it is the company's business to provide services then the price to be charged should reflect all relevant costs (including indirect costs) together with an element of profit. In the case of P, however, since its principal business is that of manufacturing and selling (and even though services are provided for the group through its headquarter's division), Revenue would be unlikely to press for the inclusion of a profit element.

Subsidiary in United Kingdom

1. UK Revenue will not, as a matter of course, accept an allocation made by P's country. However, if the basis of allocation is shown to be fair and reasonable and more especially if the allocation is supported by documentary evidence, it is likely that it will be accepted by UK Revenue. S will not, however, be permitted to make a deduction unless a charge is actually made to P.
2. Payments by S to P in respect of services are not subject to deduction of withholding tax in the UK, even if they contain a profit element. The overall payment must, of course, be reasonable.

E. Loan Guarantees and Rentals

Assumed Facts

P is a multinational company whose main business is manufacturing and selling. P plans to establish foreign sales subsidiary S located in country S. P capitalizes S with $500,000 and guarantees a loan to S of $500,000 obtained from an independent bank. Land and a warehouse which P owns in country S will be used as a site for S's operations. P plans to make this land and warehouse available to S at a fee of $1 per year for 99 years.

Parent in United Kingdom

1. On the assumption that P does not incur any expense in guaranteeing the loan to S, income will not be imputed to P. However, provision by P of land and warehouse facilities as a site for S's operations at a nominal rental would give rise to a potential imputation of income to P. Whilst UK Revenue might look sympathetically upon the rent-free provision of accommodation for an initial start-up period, it would not accept a rent-free period extending for 99 years. The imputation would be by reference to comparable market rentals for a lease of a similar term of years. A 99-year lease would be unusual but in any event the current market price concerning rent reviews (usually every five years) would need to be taken into account. It is worth observing that if P structured the arrangements differently and provided a loan to enable S to purchase the property, the loan might possibly be characterized as equity finance on the basis that it is being used for fixed capital investment (see B.1 above).
2. Following on from 1 above, it might be contended that the provision of rent-free accommodation is similar, in character, to the provision of additional equity finance and it might be possible to persuade a UK tax inspector of the validity of this argument. It is considered, however, that this contention would not normally be accepted and the only way in which the provision of property might be treated as an additional equity investment in S, is if P contributed the property as capital (not necessarily in exchange for shares) or, as mentioned in 1 above, P provided financing to enable S to acquire the property. If P did contribute the property as capital to S, there would be a deemed disposal of the property for capital gains tax purposes in the UK.

Subsidiary in the United Kingdom

1. UK Revenue will not, as a matter of course, accept an allocation made by P's country. However, if the basis of allocation is shown to be fair and reasonable and more especially if the allocation is supported by documentary evidence, it is likely that it will be accepted by UK Revenue.
2. The basis upon which a deduction would be allowed to S would be by reference to the open market rental which would be payable in a comparable uncontrolled situation. A deduction would be allowed, however, only if payment is made to P.
3. The UK tax code (S.89 Taxes Act 1970) requires that property rentals paid to non-residents be subject to a withholding tax equal to the basic rate (currently 30 per cent). Exemption (or a lower rate of tax) may, however, be prescribed by the relevant tax treaty. Guarantee fees are not subject to withholding.

PART III. TAX TREATIES

A. Some 45 of the 75 or so general tax treaties negotiated by the UK contain a mutual agreement clause – see appendix 2 for the list of countries (such treaties also contain an associated enterprises article similar to Article 9 of the OECD model). Those which do not are older type agreements which, as and when they are renegotiated, will almost certainly include such a clause. The clause generally follows the OECD model (Article 25) except that Article 25(3) is omitted. The attitude of UK tax authorities towards reallocations between related parties would not differ based on the fact that a treaty did not contain a mutual agreement clause.

B. The existence of a mutual agreement procedure under particular tax treaties does not basically affect what has been said in relation to the foregoing general considerations or specific situations. If the mutual agreement procedure is invoked in cases of dispute, the competent authorities will endeavour to reach a settlement. There are no provisions in the UK tax code which impinge upon the operation of the mutual agreement procedure neither are there published guidelines or practices. However, the normal framework of domestic law would apply and Revenue would be obliged to operate in good faith and in accordance with concepts of equity and feasibility. Since the UK has, in principle, accepted the OECD report on 'Transfer Pricing and Multi-national Enterprises', it will clearly be influenced by that report and by the arm's length principle in particular.

C./D. It is necessary in the UK for the taxpayer to initiate mutual agreement procedures in appropriate cases. Treaty protection will not be invoked automatically by the UK Revenue. There is no formal procedure for a claim and a simple letter setting out the salient facts, addressed to the Assistant Secretary, International Tax Policy Division, Board of Inland Revenue, Somerset House, London WC1B, is sufficient. It is worth noting that the 3-year time limit for claims referred to in Article 25(1) of the OECD model has not been accepted by the UK and, therefore, the usual domestic 6-year time limit will apply. Whilst it is not clear whether Revenue is entitled legally to refuse to proceed with an application, it is equally unclear whether the taxpayer can legally compel Revenue so to proceed. The mutual agreement article usually incorporates the phrase 'the competent authority *shall endeavour if the objection appears to it to be justified* to resolve the case by mutual agreement with the other competent authority'. It is difficult to see how a Court could compel Revenue to 'endeavour' to reach an agreement with a party outside the jurisdiction of that Court. Revenue would be unlikely to agree to proceed in a situation similar to that in which they had previously failed to reach agreement, neither would they be likely to take up a case which appeared to them to be of doubtful merit or small in amount.

E. If, as a result of the failure of the competent authorities to reach agreement or where Revenue has declined to proceed with an application, there is resultant economic double taxation, the UK taxpayer will seek to negotiate a settlement with Revenue which recognizes the element of double taxation.

F. There is no procedure in the UK for a taxpayer to appeal against a settlement made between two competent authorities though in practice no settlement would be imposed on the UK taxpayer if he objected to it. Failure to accept, however, would presumably result in negotiations being abandoned. An application might reveal that a taxpayer had been under-assessed on ordinary principles, in which event, any additional assessment would be subject to appeal in the ordinary way.

G. Where agreement is reached between two authorities as to the correct allocation, consequential adjustments will be made to the relevant assessments and, where appropriate, overpaid tax will be repaid. Conforming adjustments or payments will generally not give rise to any further taxation consequences except, possibly, where withholding taxes are in point.

H. Whilst no official statistics are published, it is understood that comparatively few requests have been made to Revenue in recent years to initiate mutual agreement procedures. The involvement of the UK Revenue has been mainly in relation to requests initiated in overseas countries. With greater interest being taken by the UK in transfer pricing arrangements, however, it is likely that the number of applications will increase, though it is probably true to say that most transfer pricing investigations in the UK have resulted in negotiated settlements, often conditional upon no application being made under the mutual agreement procedure.

PART IV. SPECIAL SITUATIONS

A. 1./2. In certain circumstances, UK Revenue would probably look sympathetically upon situations where either a gross loss or operating loss arises. For example, where a parent is trying to establish a subsidiary in a new territory or an attempt is being made to enter or secure a larger share of the market Revenue would almost certainly accept, for a reasonable period of time, lower transfer prices than those which would normally be obtained. Indeed, it is not unknown for lower than cost prices to be charged in these situations and it could be argued, in these particular circumstances, that this represented an arm's length price. There may also be other justifiable reasons (eg political or social) why a company should be allowed to continue in business despite the fact that losses are incurred over a relatively long period. UK Revenue will obviously wish to examine a situation where there are sustained losses but, if it can be demonstrated that losses are not being contrived for tax avoidance reasons, they are likely to take an understanding attitude.

Mention has already been made (see Part II, B.1) of the fact that Revenue has been known to concede that where pre-tax income does not cover interest charges by at least 3:1, interest should not be imputed to inter-company loans. Similarly, in the case of intangibles, a sympathetic attitude might be taken about the non-payment of royalties in a loss making situation. It is always helpful if there is provision in the relevant agreements for the waiving of interest or royalties in these circumstances. Some agreements provide that licence fees or royalties, etc., will not be charged to the extent they would create or augment a loss.

3./4. The UK Revenue will almost certainly take a close interest in transfer pricing arrangements affecting companies situated in low tax or 'tax haven' countries. They can be expected to look closely at all such situations with a view to satisfying themselves that profits are not being transferred to such countries. Legislation was introduced in April, 1984 which has the effect of imputing profits of companies in tax haven countries to UK corporate shareholders holding more than 10 per cent of the equity capital of such companies, unless the company is engaged in genuine trading activities or it distributes a prescribed proportion of its profits by way of dividend.

B. Special transfer pricing rules apply in the case of oil companies and a special office of the Inland Revenue (the Oil Taxation Office) is concerned with transfer pricing and other matters affecting taxation of such companies. As stated earlier the transfer pricing provisions of S.485 do not normally operate in relation to purchases and sales between domestic companies, but this exception will not apply if the buyer or seller (or both) is or are petroleum companies and –

a. the activities of one or both include either the exploration or exploitation of the seabed or subsoil of the UK and its territorial waters or the Continental Shelf and the profits of those activities are subject to overseas tax in circumstances where tax credit relief could be given against UK taxes; or
b. the sale is part of a transaction (or series of transactions), the terms of which are affected by the remainder or the sale is of petroleum under rights exercisable by a company other than the buyer and 20 per cent or more of that company's ordinary share capital was at that time owned by the buyer or its associates.

These special rules (contained in Schedule 9 Oil Taxation Act 1975) also provide (unlike the general rules in S.485) certain guidelines governing the fixing of an arm's length price. Briefly, they provide that it shall be assumed –

a. that the terms of a transaction are such that might be expected to secure for both buyer and seller a reasonable profit from any transactions of the same kind carried out on similar terms over a reasonable period;
b. that the seller is not bound by artificial prices fixed by law or executive action of any government; and
c. where deliveries are to be made more than 12 months after a sale contract the price for those deliveries will be regarded as equal to the price which would have been expected under a contract made in the month of delivery.

PART V. OTHER CONSIDERATIONS

In considering this topic in relation to the United Kingdom, the following further matters are of relevance.

1. Absence of tax audit in the UK

There is no tax audit in the UK such as is to be found in countries like the United States or Germany. The accounts of UK companies are required by the Companies Acts to be audited by qualified auditors and Inland Revenue have always accepted such accounts as the basis for computing a company's taxation liability. The taxpayer or his agent prepares and submits to Revenue detailed computations of the taxation liability and these are duly examined. Questions may be asked (usually by way of correspondence) by the inspector of taxes about the nature of particular items of income or expense or the reasons for certain deductions but there is no detailed examination or audit by Revenue of the underlying books or documents.

Enquiries relating to a company's transfer pricing policies or arrangements will normally be initiated by the inspector during his examination of the taxation computations. He will ask for information about the extent of transactions with non-resident members of the group and enquire into the basis upon which prices are charged. The local inspector also has available to him the services of a special S.485 unit which is located in London. This unit has special expertise in the field of transfer pricing and, in addition to assisting local inspectors, it sometimes initiates enquiries in the case of the larger multinationals. The unit has a considerable store of data and statistics from many sources, both in the UK and elsewhere.

2. The Revenue's investigatory powers

Whilst, as mentioned in 1 above, there is no tax audit in the UK, the UK tax code does contain provisions which enable Revenue to obtain production of a taxpayer's books, accounts and other relevant documents should this be necessary. In addition to provisions of a general nature, there are some quite fearsome investigatory provisions which specifically back up S.485. Briefly, Revenue can require a company to give particulars of any transactions which might fall within or have a bearing on transactions falling within S.485 and to make available for inspection its books, accounts and other documents and those of its subsidiaries (including non-resident subsidiaries). These special provisions (contained in S.17 Finance Act 1975) also permit a duly authorised inspector to enter a taxpayer's premises at any time in order to inspect books and records, etc. The existence of these rather powerful provisions are sufficient to persuade most taxpayers to comply with requests for information.

3. *Exchange of information*

In addition to the 'exchange of information' articles contained in most of the UK's tax treaties with other countries, there have been two other developments in recent years which have a bearing on the disclosure of information relating to UK taxpayers. These are –

a. The EEC directive on mutual assistance (77/799 EEC) which enables the competent authorities of the member countries to exchange information regardless of the provision of any particular treaty. The directive provides for information exchanged in response to specific requests as well as automatic exchange of information on an ongoing basis. There is evidence to suggest the competent authorities are using these provisions to a considerable extent.
b. The working arrangement set up in 1978 between the UK and the US revenue authorities for simultaneous examination of the affairs of related taxpayers in both countries. Again, there is evidence that this arrangement too has been operated quite extensively.

4. *Need for adequate documentary evidence*

The need for adequate documentation and evidence in support of transactions and particularly the basis of charge cannot be too strongly emphasized. UK Revenue are strongly influenced by the presence of contemporary documentation which clearly sets out the terms of transactions and the basis of charge or, where appropriate, reasons for the absence of any charge.

It is also desirable that pricing policies and arrangements should be reviewed on a regular basis.

APPENDIX 1. SECTION 485 TAXES ACT 1970

Transactions between associated persons

485. Sales, etc., at undervalue or overvalue

(1) Subject to the provisions of this section, where any property is sold and—

(*a*) the buyer is a body of persons over whom the seller has control or the seller is a body of persons over whom the buyer has control or both the seller and the buyer are bodies of persons and some other person has control over both of them; and

(*b*) the property is sold at a price less than the price which it might have been expected to fetch if the parties to the transaction had been independent persons dealing at arm's length,

then, in computing the income, profits or losses of the seller for tax purposes, the like consequences shall ensue as would have ensued if the property has been sold for the price which it would have fetched if the transaction had been a transaction between independent persons dealing as aforesaid:

Provided that this subsection shall not apply where the buyer is resident in the United Kingdom and is carrying on a trade therein, and the price of the property falls to be taken into account as a deduction in computing the profits or gains or losses of that trade for tax purposes.

(2) Subject to the provisions of this section, where any property is sold and—

(*a*) the buyer is a body of persons over whom the seller has control or the seller is a body of persons over whom the buyer has control or both the seller and the buyer are bodies of persons and some other person has control over both of them; and

(*b*) the property is sold at a price greater than the price which it might have been expected to fetch if the parties to the transaction had been independent persons dealing at arm's length,

then, in computing the income, profits or losses of the buyer for tax purposes, the like consequences shall ensue as would have ensued if the property had been sold for the price which it would have fetched if the transaction had been a transaction between independent persons dealing as aforesaid:

Provided that this subsection shall not apply where the seller is resident in the United Kingdom and is carrying on a trade therein, and the price of the property falls to be taken into account as a trading receipt in computing the profits of gains or losses of that trade for tax purposes.

(3) The preceding provisions of this section shall not apply in relation to any sale unless the Board so direct, and where such a direction is given all such adjustments shall be made, whether by assessment, repayment of tax or otherwise, as are necessary to give effect to the direction.

(4) Nothing in this section shall be construed as affecting the operation of any of the provisions of the Capital Allowances Act 1968.

(5) In this section, "body of persons" includes a partnership and "control" has the meaning ascribed to it by section 534 of this Act, and, for the purposes of this section, a sale shall be deemed to take place at the time of completion or at the time when possession is given, whichever is the earlier.

(5A) In determining for the purposes of this section whether any person (alone or with others) has control over a body of persons—

(*a*) there shall be attributed to him any rights or powers of a nominee for him, that is to say, any rights or powers which another possesses on his behalf or may be required to exercise on his direction or behalf:

(*b*) there may also be attributed to him any rights or powers of a person with whom he is connected (within the meaning of section 533 of this Act, but omitting subsections (5) to (7) and the exception in subsection (4)), including any rights or powers of a nominee for such a person, that is to say any rights or powers which another possesses on behalf of such a person or may be required to exercise on his direction or behalf.

(6) The preceding provisions of this section shall, with the necessary adaptations, have effect in relation to lettings and hirings of property, grants and transfers of rights, interests or licences and the giving of business facilities

of whatever kind as they have effect in relation to sales, and the references in the said preceding provisions to sales, sellers buyers and prices shall be deemed to be extended accordingly.

APPENDIX 2. LIST OF UK TAX TREATIES CONTAINING A MUTUAL AGREEMENT CLAUSE

Australia
Austria
Bangladesh
Belgium
Canada
Cyprus
Denmark
Egypt
Fiji
Finland
France
Gambia
German Federal Republic
Ghana
Hungary
India
Indonesia
Irish Republic
Italy
Japan
Kenya
Korea
Luxembourg
Malaysia
Mauritius
Morocco
Netherlands
Netherlands Antilles
New Zealand
Norway
Philippines
Poland
Portugal
Romania
Singapore
Spain
Sri Lanka
Sudan
Swaziland
Sweden
Switzerland
Thailand
USA
Yugoslavia
Zambia

United States

John W. Gunn

PART I. GENERAL RULES

A. The general rule is that US income tax authorities may distribute, apportion or allocate gross income, deductions, credits or allowances between parties under common control where it is necessary to prevent evasion of taxes or to clearly reflect income. The authority for making such adjustments is provided by statute (Section 482), related income tax regulations and court decisions. The following references are in regard to the income tax regulations:

1. Tax avoidance is not a requirement for an allocation.
2. The standard stated in the regulations is arm's length. This is the income which would have resulted if an uncontrolled taxpayer were dealing with another uncontrolled taxpayer at arm's length.

   The regulations establish safe haven prices for several types of transactions. The approach of the regulations is to 'deem' safe haven prices to be arm's length prices. For clarity, this discussion used the term 'arm's length' only to refer to prices set with reference to transactions involving uncontrolled taxpayers, unless otherwise indicated.
3. The regulations provide specific rules for five types of transactions as follows:
   a. interest rates on loans or advances,
   b. price for performance of services,
   c. rentals for use of tangible property,
   d. price for transfer or use of intangible property,
   e. price for sales of tangible property.

   The regulations provide for safe haven prices for the first three types of transaction, and guidance for pricing in the last two. See the examples in Part II following for a more thorough discussion of specific rules which apply to each type of transaction.
4. No. The same rules apply to transactions between domestic taxpayers as to transactions between residents and non-residents.

B. The US statutory rule is stated in terms of parties under 'common control' rather than in terms of related parties. US rules allow allocations between organizations, trades, or businesses which are owned or controlled directly or indirectly by the same interests. Neither the statute nor the regulations contain a definition of control for this purpose and the court decisions have interpreted the term broadly. For example, in a case involving two domestic corporations where each owned 50 per cent of a third domestic corporation, control was found to exist, allowing allocation of income from the third corporation to the other two corporations.

C. The principal approach specified in the regulations is on a transactions basis. As a practical matter, many issues are settled with tax authorities on a reasonable split of profits between the parties.

D. The same statute of limitation applies to allocations as applies to domestic income tax issues regarding adjustment of income and expense. The general rule, barring unusual circumstances, is that the income tax authorities may assert that additional income taxes are owned within three years of the filing of the tax return for the taxable year. Other periods apply for other purposes. The limitation period may be extended by agreement of the taxpayer and the tax authorities, and it is common practice to do so.

Under certain treaties, the competent authorities may grant relief notwithstanding the US statutes of limitation.

E. The regulations provide that, whenever the income of a US taxpayer is adjusted, a corresponding correlative adjustment is considered made to the appropriate other party.

The adjustment need not necessarily be directed to the income of the other party. For example, if a US corporation provides, free of charge, engineering services to its foreign subsidiary relating to construction of a building and allocation of income is made to the US corporation, the correlative adjustment should be to the foreign corporation's depreciable basis in the building rather than its income.

F. When an adjustment is made to a company located outside the US:

1. There is no provision to require consolidation of that company with domestic companies for tax purposes.
2. US income taxation of distributions from that company and calculation of associated foreign tax credits may be affected.

   As background, for purposes of calculating foreign income taxes deemed paid by a US parent, the accumulated income of a foreign subsidiary is described as its 'earnings and profits'. The earnings and profits of a foreign subsidiary are determined by calculating profits of the subsidiary following US tax and accounting standards and converting such amounts to US currency. Normally when an allocation is made for US income tax purposes the correlative adjustment is considered to be made to the earnings and profits of the foreign subsidiary. However, see E above.

   a. Treatment of distributions as dividends

      For US income tax purposes distributions from foreign corporations are generally taxed as dividends only to the extent of the earning and profits of the foreign corporation not previously distributed or, if greater, the current year's earnings and profits. To the extent that the correlative adjustment reduces earnings and profits of a foreign corporation, characterization of a distribution as a dividend may change.

b. Calculation of foreign tax deemed paid by US parent corporation

  i. General concept

  Earnings and profits of a foreign corporation are used to determine the foreign income taxes deemed paid (underlying tax) by the US parent corporation when it receives a dividend from the foreign corporation. A correlative adjustment of earnings and profits of a foreign subsidiary will affect the calculation of foreign income taxes deemed paid, and may affect the foreign tax credit to which the US parent is entitled.

Example (wholly-owned subsidiary – assume no limitations apply to the use of foreign income taxes deemed paid as credit):

	Before Adjustment	Correlative Adjustment	After Adjustment
1. Assumptions:			
Pretax earnings of foreign subsidiary (US basis) for year	100	(20)	80
Foreign income tax	(20)	—	(20)
Earnings and profits	80	(20)	60
Dividend	4		4
2. Calculation of foreign income tax deemed paid by US parent:			
Portion of earnings distributed	4/80		4/60
Foreign income tax for year	x 20		x 20
Foreign income tax deemed paid	1.0		1.3
3. Calculation of US income tax (assume no foreign tax credit limitation):			
Dividend	4.0		4.0
Gross-up for foreign income tax deemed paid	1.0		1.3
Taxed as dividend	5.0		5.3
Tax rate	x 46		x 46
Tax before credit	2.3		2.4
Foreign tax credit	(1.0)		(1.3)
US income tax on dividend	1.3		1.1

ii. Potential problem

US income tax authorities have asserted that, when there is an allocation of income from a foreign subsidiary to its US parent, the parent and subsidiary must both seek refund of the foreign income tax attributable to income allocated to the US parent. The foreign subsidiary must exhaust all 'effective and practicable administrative remedies' in seeking a refund from foreign tax authorities, and the US parent must seek competent authority consideration if a treaty makes this remedy available. Otherwise, foreign income tax attributable to the reallocated income will not be considered income tax for purposes of US foreign tax credit, and no credit for the portion of foreign income tax attributable to the income allocated will be allowed.

US income tax authorities have also asserted that, even if both parent and subsidiary exhaust all administrative remedies, the foreign income tax attributable to income allocated to a US parent may not be considered an income tax in 'egregious' situations. An example would be where the US parent sold products to its foreign subsidiary at substantially below cost, and the foreign country's income tax law provides for arm's length pricing.

Under recent regulations, advice from competent foreign tax advisors stating that all practical remedies have been pursued may be sufficient.

3. Payment of allocated amounts is not required. There are two possibilities which may allow payment of allocated amounts or other adjustments. One, available only for allocation of income by the US income tax authorities to US taxpayers, is provided by domestic procedures under which US income tax authorities allow adjustments. That approach is discussed in more detail below.

The other possibility, which applies to both allocations by US income tax authorities and to allocations by foreign income tax authorities, is adjustment and payment allowed by the competent authorities in a settlement of a competent authority proceeding. Such adjustments and payments may also be allowed unilaterally by the US competent authority. That approach is discussed in Part III, G., following.

In order to qualify for the domestic procedures allowed by US income tax authorities, such authorities must determine that the arrangement or transactions which gave rise to the allocation did not have avoidance of US income tax as one of their principal purposes. Where this requirement is met, the following remedies are available:

a. Allocation of income from foreign subsidiary to US taxpayer parent

i. The US taxpayer may enter into an agreement with the US income tax authorities to establish an account receivable from the subsidiary for whatever portion of the allocation it wishes to be paid to the parent. The account receivable must also include interest (on the portion of the allocation to be paid) from the year-end of the year for which the allocation is made until the time of payment. The payment of the account receivable must be made within 90 days after execution of the agreement. Payment of the allocation amount will have no US income tax consequences, but the interest amount will be taxable as taxable income in each intervening year and reduce earnings and profits of the subsidiary. Normally, the account receivable is paid in the form of a dividend from the foreign subsidiary.

ii. If the foreign subsidiary paid a dividend to the US parent in the same year for which an allocation is made, the US taxpayer may enter into an agreement with US income tax authorities to treat the dividend as non-taxable to the extent of the amount of the allocation. In effect, the dividend is considered a payment of the allocation.

b. Allocation of income from foreign parent to US subsidiary taxpayer The US taxpayer may agree to establish and receive payment of an account receivable from its foreign parent. In such case, the transaction which gave rise to the allocation will not be considered a dividend, and no US withholding tax will be imposed on the amount allocated to the extent payment is made. The same procedures apply to this payment as those described above.

G. Adjustments are made to the tax year in which the underlying transaction took place. However, see Part I, F. 3. a. i. above.

H. Only the US income tax authorities may make an adjustment. There is no procedure for a taxpayer to initiate a request for an adjustment, even where a foreign taxing jurisdiction has made an allocation for which the corresponding adjustment would reduce a US taxpayer's taxable income. When a US taxpayer has had income allocated, however, it may assert that the allocated amount should be reduced by the benefit it may have received from other non-arm's length transactions with the same party.

In addition, if there is an applicable tax treaty which provides for competent authority consideration, the taxpayer may request it. The US competent authority may allow a US income tax adjustment as part of a competent authority settlement. If no settlement is reached or provides only partial relief, the US competent authority may allow a unilateral adjustment by the US, but it is not required to do so.

PART II. SPECIFIC EXAMPLES

A. Sale of Goods

Assumed Facts

Assume P is a manufacturer which sells finished products to S, which is located in a different country. P sells these products to S at cost. P also sells these products to unrelated parties at cost plus 10 per cent mark-on. Both S and the unrelated parties incur the same selling and promotional expense and both resell P's products at the same price per unit.

Parent in United States

1. Income may be allocated to P by US tax authorities.
2. The US tax authorities will determine an appropriate price and assert that P's taxable income should be increased by the difference between the appropriate price and the price actually paid. The standard for an appropriate price for sales of tangible property is an arm's length price, defined in the regulations as the price which an unrelated party would have paid under the same circumstances for the property involved in the sale. Since unrelated parties normally sell products at a profit, an arm's length price normally involves a profit to the seller.

a. Discussion of regulations
   The regulations provide guidance for determining the arm's length price for various types of transactions. The regulations provide for the following approaches to determining an arm's length price for sales of tangible property:
   i. Comparable uncontrolled price method
      The best determination of an arm's length price is the price in a comparable uncontrolled transaction. This is the price actually paid in a sale between two parties not under common control. In order to be used to establish a comparable uncontrolled price, such a sale would need to involve identical property and circumstances to that for which a price is being determined, or so nearly identical as to allow a reasonable number of adjustments of price to reflect the differences. Differences which might affect the price or make sales non-comparable include quality of product, terms of sale, intangibles (such as trade names) associated with the sale, time of sale, level of distribution and the geographic market in which the sale is made.
   ii. Resale price method
      This method applies only when there is no comparable uncontrolled price. A typical situation in which this might apply is where a manufacturer sells products to a related distributor (reseller) for resale,

without further processing, to purchasers which are not under common control with P and S.

The approach is to determine an appropriate mark-up percentage based upon sales by resellers in which both the purchase is from and the resale is to parties not under common control. The anticipated resale price of the property is discounted by the appropriate mark-up percentage to determine the price to the reseller. For this method to apply, the resale price must be available. Also, the reseller should not add more than an insubstantial amount to the product; however, this requirement may be ignored if the resale price method appears to produce a more accurate determination of arm's length price than the cost-plus method.

iii. Cost-plus method

This method applies only when the previous two methods do not apply.

A typical situation in which this might apply is where a manufacturer sells products to a related entity which either performs substantial processing or adds substantial value to the product before resale to purchasers which are not under common control with P and S.

Under this method, a price is determined which will provide the seller with the same percentage return on its costs as is earned in the most similar transaction between parties not under common control

iv. Other appropriate methods

If none of the three methods above apply, then the taxpayer may use some other appropriate method. Settlement of disputes with income tax authorities are often negotiated on the basis of such another appropriate method. It is common to settle such disputes on a reasonable split of the combined net income of the two parties.

b. Specific application

If sales to uncontrolled parties are comparable to the sales to S (eg same volume, level of distribution), then the price may be a comparable uncontrolled price and should be used for the sale from P to S.

3. Effect of changing assumptions

a. No sales to independent parties

If there were no sales to uncontrolled parties or if the sales to uncontrolled parties were not similar enough to be comparable uncontrolled sales, then the comparable uncontrolled price method would not apply, and one of the other pricing methods would apply. The resale price method probably applies most commonly in situations similar to the example.

b. S incurs greater expense

The price to S may be affected by S's incurring greater expense, depending on the method used to establish prices on sales to S as follows:

i. Comparable uncontrolled price method

The price to S would be unaffected. Different promotional and selling expenses, however, might indicate that the sales are not really comparable.

ii. Resale price method

The price to S would normally be unaffected because the costs used to calculate mark-up percentages normally would not include promotional and selling expenses.

iii. Cost-plus method

The price to S would be reduced to allow S a greater profit on its greater costs.

c. Establishing a market

The regulations allow pricing at a reduced profit or even a loss to establish or maintain a market for a seller's products. However, this is allowed only in situations where P would have priced similarly in sales to uncontrolled purchasers. Greater promotional and selling expenses incurred by S might be evidence that P is pricing to maintain or establish a market.

Subsidiary in United States

1. The US will make an independent determination.
2. There is no procedure for a US taxpayer to request an allocation. However, see Part I, H.
3. If S makes a payment of the allocated amount, the payment could be considered a dividend subject to US withholding tax.

B. Loans and Advances

Assumed Facts

P and S are manufacturers located in different countries. P loans S money on open account without interest so that S can expand its operations. P is not engaged in the business of lending money.

Parent in United States

Because P loans the money on open account for S to expand S's operations, it is assumed the loan did not arise in the ordinary course of business out of sales, leases, rendition of services or the like.
1. Interest income may be allocated to P. If the loan is denominated in US dollars and if P is not in the business of making loans or advances of the same general type, interest income may be allocated to P at a rate of 12 per cent, or at such other appropriate arm's length rate as the US taxpayer is able to establish.

Otherwise, the amount of interest income allocated to P will be calculated at an arm's length rate, based upon interest charged in transactions between unrelated parties.

However, if P borrowed the funds for the loan at the 'situs of S' (generally interpreted to mean in the same country as S) then interest income to be allocated to P will be calculated at the same rate for which it was borrowed, plus an amount to reflect P's costs or deductions incurred in borrowing and relending the money.

If P was to merely guarantee the borrowings of S in S's country, there could be an income allocation to P. The same would be true where P incurred costs to have a bank provide letters of credit to assist S with its financing.

2. The amount of interest allocated would be unaffected by the existence of a non-interest bearing note with a fixed maturity date.

3. This is an unsettled area in US law. The loan could be considered an equity investment by P under certain circumstances. Under proposed regulations, non-payment of interest and existence of a note would be factors but not the only factors in determining whether a loan could be considered an equity investment. Proposed regulations have been rewritten and the effective date postponed several times. The tax authorities have also announced that the current set of proposed regulations will not apply to loans to or by a non-US entity.

If the loans are considered to be an equity investment, repayment of the loans could be taxed as dividends.

Subsidiary in the United States

1. The US will make a separate determination.

2. The transaction could be characterized as an equity investment (see 3 above).

3. There are no procedures for a US taxpayer to request an allocation. However, see Part I, H.

4. If P's country allocated a greater amount than S's country and S pays the amount allocated by P's country, the payment amount could be considered a dividend for US income tax purposes, subject to US withholding tax.

C. Intangibles

Assumed Facts

P and S are manufacturers located in different countries. P performs research and development which has led to P's ownership of certain intangibles consisting of patents, trademarks and know-how. P makes available to S

exclusive right to use in S's country all of P's intangibles. P does not charge S for the use of P's intangibles.

Parent in United States

1. If the right to use the intangibles has not been transferred by P to S, then income may be allocated to P. The amount of the allocation will be the amount which would have been paid by an unrelated party for similar property under similar circumstances.

Under recent legislation, P will not generally be able to transfer certain rights to the intangibles to S free of US tax. If a transfer occurs, it may be treated as a licence arrangement with an arm's length royalty to the US parent, but the income from such licence will be considered US source rather than foreign source.

2. The regulations provide that the form of allocation shall be consistent with the form of payment which would be adopted in a transaction between unrelated parties. However, where S actually pays no consideration for the intangibles and P retains a substantial interest in the intangibles, the allocation shall be presumed not to take the form of a lump sum payment. In the example, if P retained a substantial interest in the rights, then the allocation might be in the form of royalties based upon S's output, profits or similar measures. P could have retained a substantial interest in the intangibles by reserving the right to use them directly or the right to receive royalties at some later date.

Under the regulations, if P did not retain a substantial interest in the intangibles transferred, a lump sum allocation could be appropriate. However, under subsequent legislation, even if the intangibles were transferred with P retaining no substantial rights, the transfer will be treated as a licence arrangement for an arm's length royalty to the US parent. However, in such a case, the income from the licence will be considered US source rather than foreign source.

The standard for determining the amount of allocation is the amount which would have been paid by a party not under common control for the same intangible property in similar circumstances. If P has made similar transfers to parties not under common control, the price actually charged is the best indication of an appropriate price. Otherwise, the price may be determined in accordance with market conditions. The regulations list twelve factors which may be considered.

If P can show that payment for the use of the intangible was prevented because of currency or other restrictions imposed under foreign law, P may elect to defer US income tax recognition of any allocated amount until the restrictions cease to be in effect. However, P will also be required to defer taking any deductions attributed directly or indirectly to the deferred income amount.

Whether or not S's country allows a tax deduction for payments for the use of intangibles is not relevant to determination of whether there should be an allocation.

3. In effect, the regulations provide for two approaches for compensating a party which develops intangible property. One alternative is for the parties to enter into a *bona fide* cost sharing arrangement for the development of intangible property, and provide for a sharing of the costs and risks of development. To result in a sharing of risks, presumably the agreement would be entered into before it was clear that anything of value would develop. The other alternative is for the user of the intangible to pay an arm's length price to the party which developed the intangible.

Because, in the example, the intangible has already been developed, a cost sharing arrangement for that intangible would probably not be accepted by US tax authorities. P and S might consider entering into such an arrangement for the future development of intangibles.

4. The regulations provide that, where there is a *bona fide* cost sharing arrangement, the tax authorities will not make allocation with respect to the intangible involved other than to adjust the cost sharing amounts to reflect each participant's share of costs and risks. In order for an agreement to qualify as a *bona fide* cost sharing arrangement, the agreement must be in writing and must reflect an effort in good faith by each participant to bear their respective shares of costs and risks on an arm's length basis.

Subsidiary in United States

1. The US will make a separate determination.

2. There is no procedure for a US taxpayer to request an allocation. However, see Part I, H.

3. Assuming the payment is not accepted by US tax authorities as compensation for the intangible property, the payment could be considered a dividend subject to US withholding tax.

D. Services

Assumed Facts

P is a large multinational concern which wholly owns foreign subsidiary S. Both P and S are engaged in manufacturing and sales activities. P's headquarters division performs general management services for P's multi-national operations including services which directly relate to S. The services performed for S include periodic visits by P's executives to review S's operations, financial analysis of S's future requirements, engineering services in connection with S's manufacturing activities and marketing services in connection with S's sales activities. P does not charge S for such service.

Parent in United States

1. Whether there will be an allocation depends upon the nature of the benefit to the recipient, and whether the services duplicated activities of the recipient. The regulations provide that no allocation shall be made if the probable benefits to the recipient or a group of recipients are so indirect or remote that unrelated parties would not have charged for the services. Even if the services directly benefit the recipient, allocations will generally not be made if the services are duplication of services independently performed by the recipient.

On the facts in the example:

a. Visits – Periodic visits by P's executives to review S's operations would likely be considered stewardship expenses for P's benefit as a shareholder rather than for S's benefit. Thus, no allocation would be appropriate.

b. Financial analysis (assume provided directly for S's benefit) – if S does not have the qualified staff to perform the financial analysis, then an allocation would be appropriate. If S has a qualified staff which prepares the analysis which P merely reviews no allocation for that review would be appropriate.

c. Engineering services – An allocation would be appropriate for engineering services, provided that the services were performed for S's direct benefit and are not a duplication of services independently performed by S.

d. Marketing services – An allocation would be appropriate for marketing services, provided that all the services were performed for S's direct benefit and are not a duplication of services independently performed by S.

2. The regulations provide that the method to calculate the amount of an allocation for services depends upon the nature of the services performed in relation to the total activities of P and S.

If the services are an integral part of the business activity of either the renderer of the services (P) or the recipient of the services (S), then the allocation will be based on an arm's length charge for the services. Normally, an arm's length charge would include a profit element. The regulations provide detailed rules for determining when services are an integral part of the activity of the renderer or recipient. For example, the provision of engineering services would be considered an integral part of the activities of P, if P were in the business of providing engineering services to unrelated parties.

If the services are not an integral part of the business activity of either P or S, P may choose to charge S only its costs incurred in providing the services, or P may establish a more appropriate charge, based upon an arm's length standard. The regulations provide detailed rules for determination of cost for this purpose, which must include overhead and other indirect costs.

Subsidiary in United States

1. The US will make a separate determination. In determining whether to make an allocation and the amount of an allocation, the US applies the same rules to foreign subsidiaries of a US taxpayer as it does to US subsidiaries of a foreign shareholder. There is no procedure for a US taxpayer to request an allocation. However, see Part I, H.

2. If payments of the allocated amounts are made, and the payments are not accepted by the US tax authorities as being for services, the payments could be considered to be a dividend subject to US withholding tax. If the payments were accepted by the US tax authorities as *bona fide* payments for services, then there would be no US withholding tax where the services were performed outside the US. Where the services were performed inside the US, US withholding tax would be applied if P had no permanent establishment in the US, and US profits tax would apply if P did have a permanent establishment in the US.

E. Loan Guarantees and Rentals

Assumed Facts

P is a multinational company whose main business is manufacturing and selling. P plans to establish foreign sales subsidiary S located in country S. P capitalizes S with $500,000 and guarantees a loan to S of $500,000 obtained from an independent bank. Land and a warehouse which P owns in country S will be used as a site for S's operations. P plans to make this land and warehouse available to S at a fee of $1 per year for 99 years.

Parent in United States

1. Income could be allocated to P for both the loan guarantee and the use of the property. The loan guarantee would likely be considered a service and, if not an integral part of the business activities of P or S, could be allocated at cost or an arm's length rate. See D. above.

The method to calculate an allocation for rentals depend upon whether the owner (P) or user (S) is in the trade or business of renting property. The regulations provide that if either are in such a business, then the allocation would be based on an arm's length rental for the property. If neither is in such business, then the allocation is based on a safe haven rental provided in the regulations, or the taxpayer may establish a more appropriate charge, based on an arm's length standard. The safe haven rental is determined as the sum of straight-line depreciation on the adjusted tax cost of the property, plus 3 per cent of adjusted tax cost of the property, plus all costs connected with owning

and renting the property. The regulations provide detailed rules for determining costs for this purpose.
2. P could be treated as having made an additional equity investment in S. See Part II, B (as to P, 3). If P is treated as having made an additional equity investment in S, then the future relinquishment of the property to P could be considered a dividend. If S were to begin paying rent, such payments could be considered dividends to P.

Subsidiary in United States

1. The US will make a separate determination.
2. There is no procedure for a US taxpayer to request an allocation and it is unlikely that US tax authorities would make an allocation which would reduce the income of a US taxpayer.
If an allocation were made the same rules described above would apply.
3. Assuming the payment is not accepted by US tax authorities as service fees or rentals, the payment could be considered a dividend subject to US withholding tax. Even if the payments are accepted by the US as deductible rental payments, there would be US withholding tax on the rentals as the real estate is located in the US. Withholding might be avoided if P elects to be subject to US profits tax on the net rental income. There is no US withholding tax on guarantee fees.

PART III. TAX TREATIES

A. All treaties with the US contain a provision for mutual agreement, except the treaty with Ireland and the old UK treaty, which still applies to certain countries.

B. The treaty provisions affect prior answers. An important modification is that a US taxpayer may get relief from double taxation through the competent authority of the US, even when no agreement is reached between the competent authorities. For example, assume a US taxpayer has received services, for which it was not charged, from a foreign subsidiary, and that the foreign tax authorities have allocated a fee to the foreign subsidiary for the arm's length value of the service. The US taxpayer wishes to take a US tax deduction for the allocated amount. There is no procedure under domestic law for the US taxpayer to request an allocation of income. However, if an appropriate treaty provides for competent authority consideration, the US taxpayer may request it. A correlative adjustment of US taxable income may be made as a part of the competent authority agreement. If no settlement is reached or only partial relief is afforded by the settlement, the US competent authority may grant unilateral relief although it is not required to do so. The unilateral relief provided by the competent authority may provide a remedy not otherwise available under domestic law.

The US tax authorities have announced information regarding the competent authority procedure. It is stated that the US competent authority will be guided by 'the standards of arm's length dealing . . . and the equivalent standard of arrangements or conditions which would have been made between independent persons . . .'. The US competent authority is not required to adhere to US income tax law, although as a practical matter it will normally attempt to do so.

C. The mutual agreement provisions are normally invoked by the taxpayer, who must seek competent authority consideration. However, the audit manual used by US income tax auditors indicates that the US competent authority may initiate competent mutual agreement procedures when notified of a potential issue by the auditors, regardless of whether the US taxpayer requests it.

D. US tax authorities have announced procedures to be followed by a US taxpayer seeking competent authority consideration. The procedures to be followed on an issue involving allocation of income depend upon whether the US or the treaty country proposes the allocation.

If the treaty country first proposes an allocation, the US taxpayer should request competent authority consideration as soon as practicable after the treaty country's position on the adjustment has become sufficiently developed to permit consideration. The request should be made whether or not the allocation has been formally proposed by the treaty country, but no later than 90 days after the treaty country's adjustments have been formally communicated. If the US proposes the allocation, the taxpayer is encouraged to exhaust all administrative appeals in dealing with US tax authorities before requesting competent authority consideration.

1. the taxpayer is not entitled to relief (for example, double taxation does not exist);
2. the taxpayer indicates unwillingness to accept a reasonable competent authority settlement;
3. the taxpayer does not accept the concept that the negotiation does not include the taxpayer's participation; and
4. the taxpayer does not provide sufficient information or otherwise does not comply with procedural requirements (such as filing the request on a timely basis);
5. the request is from a taxpayer under jurisdiction of another competent authority; or
6. the taxpayer refuses to consent to an extension of the statute of limitations for the year under consideration.

As a practical matter, the competent authority accepts most requests which are filed on a timely basis. However, it has been announced by US and Canadian income tax authorities that the competent authorities will no longer consider requests for relief arising from 'thin capitalization adjustments' made by either country under debt/equity rules.

If the competent authority denies a request for assistance, the taxpayer may request an administrative hearing with the tax authorities and appeal the denial, but may not contest the panel's decision in the courts.

E. If the competent authorities fail to reach agreement, the taxpayer may be subject to double taxation. The US competent authority may make a unilateral adjustment but is not required to do so. If the taxpayer does not achieve relief from the competent authority or does not accept the measure of relief achieved, the taxpayer may withdraw the request for competent authority consideration and pursue administrative and judicial review otherwise available in the US and the treaty country.

F. The US competent authority will notify a taxpayer of any agreement or partial agreement that the competent authorities reach. The taxpayer may accept the agreement or withdraw the request for competent authority consideration, in effect, rejecting the agreement. If the taxpayer accepts the agreement, it is not subject to judicial review in the US.

G. Normally, payments of allocated amounts and conforming adjustments (such as recharacterizing a dividend as a non-taxable payment of an allocated amount) are arranged for in any settlement made by the competent authorities. Any payments are usually made free of further income tax effect in the US.

US tax authorities have also provided separate domestic procedures to allow conforming adjustments and payments of amounts of income allocated to a US taxpayer. See Part I, F. 3 for a detailed discussion of these procedures. These procedures apply regardless of whether there is an applicable treaty. Certain procedural and factual requirements must be met to use these procedures, and payment of allocated amounts may not be entirely free of US tax consequences. For example, a condition for making payment of an allocated amount is that the taxpayer must accrue interest income on the allocation from the year-end of the year from which the allocation arose until the payment is made. Such a requirement would be unlikely in an agreement between competent authorities.

H. Our experience is that competent authority consideration is an expensive and time-consuming procedure. We understand that approximately 86 per cent of cases are settled with full relief from double taxation, 8 per cent with partial relief, and 6 per cent with no relief. There is a wide variation of time required, depending upon the complexity of the issues. The most common cause for delay is inadequacy of information provided to the competent authority, and changes to the procedures have increased the amount of information required to be filed with the request.

PART IV. SPECIAL SITUATIONS

A. Modification of Normal Rules

1. The regulations specifically state that there may be an allocation from one member of a group to another even if the first member did not realize any gross income during the year. Although early case law held to the contrary, current case law supports the position stated in the regulations.
2. The answer is the same as 1 above.
3. Although the relative tax rates of the two countries should not affect the amount of the allocation, the regulations state that transactions will be subjected to special scrutiny to ascertain whether transactions are being used to avoid taxes. The tax authorities are much less active in seeking an allocation where a change in pricing would not have substantially affected the overall tax burden.
4. The answer is the same as 3 above.

B. Situations of Special Interest

Tax authorities will closely examine transactions with companies which pay reduced rates of tax or have tax holidays.

PART V. OTHER CONSIDERATIONS

It is important for a foreign subsidiary of a US corporation to advise the US corporation of any proposed allocations and changes in its tax liability which may result. If an adjustment is proposed, the foreign subsidiary and US parent must exhaust all administrative remedies to attempt to oppose the adjustment in order to protect the US parent's right to a deemed paid credit (underlying credit) upon receiving a dividend from the subsidiary. See Part I, F (2)(b)(ii).

If the foreign income tax liability changes, the US taxpayer must notify the US tax authorities if the US taxpayer has taken a foreign tax credit with respect to those taxes of that year. If the US taxpayer fails to provide the notice, a penalty may be imposed.

The audit manual used by the US income tax auditors requires the auditors to ask if there have been any 'foreign adjustments' that resulted in reduction of US income tax. For treaty countries, the information is required to be forwarded to the competent authority, which may initiate mutual agreement negotiations or wait for the taxpayer to request it to do so.

Venezuela

Francisco Salazar

PART I. GENERAL RULES

A. 1. The Venezuelan tax law has no specific provisions dealing with transactions between related companies. It is, however, a generally accepted principle that prices for transactions between related companies shall be the same as those between independent parties in order to be acceptable for tax purposes. The general rule for making allocation of income for both related and non-related parties is the selling price of the products or services sold.
2. No, tax avoidance need not be established.
3. As a general rule, all loans are supposed to have a minimum interest of 8 per cent. Venezuelan corporations owned 51 per cent or more by foreign corporations cannot pay royalties for technological services, technical assistance or management fees to parent or related companies. There are no safe haven rules.
4. Dividends received by Venezuelan corporations are not taxable. Dividends received by foreign individuals or corporations are 20 per cent taxable.

B. 'Related Persons' include those under common management control, or those owning 51 per cent of a company's shares.

C. The principal approach to making adjustments is on a transaction basis.

D. The statute of limitations is four years after fiscal year end.

E. No, a correlating adjustment is not made with respect to the foreign taxpayer where an adjustment is made by Venezuela.

F. When an adjustment is made to a company located outside Venezuela:
1. That company is not taxed on a consolidated basis with domestic companies.
2. Profits and dividends from a corporation located outside of Venezuela are not taxable.

3. No, payments of allocated amounts are not required.

G. Adjustments are made to the transaction year.

H. As a general rule, at any time the taxpayer must present a substitute tax return to correct any error in its original tax declaration.

PART II. SPECIFIC EXAMPLES

A. Sale of Goods

Assumed Facts

Assume P is a manufacturer which sells finished products to S, which is located in a different country. P sells these products to S at cost. P also sells these products to unrelated parties at cost plus 10 per cent mark-on. Both S and the unrelated parties incur the same selling and promotional expense and both resell P's products at the same price per unit.

Parent in Venezuela

1. No income will be allocated.
2. Not applicable.
3. No, the answer would not differ based on S assuming incurring greater promotional expenses, etc.

Subsidiary in Venezuela

1./2. Allocation will only be accepted if charged as additional cost of the merchandise.
3. Yes, if not properly billed, the excess payments from S will be regarded as a dividend subject to withholding tax of 20 per cent.

B. Loans and Advances

Assumed Facts

P and S are manufacturers located in different countries. P loans S money on open account without interest so that S can expand its operations. P is not engaged in the business of lending money.

Parent in Venezuela

1. Under the territoriality concept contemplated in the Income Tax Law, income and expenses obtained or incurred outside of Venezuela are not taxable/non-deductible.
2. No, the existence of a non-interest bearing note makes no difference.
3. The loan is not considered additional equity. The Law that regulates foreign investments in Venezuela prohibits any Venezuelan corporation owned 51 per cent or more by a foreign corporation to have investments or to make loans outside the country.

Subsidiary in Venezuela

1./2. Remains a loan, not an equity investment.
3. Yes. Interest is a deductible expense for S. The rate of interest cannot exceed 3 points above the prime rate in P's country.
4. Retroactive payments are not permitted by exchange control and are thus not deductible.
5. Remains a loan, not equity.

C. INTANGIBLES

Assumed Facts

P and S are manufacturers located in different countries. P performs research and development which has led to P's ownership of certain intangibles consisting of patents, trademarks and know-how. P makes available to S exclusive right to use in S's country all of P's intangibles. P does not charge S for the use of P's intangibles.

Parent in Venezuela

1./4. By application of the territorial concept, no income will be allocated to P or costs allocated to S. The existence of a cost-sharing agreement would not change the result.

Subsidiary in Venezuela

1./3. All contracts for the transference of patents, trademarks, know-how, technical assistance, etc., and the payment of a fee between a foreign and a Venezuelan corporation must be approved by the Superintendent for Foreign Investments. If not approved, any payment made is illegal and the expense is not deductible. Venezuelan corporations owned 51 per cent or more by foreign corporations cannot make any payment for these concepts to parent or related companies. Expenses are deductible if contract is approved. If payments are approved, taxes must be withheld by application of Tariff No.2 on net taxable income which is presumed to be as follows:

1. 30 per cent of gross income obtained from supply of technical assistance.
2. 50 per cent of gross income from supply of technological services.
3. 90 per cent of gross income for use of brand names, emblems, symbols.

Tariff No.2 From	Taxable Income To	Per cent
Bs 001	Bs 300,000	18
300,000	2,500,000	30
2,500,000	5,000,000	35
5,000,000	5,000,000	45
over	20,000,000	50

D. Services

Assumed Facts

P is a large multinational concern which wholly owns foreign subsidiary S. Both P and S are engaged in manufacturing and sales activities. P's headquarters division performs general management services for P's multi-national operations including services which directly relate to S. The services performed for S include periodic visits by P's executives to review S's operations, financial analysis of S's future requirements, engineering services in connection with S's manufacturing activities and marketing services in connection with S's sales activities. P does not charge S for such service.

Parent and Subsidiary

Basically, no allocations would be made to P or accepted by S in Venezuela as these types of payments are illegal. In accordance with income tax regulations, management services are considered to be technical assistance, and it is illegal to make such payments to related companies outside Venezuela.

E. Loan Guarantees and Rentals

Assumed Facts

P is a multi-national company whose main business is manufacturing and selling. P plans to establish foreign sales subsidiary S located in country S. P capitalizes S with $500,000 and guarantees a loan to S of $500,000 obtained from an independent bank. Land and a warehouse which P owns in country S will be used as a site for S's operations. P plans to make this land and warehouse available to S at a fee of $1 per year for 99 years.

Parent in Venezuela

1. Income will not be allocated to P for the guarantee to the loan to S. By application of the territoriality concept, any income or loss from P's investment in S abroad will not be taxable or deductible in Venezuela. Therefore, P will not be allowed to deduct depreciation for the warehouse.
2. P will not be considered as having made an additional equity investment in S.

Subsidiary in Venezuela

No allocation to S or payments by S will be permitted.

PART III. TAX TREATIES

None exist.

PART IV. SPECIAL SITUATIONS

Venezuela would not alter its rules in any of the situations described.

Summary Charts

Cross-Border Transactions Between Related Companies (Tax Aspects)

These charts are very abridged summaries of each country's responses to the questionnaire. Readers should refer to the country reports for more detail. Readers can also refer to the questionnaire for clarification of the questions if necessary.

GENERAL RULES

	A.		
	1. What is the general rule? What standard is used?	2. Must tax avoidance be established to permit the adjustments?	3a) Are any transactions specifically covered?
AUSTRALIA	Arm's length	No, Int'l trans. Yes, domestic trans.	No
BELGIUM	Arm's length	No	Payments to tax havens
BRAZIL	Arm's length; allocations rare; strict exchange cont.	Yes	Yes
CANADA	Arm's length	No	No
DENMARK	Arm's length	No	No
FINLAND	Arm's length; arbitrary assessments can be used after first 5 yrs. See special reserves and incentives	No	Management fees, interest
FRANCE	Arm's length	No	Payments to tax havens
WEST GERMANY	Arm's length; conscientious unrelated parties; many rules codified in statutes or regulations	No	Yes
HONG KONG	Unreasonable expenses denied or entire receipts of N.R. taxed-rules rarely used	Yes	No
IRELAND	Arm's length	No	No
ITALY	Arm's length See note on tax amnesties	No	No
JAPAN	Arm's length; rules rarely used	No	Real property rental
MEXICO	Arm's length; authorities have discretionary powers	No	No
NETHERLANDS	Arm's length	No	No
NEW ZEALAND	Arm's length; discretionary assessments used; reserve bank approval needed	No	Yes-NR pays profits tax on all income from N.Z., very broad rules
NORWAY	Arm's length	No	Yes; oil prices
SAUDI ARABIA	Allocation concept N/A; tax based on AFS; the NR subject to Saudi profits tax on profit of 15%-100% of most payments originating in the Kingdom	N/A	Yes
SINGAPORE	Arm's length	No	Yes; some payments deemed to have source in Singapore
SOUTH AFRICA	Arm's length; exchange controls prevent certain payments	Yes	No
SPAIN	Arm's length; very new law not yet in effect	No	No
SWEDEN	Arm's length; onus on tax authorities	No	Yes
SWITZERLAND	Arm's length	No	No
UNITED KINGDOM	Arm's length	No	Yes; oil prices
UNITED STATES	Arm's length; most rules codified in statutes or regulations	No	Loans, services, rentals, intangibles and tangibles
VENEZUELA	Arm's length; exchange controls prevent allocations	No	Loans-8%; no royalties or mgmt fees for foreign parent

		B.	C.
3b) Are safe havens provided for?	**4.** Do different rules apply to transactions between domestic taxpayers and those between residents and non-residences?	What is a related person for these purposes?	Is the principal approach to making adjustments a transaction or net income basis?
No	Yes	Non-arm's length	Transactions
No	Yes, caps on interest rates	Common mgmt. control or capital	Net income
No, generally	No	Common control; some extended rules	Transactions
Interest prescribed-rate changes quarterly	Minor differences	Common control	Transactions
No	Yes	Effective control	Transactions
No	No, but NR corps. pay net worth tax of 1%; subvention payments exist for domestic corps.	One who financially participates or who has influence on management	Transactions
No	Yes	Effective control; all dealings with tax havens	Transactions
No	No, but domestic trans not watched	25% of greater common ownership	Transactions
No	Yes	Common control; commissioners have discretion	Transactions
No	Minor differences	Common control	Transactions
No	Yes	Potential or actual influence over management decisions	Transactions
No	No	50% or more of shares owned by 3 or fewer unrelated persons	Transactions
No	No	Common control	Transactions
Advance rulings possible for interest and royalties	Yes, in practice	Effective control	Transactions
No	Yes, arbitrary assessments against NR plus other specific rules	Common control; be careful, directors may control	Commissioner has choice
No	No	Participating interest; greater than 30%	Transactions
No	Yes	Affiliated parties	Transactions
No	Minor differences	Common control	Transactions
No	No (exchange control)	Not defined; includes close corportate relationships	Transactions
No	No	25% or greater common ownership	Transactions
No	Yes, domestics use subvention payments	Common ownership or management	Transactions
No	No	Common control (over 50%)	Net income (transaction basis on cross-border loans)
No	No, but only used for cross-border trans.	Common control	Transactions, but net income important
As in 3(a)	No	Common control	Transactions
No	Yes, Only NR taxed on dividends	Common control; common management	Transactions

	D.	E.
	Is there a statute of limitations for these allocations?	Where adjustment is made by your country is a correlating adj. made with respect to foreign taxpayer for purposes of subsequent dvds, frgn. tax credit, etc. in your country?
AUSTRALIA	None	No
BELGIUM	3 years after part. year	No
BRAZIL	5-7 years after relevant year	No
CANADA	3 years after return first assessed	No
DENMARK	5 years after year of assessment	No
FINLAND	None	No
FRANCE	4 years after end of taxable year	No
WEST GERMANY	4 years after end of year return filed	No
HONG KONG	6 years after year of assessment	No
IRELAND	10 years after end of taxable year	No
ITALY	5 years	No
JAPAN	None	No
MEXICO	5 years	Yes
NETHERLANDS	3-5 years on P&L items; no limit on B/S adj.	No
NEW ZEALAND	4 years after end of year of assessment; treaties can reduce	No
NORWAY	None	No
SAUDI ARABIA	N/A	N/A
SINGAPORE	12 years	No
SOUTH AFRIKA	3 years	No
SPAIN	5 years	No
SWEDEN	6 years prior to current year	No
SWITZERLAND	Auth. assess within 5 years, if not objected to the assessment is final	No
UNITED KINGDOM	6 years after end of taxable year	No
UNITED STATES	3 years after return filed; some treaties extend	Yes, see details
VENEZUELA	4 years	No

F. What effect does an adjustment have when made to a company located outside your country? For example:			G.	H.
1. Is that company taxed on consolidated basis with domestic companies?	2. Are dividends or foreign tax credits from that company effected?	3. Is payment of allocated amounts required?	Are adjustments made to the underlying transaction year or to a more current year?	Can a taxpayer initiate an adjustment under the allocation rules by request to your tax authorities? If so, when?
No	No	No	Transaction year normaly	No, only comp. auth.
No	No	No	Adjustment year	No
No	No	No	Transaction year	No
No	No, normaly	No	Transaction year	Not legally, perhaps administratively
Optional	Yes, FTC	No, unless for exchange auth. require	Transaction year	No, normaly
No	No	No	Transaction year normaly	Yes
No	No	No	Transaction year	No
No	No	No, German tax on such payments very severe	Transaction year	Only comp. auth. requests heard
No	No	No	Transaction year	No, unless error in prior year
No	Yes, FTC	No	Transaction year, current year by agreement	No, normaly
No	No	No	Transaction year	No
Yes, mandatory if a tax haven	Yes, FTC if consolidation required	No	Transaction year	No
No	Yes, FTC	No	Transaction year	No
No	No	No	The earliest open year	Taxpayer merely makes adjustment in current tax return
No	No	Yes	Transaction year	Yes
No	No	No	Transaction year	No
No	No	N/A	Transaction year	No
No	No	No	Transaction year	No, what went into AFS is final
No	No	No	Transaction year	No
No	No	No	Transaction year	Yes
No	No	No	Transaction year	Yes
No	No	No	Transaction year normaly	Yes, administratively
No	Yes, FTC	No	Transaction year (current year by agreement)	No, legally, often yes administratively
No	Yes, if earnings & profits or taxes of foreign corp. affected	No, but rules encourage payments back to the U.S.	Transaction year (see special rules re: payment of allocation)	No, legally, only under comp. auth.
No	No (exempt)	No	Transaction	Yes, in principle

SALE OF GOODS

Assume P is a manufacturer which sells finished products to S which is located in a different country. P sells the products to S at cost. P sells the products to unrelated parties at cost plus 10%. Both S and unrelated parties incur same selling and promotional expenses and both resell P's products at same price per unit.

	As to P		
	1. Will income be allocated to P?	**2.** If yes, how will allocation be made? What factors are considered?	**3.** Would answer differ if no sales to independent parties or if S incurred greater selling/ promotional expenses or resold P's products at lower price per unit to establish market?
AUSTRALIA	Yes, legally but rarely applied	Arm's length tests	These factors considered
BELGIUM	Yes	Arm's length tests	These factors considered
BRAZIL	No	Prices approved by exchange control	Exchange auth. will consider
CANADA	Yes	Arm's length tests; see U.S. rules and OECD report	These factors considered but still A.L. prices
DENMARK	Yes	Arm's length tests, but smaller markup of sales to S acceptable	These factors considered
FINLAND	Yes	Arm's length tests (but tax auth. may not be alarmed by 10% discount)	These factors considered but still A.L. prices
FRANCE	Yes	Arm's length tests	These factors considered; lower price s/b acceptable
WEST GERMANY	Yes	Arm's length tests; see U.S. rules, OECD report & new German regs.	Yes, but marketing costs must be borne by P
HONG KONG	Not unless extreme abuse	All S's income from HK subject to HK profits tax; collected from P	Yes, results would differ
IRELAND	Not likely-Export Sales Relief	Arm's length tests	These factors considered
ITALY	Yes, if amount is significant	Arm's length tests	These factors considered
JAPAN	Yes, P asked to make charge to S	Arm's length tests; onus on tax auth.	These factors considered
MEXICO	Yes	Arm's length tests; normal gross profit margin of P	Yes-probably negates any allocation
NETHER-LANDS	Yes	Arm's length tests; see OECD report	These factors considered
NEW ZEALAND	Yes	Arm's length tests	These factors considered
NORWAY	Yes	Arm's length tests	These factors considered
SAUDI ARABIA	Not likely	N/A	N/A
SINGAPORE	Yes	Arm's length tests	These factors considered
SOUTH AFRICA	Not normally	Arm's length tests	These factors considered
SPAIN	Yes	Arm's length tests	These factors considered
SWEDEN	Yes	Arm's length tests	Yes, can lower price to establish market
SWITZER-LAND	Yes	Arm's length tests	These factors considered but still A.L. prices
UNITED KINGDOM	Yes	Arm's length tests	Yes, can lower price to establish market
UNITED STATES	Yes	1. Comparable uncontrolled prices 2. Resale price method 3. Cost plus method 4. Other reasonable method	Can lower price to estab. mkt if also do so with arm's length buyers
VENEZUELA	No	N/A	No

As to S		
1. Will allocation in P's country be accepted by S's country, or will S's country make independent determination?	**2.** Under what circumstances can S deduct the allocation?	**3.** If S make payment of the allocated amount to P, will S's country treat the payment as a divident subject to withholding?
Independent determination	Only if S pays amount & argues there was a binding contract to do so	No, even if not deductible under 2
Independent determination	Arm's length charge deductible	No, if evidence from P's tax auth. to support
No allocation	No deduction	Payment rarely permitted; W/H tax would apply
Independent determination	If reasonable & year not statute barred	No, if deductible under 2
Independent determination	No deductions unless passed in fiscal accounts	No, if deductible under 2
Independent determination	Only if P charges S & S proves charges based on open market prices	No, if deductible under 2
Independent determination	Only under comp. auth.	No, if deductible under 2
Independent determination	Only under comp. auth. (rare)	Yes, unless pursuant to comp. auth.
Not normally accepted in HK	Normally no deduction	No
Independent determination	Only under comp. auth. (not probable)	No deduction but no W/H-watch new A.C.T.
Independent determination	Only under comp. auth.	No, but exchange control very strict
Independent determination	If reasonable & binding obligation existed	Only is S being reorganized
Will deny for profits tax but would collect import duty on higher price	No deduction	Yes
Independent determination	If reasonable	No, if deductible under 2
Independent determination	If reasonable and amounts paid by S	Not normally
Independent determination	If reasonable and P invoices S	Yes
No allocation	P only exempt from profits tax on original selling price if P's auditor certifies it was FMV	NA
No allocation	No retro. adj. accepted but current year adj. might be negotiated	No
Independent determination	Normally, if P actually charges S	No, normally
No allocation-higher price may be used for import duty	Not deductible	Yes
No allocation	Not deductible	Yes
Independent determination	Charges based on 3rd party prices accepted; others negotiated; must be booked by S in relevant year	No, to extent deductible under 2
Independent determination	Only to extent UK auth. accept (negotiations)	No to extent deductible under 2
Independent determination	Only under comp. auth. settlements	No to extent deductible under 2
If charged as cost of goods	As in 1	Yes

LOANS AND ADVANCES

P and S are manufacturers located in different countries. P loans money *on open account without interest* so that S can expand its operations. P is not engaged in the business of lending money.

	As to P			As to S
	1. Will interest income be allocated to P? If yes, at what rate?	2. Would your answer differ if loan was evidenced by non-interest bearing note with fixed maturity date?	3. If interest income is not allocated could the loan be considered additional equity investment in S? If yes, what happens when the loan is repaid?	1. Will the characterization of the transaction of P's country be accepted by S's country?
AUSTRALIA	Normally yes, arm's length rates	No, but rate may change	Remains a loan	Remains a loan
BELGIUM	Yes, open market rates	No	Remains a loan	Remains a loan
BRAZIL	No, but loan & interest pre-approved by exchange control	No	Remains a loan	Yes, if approved by Central Bk. zero interest & term of at least 8 years accepted
CANADA	No (yes in other circumstances)	No	Remains a loan	Remains a loan
DENMARK	No if necessary for advancement of subsidiary	No	Remains a loan	Remains a loan
FINLAND	Yes, open market rates	No	Perhaps, but overall tax treatment not affected	Independent determination
FRANCE	Yes, arm's length or Bank of France rates	No	Remains a loan	Remains a loan
WEST GERMANY	Yes, open market rates	No	Remains a loan	Remains a loan
HONG KONG	Possibly to extent of dividends received	No	Remains a loan	Remains a loan
IRELAND	Not likely unless exchange control insisted	No	Remains a loan	Remains a loan
ITALY	Yes, Bank of Italy discount rate	No	Remains a loan	Remains a loan
JAPAN	Yes, equal to P's L.T. borrowing rate; otherwise 10%	No	Remains a loan	Remains a loan
MEXICO	No, but expenses denied	No	Remains a loan	Remains a loan (S may lose a tax incentive)
NETHER-LANDS	Could be equity (no allocation) or loan (alloc.)	Now clearly a loan; allocation required	Yes, no Dutch tax on repayment	Independent determination
NEW ZEALAND	No, if ultimate benefits accruing to P; expenses might be denied	No	Remains a loan	Remains a loan
NORWAY	Yes, open market rates	No	Yes, repayment then taxed at 50.8% as a dividend	Most likely a loan
SAUDI ARABIA	Not presently	No	Remains a loan	Remains a loan
SINGAPORE	No but expenses denied	No	Remains a loan	Remains a loan
SOUTH AFRICA	No, exchange controls	No	Remains a loan	Remains a loan
SPAIN	Yes if not approved by exchange auth.; No otherwise	No	Remains a loan	Remains a loan; if not originally approved repayment can be denied
SWEDEN	Yes, open market rates; may not do so in practice	No	Remains a loan	Remains a loan
SWITZER-LAND	Yes, 6 1/2% to 7 1/2% for Swiss franc loans; others based on open market rates	No	Perhaps if equity 3% stamp tax applies; No tax on repayment	Independent determination
UNITED KINGDOM	Yes, open market rates; no imputing if S's equity not greater than external debt, or to extent S's income does not exceed total interest expense by more than 3 to 1	No	Remains a loan	Remains a loan
UNITED STATES	Yes at 12% if loan in US $; if P borrowed in country S then inputed income equal to borrowing cost	No	Perhaps if equity then repayment may be taxed as a dividend	Independent determination
VENEZUELA	No	No	Remains a loan	Remains a loan

As to S			
2. Would S's country ever treat as an equity investment?	**3.** If a loan, will interest be allocated? If yes, at what rate?	**4.** What if P's country allocates more than S's country and S pays the larger amount?	**5.** If transaction regarded by S's country as equity what happens on repayment? What if P's country treats as a loan & S pays the amount allocated by P's country?
Remains a loan	No, a legal obligation to pay required	No ded. plus W/H tax may apply	Remains a loan
Remains a loan	Yes, open market rates	No. ded. plus W/H tax	Remains a loan
N/A	N/A	N/A	N/A
Remains a loan	No, a legal obligation to pay required	No ded. plus W/H tax	Remains a loan
Remains a loan	No, a legal obligation to pay required	No ded. plus W/H tax	Remains a loan
Probably treated as equity if no mat. date fixed	Yes, generally up to open market rates	No ded. plus W/H tax	If treated as equity repayment can occur tax free in S; interest payments then treated as non-ded. dvdns.
Remains a loan	No allocation	No ded. plus W/H tax	Remains a loan
Remains a loan	No, unless a comp. auth. decision; they use market rates	Any retro. payment without comp. auth. decision attracts severe tax	Remains a loan; principal repayments no tax; interest attracts severe tax
Remains a loan	No, a legal obligation required	No ded. W/H only if credit arranged in HK	Remains a loan
Remains a loan	No,normally; may allow if interest actually paid (see 4)	If S a 75% sub then interest paid is non-deduct. dividend (subject to treaties); otherwise deductible	Remains a loan
Remains a loan	No allocation	No payment permitted	Remains a loan
Remains a loan	Only if legal obligation exists; same rates as P's	Excess no ded. but no W/H	Remains a loan
Remains a loan	No allocation	Deductible but 55% W/H tax	Remains a loan
Can be equity or loan	Yes, open market rates	No ded. plus W/H tax	Repayment of equity can attract W/H as dividend
Remains a loan	No, not unilaterally but may accept P's allocation if S pays it, etc.	No ded. plus P subject to NZ profits tax regardless	Remains a loan
Most likely a loan	Yes, if P charges a fair amount	No ded., plus W/H tax	N/A
Remains a loan	No allocation	S can deduct reasonable interest but not retro; P pays profits tax	Remains a loan
Remains a loan	No allocation	No ded., but no W/H	Remains a loan
Remains a loan	No allocation unless legal obligation & actual charge made	No ded. plus W/H tax	Remains a loan
Remains a loan	No allocation	N/A Legal offence	Remains a loan; cannot repay unless exchange approval
Remains a loan	Perhaps allocation for reasonable amounts	No ded., plus W/H tax	Remains a loan
Normally a loan	Will accept rates above	No ded. plus 35% W/H tax	If equity, repayment still tax free; interest then non-ded. dividend
Remains a loan	No allocation	Ded. allowed provided it doesn't exceed comm. rate; excess payments treated as dividend distribution	Remains a loan
Could be equity or loan; many factors to consider	Interest only deductible if comp. auth. decides	No deduction plus W/H tax	If U.S. considers equity, then repayment a dividend to extent of earnings and profit
Remains a loan	If exchange controls permit can deduct prime + 3%	No ded. as no payment permitted	Remains a loan

P and S are manufacturers located in different countries. P performs research and development which has led to P's ownership of patents, trademarks, knowhow, etc. P gives S exclusive right to use these intangibles in S's country. P does not charge S.

	As to P		
	1. Will income be allocated to P? Could P be treated as contributing the intangibles to capital of S?	2. If allocation, will it be annual royalties or lump sum? How is allocation computed? Does it matter if S's country denies a deduction or denies the payment itself?	3. Alternatively, could a portion of the R & D costs be allocated to S?
AUSTRALIA	Not likely	Annual royalty; S's treatment N/A	No but some danger of P's costs being denied
BELGIUM	Yes	Annual royalty; S's treatment N/A	Not normally
BRAZIL	No allocation	No allocation	No
CANADA	Yes	Annual royalty normally; S's treatment N/A	Only if S was legally obligated
DENMARK	Yes	Lump sum or annual royalty; S's treatment N/A	Yes
FINLAND	No, normally	N/A	Yes
FRANCE	Yes, not treated as capital	Annual royalty; S's treatment N/A	Yes
WEST GERMANY	Yes	Lump sum or annual royalty; S's treatment N/A	Yes
HONG KONG	No – but expenses dissalowed if intang. not used in HK	N/A	No, but costs may be denied
IRELAND	No, but expenses may be denied	N/A	Yes
ITALY	Yes	Annual royalty; S's treatment N/A	Yes, possibly
JAPAN	No, assumed P will eventually benefit	N/A	Permitted, not required
MEXICO	No, & expenses deductible	N/A	Possible, profit element prob. regd.
NETHER-LANDS	Yes	Lump sum or annual royalty; S's treatment N/A	Yes
NEW ZEALAND	No, but expenses may be denied	N/A	Yes
NORWAY	Yes, legally; in practice may be	Lump sum annual royalty; S's treatment N/A	Yes
SAUDI ARABIA	Not likely	N/A	N/A
SINGAPORE	No, but expenses denied	N/A	Yes, current year only
SOUTH AFRICA	Not likely	Probably annual royalty; S's treatment N/A	Not likely
SPAIN	Yes, in principal; can apply for capital cont. treatment	Probably lump sum; S's treatment N/A	No
SWEDEN	Yes, in principal	Probably annual royalty; S's treatment N/A	Yes
SWITZER-LAND	Only if P in business of selling such intangibles, & material to P's income	Lump sum or annual royalty; S's treatment N/A	Yes
UNITED KINGDOM	Yes, unless P compensated with higher product prices etc.	Form depends on facts; S's treatment N/A	Yes
UNITED STATES	Yes, unless P got ruling to transfer substantial rights tax free to S	Annual royalty if P retains substantial interest, otherwise lump sum; S's treatment N/A	Only if a contract existed before costs incurred
VENEZUELA	No	N/A	No

	As to S		
4. Would answers change if P & S entered a bona fide cost sharing arrangement with respect to R & D costs?	**1.** Will S's country accept the allocation from P or make separate determination?	**2.** Will S be allowed a deduction for the lump sum, royalty or expenses allocations to P? How is deduction computed?	**3.** Will S's country levy withholding tax if S pays lump sum, royalty or cost sharing?
Contract governs	Independent determination	Can deduct non-capital outlays; lump sums amort.; legal obligation to pay required	P Subject to profits tax unless treaties reduce to W/H tax
Contract governs	Independent determination	Yes, if reasonable; lump sum can be expensed or amort	Yes, unless treaties exempt
Prospective contract app. by exchange auth.	No allocation	No deduction	No payment allocated
Contract governs	Independent determination	Yes, normally if reasonable	Royalties attract W/H, purchase of rights does not
Contract governs	Independent determination	No unless S receives charge from P	No, W/H only on dividends
No	Independent determination	Can deduct if P charges S & S demonstrates charge equal to open market rates; lump sums amort over economic life up to 10 years	Yes
Contract governs	Independent determination	No deduction	No ded. plus W/H tax
Contract governs	No acceptance unless comp. auth. (not likely)	No, unless comp. auth.	If comp. auth. agrees then only W/H tax; ontherwise severe tax
Contract governs	P's allocation rarely accepted	S must show prior error to get ded. (not likely)	1.85% W/H if P's allocation accepted, otherwise no W/H
Contract governs	No allocation unless comp. auth.	No deduction except for prospective expenses	Royalty-W/H, dividend-no W/H (new A.C.T. system)
Contract governs	Independent determination. See specific guidelines	No allocation likely; exchange controls	No payments permitted; exchange controls
Contract governs	Independent determination	Deductible if reasonable	Yes on lump sum, royalty or services; no on cost-sharing
Contract governs	No allocation	Only deductible if prospective royalty contract approved by foreign investment authority	Yes, at 42% unless approved
Contract governs	Independent determination	Yes if reasonable	No
Contract governs	Independent determination	Yes if Res. Bank approves, S makes payment, contract existed & S acquired rights to use property in New Zealand	P subject to profits tax in NZ unless treaty reduces to W/H tax
Contract governs	Independent determination	Yes, if reasonable and charge received from P	Yes unless deductible by S
Contract probably governs	No allocation	Allocation not acceptable; royalties taxed as in 3	Royalty payments deemed to be 100% profit-profit tax applied
Contract governs	No allocation	S deducts only prospective royalty or cost sharing	Yes on royalties & even on cost recovery payments
Contract governs	Independent determination	Royalty probably deductible; lump sum probably no; actual charge req'd	Yes, subject to profits tax
Contract governs	No allocation unless exchange auth. approves	No ded. unless exchange auth. approves & cost sharing contract existed	Yes, if a royalty; no payment without approval
Contract governs	No allocation	Perhaps allocation if reasonable amounts	Yes
Contract governs	Independent determination	Deductible if royalty agreement exists and amount negotiated with tax auth.	No
Contract governs	Independent determination	Yes, if reasonable and S makes payments	Yes, but only in respect of UK patents
Contract governs	Independent determination	Only if U.S. comp. auth. accepts	Yes, unless U.S. accepts as a purchase of intangible property
No	Payments illegal	N/A	Yes, if payments permitted

SERVICES

P is a large multi-national concern which wholly-owns foreign subsidiary S. Both P and S are engaged in manufacturing and sales activities. P's headquarters performs general management services for P's multi-national operations including services which directly relate to S. The services include periodic visits by P's executives to review S's operations, financial analysis of S's future requirements engineering service re: S's manufacturing operations and marketing services. P does not charge S.

	As to P	
	1. Will income be allocated to P? Does the nature of services matter?	**2.** How is allocation computed, recovery of direct costs, indirect costs, profit element?
AUSTRALIA	No-Stewardship Rarely-others	Cost recovery, must be negotiated
BELGIUM	Yes, type of service matters	Arm's length price
BRAZIL	No allocation	N/A
CANADA	No-stewardship Yes-others	Reasonable price
DENMARK	No-Stewardship Yes-others	N/A
FINLAND	No, normally	N/A
FRANCE	No-Stewardship Yes-others	Cost recovery
WEST GERMANY	No-Stewardship Yes-others	Cost plus for some cost recovery for others
HONG KONG	No, may deny expenses	N/A
IRELAND	No, may deny expenses	N/A
ITALY	No-Stewardship Yes-others	Full cost recovery, may be profit
JAPAN	Yes, only for costs directly related to S; type of service N/A	Recover direct cost only
MEXICO	Yes, nature of service matters	Cost recovery, plus profit if services sold to 3rd parties
NETHERLANDS	No-stewardship;Yes-others; No-where certain costs disallowed (interest)	Cost recovery, sometimes arm's length price (negotiation)
NEW ZEALAND	Very unlikely	N/A
NORWAY	Yes, legally; no in practice	Ams's length rates
SAUDI ARABIA	Not likely	N/A
SINGAPORE	No, expense denied	N/A
SOUTH AFRICA	No allocation	N/A
SPAIN	Yes, or expenses dinied	Full cost recovery
SWEDEN	Yes, nature of services N/A	Arm's length rates
SWITZERLAND	Only if P is in business of selling such services, & material to P's income	Negotiated
UNITED KINGDOM	No, expenses denied unless in P's overall interest	Recover only direct costs unless in business, then arm's length prices
UNITED STATES	Yes, for services of direct benefit to S & not already performed by S	Full cost recovery unless P in business, then arm's length prices
VENEZUELA	No allocation	N/A

	As to S	
	1. Will S's country accept allocations from P's country? How would S's country determine the allocations? Is S allowed a deduction?	2. Will S's country levy a withholding tax on payments to P?
AUSTRALIA	Independent determination; reasonable amounts accepted	No, but profits tax may apply to P
BELGIUM	Independent determination; reasonable amounts accepted	No
BRAZIL	No allocation	No payment allowed
CANADA	Independent determination; reasonable amounts accepted	No W/H if only reimbursing P's costs
DENMARK	Ind. determination; reasonable amounts accepted if an actual charge from P	No
FINLAND	To deduct must be: charged by P, of direct benefit to business of S, etc.	No
FRANCE	No allocation; prospective legal obligation reg'd	Yes
WEST GERMANY	Allocation unlikely unless comp. auth. agrees to review	No, if comp. auth. approves, otherwise severe tax
HONG KONG	P's allocation rarely accepted	No
IRELAND	No allocation; might become ded. if paid in future years with current expenses	No
ITALY	No allocation likely	No W/H if only re-imbursing P's costs
JAPAN	Ind. determination; S must show legal oblig. existed & service actually received	No, if service rendered from P's country
MEXICO	No allocation; S must get prospective payments approved to deduct	Yes, at 21%
NETHERLANDS	Ind. determination; supportable arm's length price accepted, otherwise cost recovery	No, if deductible under 1
NEW ZEALAND	Normally accept position of P's tax auth. if S makes payment, etc.	Yes, if royalties; no if contract signed & performed outside N.Z.; No if performed inside N.Z. & only cost recovery
NORWAY	No allocation likely	Yes, unless deductible by S
SAUDI ARABIA	No allocation	No Saudi tax on P if proven services performed wholly outside of Kingdom; otherwise taxable profit element deemed to be 15% or more
SINGAPORE	No allocation; no deduction in original AFS	No-cost recovery Yes-profit element
SOUTH AFRICA	May accept if actual charge made; exchange controls	No; exchange controls
SPAIN	Nothing accepted without prior approval of exchange auth.	Yes
SWEDEN	No allocation likely	Yes, unless deductible under 1
SWITZERLAND	Ind. determination; an amount based on turnover or cost in S is normally deductible	No
UNITED KINGDOM	Independent determination; reasonable amounts accepted	No
UNITED STATES	Independent determination; using same rules as for P	Yes, unless deductible in U.S. and services rendered outside U.S.
VENEZUELA	No allocation	Payments illegal

LOAN GUARANTEES AND RENTALS

P is a multi-national company whose main business is manufacturing and selling. P plans to establish foreign sales subsidiary S located in country S. P capitalizes S with $ 500,000 and guarantees a loan to S of $ 500,000 obtained from an independent bank. Land and a warehouse which P owns in country S will be used as a site for S's operations. P plans to make this land and warehouse available to S at fee of $ 1 per year for 99 years.

	As to P		
	1. Will income be allocated to P for P's guarantee of loan to S or for S's use of P's land and warehouse? If yes, how would amount of allocation be determined?		**2.** If income not allocated, as alternative could P be treated as having made an additional equity investment in S? If yes, what would be tax consequences of such treatment?
	a. Guarantee?	**b.** Real Estate?	
AUSTRALIA	No	Yes, arm's length rental	No
BELGIUM	No	Yes, arm's length rental	No
BRAZIL	No	No but related costs probably denied	No
CANADA	No	Yes,arm's length rental	No
DENMARK	No	Yes, arm's length rental	No
FINLAND	No	Yes, open market rates	No
FRANCE	Yes	Yes, both at arm's length rates	No
WEST GERMANY	No	Yes, deemed sold at FMV	No
HONG KONG	No	No, but expenses may be denied	No
IRELAND	No	No, but expenses may be denied	No
ITALY	No	Yes, arm's length rates	No
JAPAN	No	Land-8% of market value Whse-fair rental	No
MEXICO	No	Yes, arm's length rental	No
NETHER-LANDS	Yes-arm's length. Fee	Yes, arm's length rental	Yes, additional paid in capital results
NEW ZEALAND	No	Yes, arm's length rental	No
NORWAY	Yes, legally. No in practice	Yes, legally. No in practice	No
SAUDI ARABIA	No	No-costs denied	No
SINGAPORE	No-costs denied	No-costs denied	No
SOUTH AFRICA	No	No	Not likely. If done, P is taxable
SPAIN	No	Yes-open market rentals	No
SWEDEN	No	No-until S establishes a market	No
SWITZER-LAND	No	Yes, open market rates	Yes, if equity 3% stamp tax applies. No tax on repayment
UNITED KINGDOM	No-if no cost to P	No	Only equity if P contributes real estate to S, triggers income to P
UNITED STATES	No-if no cost to P	See safe haven rentals	Might be equity. If so, payments received can be treated as dividends
VENEZUELA	No	No, but related costs denied	No

As to S		
1. Will characterization of the transaction by P's country be accepted by S's country or will S's country make a separate determination?	**2.** If S's country makes separate determination what would that determination be? If income is allocated to P, how would amount of allocation be determined?	**3.** If income is allocated to P and S makes payment of the allocated amounts to P, will S's country subject the payment to a withholding tax?
Independent determination	Arm's length rental	No, but profits tax on P
Independent determination	Arm's length rental	No
No allocation	No deduction	No payment allowed
Independent determination	Reasonable charges probably acceptable	Yes, but watch treaties on guarantee fees.
Independent determination	No deductions unless legal oblig. existed and reasonable	No, but profits tax on P's rentals
Independent determination	Deductible if P charges S & not in excess of open market rates	No, but profits tax on P's rentals.
Independent determination	No allocation likely	Yes, if not deductible under 2
Independent determination	No ded. unless comp. auth. decision. They would use fair rental or deprec.	No W/H if comp. auth. decision, but profits tax on rentals.
No allocation	S requires prospective contract to get deductions	No
No allocation	N/A	Rent-W/H. Guarantees-No W/H
No allocation likely	No deduction likely	No, but P pays Italian profits tax
Independent determination	Yes, see special rules	Rent-W/H. Guarantee-No W/H
No allocation	No deductions unless a contract approved by auth.	Yes, at 21%
Ind. determination. P's allocation often accepted	Arm's length tests	No, except where payments unreasonable
Normally accept P's allocation if S makes payment	Arm's length tests	No, but P pays N.Z. profits tax on rentals.
No allocation likely accepted	No deductions	Yes
No allocation	S deducts only current rentals & P pays profits tax thereon	Yes, profits tax on P
No allocation	Only current expenses can be deducted	No
Independent determination	Actual charge may be accepted if reasonable	No
No allocation	S must establish legal oblig. to get deduction	Yes, plus exchange approval required
No allocation, but see next points	S could deduct by including with future payments	Yes, if not deductible under 2. No, otherwise
Independent determination	Open market rates normally accepted	No
Independent determination	Arm's length rentals accepted if S makes payment	Yes-rentals, No-guarantee fees
Independent determination	No allocation likely here	Yes-rentals No-guarantee fee
No allocation	No deduction	No payment allowed

TAX TREATIES

	A. Do the tax treaties that your country has entered into contain provision for mutual agreement procedure in this area?	B. Might these treaty provisions in any way modify your previous answer? If yes, what are principle modifications? e.g., what guidelines does your competent authority use when seeking to negotiate settlement concerning allocation of income and expenses? Is he required to apply domestic law?	C. How are these treaty provisions invoked? e.g., must taxpayer seek protection under treaty or will treaty protection be invoked automatically by tax authorities when they know a treaty country is involved?	D. What is procedure for applying to comp. authority in these situations? Are any guidelines established which define when application to competent auth. will be accepted?
AUSTRALIA	Yes	Yes, comp. auth. can override domestic law	Australian resident must apply	Letter
BELGIUM	Not always	No changes	Belgian resident must apply	Letter
BRAZIL	Yes	Yes in theory; no in practice	Not permitted	N/A
CANADA	Yes	No significant modifications; they apply domestic law	Canadian resident must apply	Letter
DENMARK	Recent treaties only	Little experience yet	Danish resident must apply	Make claim in tax return
FINLAND	Yes	Yes, often exceptions to domestic rules	Finnish resident must apply	Letter from resident of Finland
FRANCE	Yes	No changes	French resident must apply	Letter
WEST GERMANY	Yes	Many relief measures not posible without comp. auth.; they try to apply domestic law	German resident must apply; application goes first to P's country	Letter
HONG KONG	No treaties			
IRELAND	Yes	No differences; must apply domestic law	Irish resident must apply	Letter
ITALY	Yes	Little experience as comp. auth. procedure not fully functioning	Italian resident must apply	Letter
JAPAN	Yes	Yes, but tax auth. follow no specific guidelines	Japanese resident must apply	Specific statutory procedures
MEXICO	No treaties			
NETHER-LANDS	Yes	No, comp. auth. must apply domestic law	Dutch resident must apply	Letter
NEW ZEALAND	Yes	Yes, profits tax on royalties & other payments to N.R. reduced to W/H tax	N.Z. resident must apply	Make adj. in tax return
NORWAY	Yes	Yes, will be obliged to accept some allocations	Norwegian resident must apply	Letter
SAUDI ARABIA	No treaties			
SINGAPORE	Yes	Minor differences	Singapore resident must apply within 3 years	Letter
SOUTH AFRICA	Yes	No, must apply domestic law	S. African resident applies	Letter
SPAIN	Yes	W/H rates reduced & cap. gains tax on moveables exempted	Spanish resident must aplly	Letter
SWEDEN	Yes	Yes, must apply domestic law but will accept more alloc's	Swedish citizen normally applies Swedish authorities can initiate	In writing with 3 years of first notification of problem
SWITZER-LAND	More recent treaties only	No, comp. auth. applies domestic law	Swiss taxpayer must apply	Letter
UNITED KINGDOM	Mainly yes	No, they try to apply domestic law	U.K. resident must apply	Letter
UNITED STATES	Yes	Yes, comp. auth. applies arm's length tests; they grant unilateral relief to US taxpayers	US resident normally applies; the comp. auth. can initiate	Letter must notify promptly if frgn. country's reassessment proposed; US waivers will be required
VENEZUELA	No treaties			

E. What is effect of failure to reach settlement between the competent authorities of the two treaty countries?	F. Can taxpayer appeal settlement made between two competent authorities?	G. Where agreement is receached as to correct allocation, will conforming adjustments and payments be allowed without further tax consequences?	H. Generally, what has been your experience with comp. authority negotiations in this area? Has settlement usually been reached? How long do comp. auth. negotiations normally carry on?
Double taxation – very little experience	No appeal	Yes	Little experience, long delays
Double taxation	No appeal	Yes	Rarely used
Double taxation	No appeal	No	Poor
Double taxation	No appeal	Yes, except for normal W/H tax	Normally positive; over 1 year often required
Double taxation, unilateral relief may apply	No appeal	Yes	Little experience yet
Double taxation	No domestic appeal; query jurisdiction of int'l court	Yes	Normally positive
Double taxation	No appeal	Yes	Normally positive; several years
Double taxation	No appeal	Yes, except for net asset & trade tax	Authorities very tough if comp. auth. requested
Double taxation	No appeal	Yes	Satisfactory, authorities normally settle
Double taxation	No appeal	Yes	Poor; no known decisions of comp. auth.
Double taxation	No appeal	Yes	Japan auth. rarely concede; 1-2 years required
Double taxation	No appeal	Yes	Normally positive; 2 to 7 years required
Double taxation	No appeal	Yes	Rarely used; Commissioner settles most disputes
Double taxation	No appeal	Yes	
May grant unilateral relief in hardship cases	No appeal	Yes	Satisfactory, up to 4 years required
Double taxation	No appeal	Yes	Normally positive, slow process
Double taxation	No appeal	Yes	Rarely used
Double taxation	No appeal	Yes	Satisfactory, 1 to 3 years
Double taxation	No appeal	Yes	Normally positive, 1 to 5 years required
Double taxation	No appeal	Yes, but W/H tax may apply	Not much experience; most are settled without comp. auth.
Double taxation (unless unilateral relief)	No appeal	Yes, usually but U.S. insists on interest being accrued on amounts owing to U.S. taxpayer	Normally positive; average over 2 years required

SPECIAL SITUATIONS

	A. Are the normal allocation rules described in Part I, illustrated in Part II, modified or applied differently in any of the following situations:		
	1. If either of the related companies does not have any gross incomed?	2. If either of the related companies has an operating loss for the year?	3. Where the tax rates of the countries involved are substantially equal?
AUSTRALIA	No	No	No
BELGIUM	No	No	No
BRAZIL	No	No	No
CANADA	No	No	No
DENMARK	No	No	No
FINLAND	Expenses may be denied in company with no gross revenue	No	No
FRANCE	Yes, in practice. If French corp, has no gross income or sufficient loss		No
WEST GERMANY	No	No	No
HONG KONG	No	No	No
IRELAND	No	No	No
ITALY	Allocations to Italian entity very rarely accepted if no gross revenue or losses in Italy		No
JAPAN	No	No	No
MEXICO	No	No	No
NETHER-LANDS	No	No	No
NEW ZEALAND	No	No	No
NORWAY	No	No	No
SAUDI ARABIA	No	No	No
SINGAPORE	No	No	No
SOUTH AFRICA	No	Yes, offset may be denied	No
SPAIN	No	No	No
SWEDEN	No	No	No
SWITZER-LAND	No	No	No
UNITED KINGDOM	Yes, can sell at loss to establish or enlarge a market	As before	No
UNITED STATES	No	No	No
VENEZUELA	No	No	No

	B.	
4. Where the tax rate of the country to which the income is to be allocated is substantially lower than the rate of tax in the country where the income was originally reported?	Are there any special types of companies or transactions which your tax auth. will closely examine for purposes of allocating income and exps. between related parties? If yes, please describe these situations	Please include description of any additional considerations which you think are important
No	Oil prices and royalties	None
No	All types of charges from foreign affiliates	None
No		
No	Tax havens, management fees	Some provinces do not automatically follow federal rules. Joint audits with foreign tax auth. gaining in popularity
No	Tax havens	None
No	Cross border management fees, services, marketing fees, transfer pricing, royalties, interest	
No	Management fees	
No	U.S. subpart F type rules	Profits in tax haven S taxed currently if P owns 25% of S
No	No	Authorities' attitudes tightening
No	No	Low tax rates in Ireland mean Irish auth. very inactive in int'l area
No	All charges against Italian entity	
Low-rate countries designated as tax havens & consolidated with Japanese parent	Financial inst. allocation of interest costs	Auth. watch exchange rates, must use transactions date or average for month
No	No	No deduction for interest to a related foreigner if debt on demand, convertible, dependent on profits etc.
No	Tax havens holding cos, finance cos, royalty cos	Auth. asking for ultimate ownerships of exempt Dutch H.C.
No	Tax havens	Contractors working in N.Z. face special rules, basically 15% on gross
No	Oil producing companies	None
No	No	Saudi considering disallowing all interest payments from S to P
No	Financial Institutes transfer price of foreign-owned mfg. corps. in Singapore	Local service corp. should earn profit of 5% over costs and then no questions
No	New income of loss companies	Exchange controls closely monitor royalties, interest, management fees
No	Tax havens	Law too new, too vague to say very much. Exchange controls are dominating factor
No	Foreign H.C. are taxed in Sweden	No income imputed to P in Sweden if only helping S to avoid losses. Multi-nationals closely reviewed
No	Multi-national companies and special status cos	
No, but closer scrutiny	Tax havens. Special rules for petroleum products	No field tax audits in U.K. Special transfer price assessors exist. All EEC countries exchange information. Joint audits. Documentary evidence very persuasive with assessors
No	Tax havens	Foreign subs must resist all tax reassessments to keep the tax creditable in the U.S.
No		Authorities' attitudes tightening; a thin cap rule of 1 to 1 being proposed